Drugs and Foreign Policy

Drugs and Foreign Policy
A Critical Review

EDITED BY
Raphael F. Perl

LONDON AND NEW YORK

First published 1994 by Westview Press

Published 2018 by Routledge
52 Vanderbilt Avenue, New York, NY 10017
2 Park Square, Milton Park, Abingdon, Oxon OX14 4RN

Routledge is an imprint of the Taylor & Francis Group, an informa business

Copyright © 1994 by Taylor & Francis

All rights reserved. No part of this book may be reprinted or reproduced or utilised in any form or by any electronic, mechanical, or other means, now known or hereafter invented, including photocopying and recording, or in any information storage or retrieval system, without permission in writing from the publishers.

Notice:
Product or corporate names may be trademarks or registered trademarks, and are used only for identification and explanation without intent to infringe.

Library of Congress Cataloging-in-Publication Data
Drugs and foreign policy : a critical review / edited by Raphael F. Perl.
　p. cm.
Includes bibliographical references.
ISBN 0-8133-8786-8 (hard)
1. Narcotics, Control of—United States. 2. Narcotics, Control of—International cooperation. 3. United States—Foreign relations—1989– . I. Perl, Raphael F.
HV5825.D7875 1994
363.4'5'0973—dc20　　　　　　　　　　　　　　　　　　　　　　93-45314
　　　　　　　　　　　　　　　　　　　　　　　　　　　　　　CIP

ISBN 13: 978-0-367-01193-2 (hbk)
ISBN 13: 978-0-367-16180-4 (pbk)

"There is no foreign policy issue short of war or peace which has a more direct bearing on the well-being of the American people."

—Former Secretary of State
James A. Baker III

Contents

Preface, Raphael F. Perl — IX

1 The Global Drug Phenomenon: Lessons from History and Future Challenges, *David F. Musto* — 1

2 U.S. Narcotics Foreign Policy in the Twentieth Century: An Analytical Overview, *William O. Walker III* — 7

3 U.S. Foreign Policy and International Narcotics Control: Challenges and Opportunities in the 1990s and Beyond, *Melvyn Levitsky* — 41

4 International Drug Policy and the U.S. Congress, *Raphael F. Perl* — 61

5 The Role of Law Enforcement, *David L. Westrate* — 79

6 The Role of the Military, *Donald J. Mabry* — 101

7 The Role of Economic Development: Policy Options for Increased Peasant Participation in Peru and Bolivia, *Kevin Healy* — 131

8 World-Wide and Regional Anti-Drug Programs, *Irving Tragen* — 155

9 Drugs in Post-Communist Societies, *Rensselaer W. Lee III and Scott MacDonald* — 185

10 The Limits and Consequences of U.S. Foreign Drug Control Efforts, *Peter Reuter* — 209

About the Contributors — 223
About the Book — 227

Preface

International narcotics control poses complex challenges and dilemmas for policymakers. Efforts to greatly reduce the flow of illicit drugs from abroad into the United States have so far not succeeded. There have been tactical victories: Seizures of drugs, assets, and major traffickers have increased notably; and efforts of the international community have gained momentum and maturity—forcing traffickers to respond defensively rather than concentrate on expanding markets. Most important, illicit drug use in the United States has stopped growing and, according to some indicators, may be declining. We have learned much, yet over the past decade worldwide production of illicit drugs has increased dramatically: Opium and marijuana production has roughly doubled, and coca production tripled.

Despite a national political resolve to deal with the drug problem, serious contradictions regularly appear between U.S. anti-drug policy and other policy goals and concerns. U.S. narcotics policy seeks reduction of the supply of illicit drugs to the United States and reduction of user demand within the United States. On the other hand, important aspects of U.S. foreign policy aim at promoting the political and economic stability of U.S. friends and allies and avoiding excessive involvement in their internal affairs. Pursuit of anti-drug goals can undermine foreign policy interests and bring political instability and significant economic loss to countries where narcotics production has become entrenched economically and socially. Drug supply interdiction programs and systematic U.S. efforts to facilitate the international movement of goods, people, and wealth are often at odds. U.S. international narcotics policy requires cooperative efforts by many nations and must operate within the context of their perspectives and priorities as well as within the context of competing U.S. foreign policy goals.

The contributors to this volume examine U.S. foreign drug policy, its origins, themes, implementation, and prospects for success. Through perspectives of leading authorities in government, academia, and the private sector, central issues of ongoing concern are analyzed.

Raphael F. Perl

1

The Global Drug Phenomenon: Lessons from History and Future Challenges

David F. Musto

Global efforts to curb illegal traffic in dangerous drugs are front-page news and televised features in most lands. Nations patrol their borders with ships and inspect visitors who are suspected of carrying contraband. The United States spends billions of dollars annually in an attempt to interdict opium and opiates from Asia and cocaine and marijuana from South and Latin America. Agreements between nations and overall supervision of control treaties by the United Nations are the subject of daily comment in newspapers. The crusade includes the efforts of thousands of government officials across the world.

The energy and money devoted for much of this century to combatting drug trafficking is impressive. Yet, from the Shanghai Opium Commission of 1909 to the Vienna Anti-Drug Trafficking Convention of 1988 those most concerned about drugs have complained about frustration in achieving international consensus against drug use. Americans have been particularly dismayed by the slow pace of other nations attaining the strict regulation and policing promoted by the United States. American attitudinal change, though, has not been particularly swift: both in the 1880s and the 1960s it has required decades to move from a broad toleration of drugs to later intolerant stands which are then firmly recommended to the rest of the world.

In 1906 the United States did set in motion the global anti-narcotic movement. In that year the United States extended invitations to a meet-

---

Copyright © 1993 David F. Musto. Reprinted here with his permission. All rights reserved. No portion of this chapter may be reprinted without permission of the author.

ing in Shanghai that would consider ways to help China in its campaign against opium. Never before had the major powers been convened to consider the question of narcotics traffic. The United States was acting in a brief window of diplomatic opportunity between the end of the Russo-Japanese War in 1905 and the explosion of August 1914. During those few years, nothing totally obstructed discussion or even cooperation between major nations which had recently been at war and would soon, sadly, be caught up in the First World War. In addition, China and Britain had adopted new and energetic anti-narcotic policies that prepared the way for the American initiative. Finally, the push of American domestic antagonism toward opiates and cocaine, and the pull of needing a solution to the smuggling of opium into the newly acquired Philippines, created the impetus for convening the International Opium Commission at Shanghai.

The circumstances of an institution's creation can stamp the character of its actions far into the future and this is certainly the case with the international crusade against dangerous drugs. The multiple motivations of the United States for inviting other powers to convene in Shanghai—and of the nations that accepted—can be found again with variations and shifting emphases over a history of drug policy extending more than eight decades. Motivations ranged from furthering economic interests, to defacing the image of rivals, to promoting other national goals such as national security. Nations do, of course, wish to control drug use and curb domestic drug abuse for moral, public health and law enforcement reasons, but the simple desire to stop the flow of drugs has rarely stood alone as a motivating force, while the declaration of an unequivocal anti-drug stance has often screened contradictory actions.

Examining the context of the Shanghai Commission and focussing narrowly on the United States, we can see that the elements of American action were quite complex. The U.S. government decided in 1905 that opium use—which had been sanctioned in the Philippines by a Spanish opium monopoly prior to 1898—must stop except for strictly medicinal purposes. This chiefly meant an end to legal purchase of smoking opium. Yet to stop smuggling the United States had merely one ship assigned to patrol the enormous Philippine archipelago. International control of opium would be needed to solve this smuggling problem.

In 1906 the Chinese Empire instituted its own attack on opium smoking and other forms of consumption. The stern methods indicated an extremely dedicated onslaught. Also in 1906 the British Liberal Party gained control of Parliament. The Liberal Party had long opposed India's export of opium to China. Steps were taken by the British government to effect an end of the opium trade, but only with the assurance that China would not make up for the loss of Indian opium by increasing its own production.

Meanwhile, the United States was experiencing a growing domestic fear of drugs. The passage of the Pure Food and Drug Act in 1906 was just one expression of a new consciousness of drug dangers. Opiates and cocaine had their origin in other countries and therefore international control would greatly relieve America's own problem.

Other complicating factors were the desire of the United States to participate in large construction schemes, especially railway construction, in China; and the anger of Christian missionaries in China over the Western nations' complicity in opium trade.

Then, still in 1905, as a result of American mistreatment of Chinese nationals in the United States, merchants and consumers in China began a voluntary boycott of American goods. This alarmed American manufacturers and government and military action was threatened by the U.S. government.

When the United States convened the Shanghai Commission in February, 1909 to help China with its opium problem, all these concerns were present in one way or another. In addition, the United States embarrassed the nation's major trading rival in the area, Britain, by siding with China in an effort to end the Indo-Chinese opium trade.

Other nations were not unaware of Americans' multiple motives cloaked under a simple moral message. Irritation over the U.S. stance with its overtones of highmindedness and superior virtue was intensified by the expectation that while the great burden of the international control effort would be borne by other nations, the United States would be the beneficiary.

During those few productive years before World War One the United States challenged the world with the imperative that no drugs should be used except for medical purposes. Americans, however, had not always felt this way. Until about the mid-19th century, opium and morphine were seen more benignly, and when cocaine was introduced to the United States in 1884 the drug was hailed as a safe and powerful tonic. But as the American people grew more intolerant not only of alcohol (a movement that would lead in 1920 to total prohibition) but also more fearful of opiate addiction and cocaine, the national consensus turned around and opposed non-medical use of these substances.

Debate over alcohol continued right up the to ratification of the 18th Amendment to the Constitution, but opiate and cocaine control elicited little opposition in the decade prior to American involvement in the Great War. Thus, when U.S. delegates advocated a policy of strict opposition to any non-medical use of these drugs, not only were they comfortable with their position, they also believed it to be a global principle transcending regional and cultural differences. If the people of some regions permitted opium smoking as a harmless practice or not worth attacking or if Andean natives had been chewing coca leaves for millennia, those people were in error and should abstain.

For nations who disagreed or fell short, this rigid standard presented problems of appearance and compliance. Change came slowly. By the 1920s the United States was extremely impatient with those countries that would not take quick and direct action to root out smoking opium or control the production of raw materials in their lands. The refusal of more developed nations to stop the manufacture of heroin also angered American officials. In 1925 the United States walked out of the Second Geneva Opium Conference and withdrew from almost any cooperation with the League of Nations which then administered the Hague Opium Convention.

This *volte-face* was in keeping with Americans' great distrust of foreign nations in the years after World War One. The narcotics policy of the United States paralleled other more dominant themes in American foreign policy. Several elements shaping the pre-war understanding of the drug problem now changed. The United States no longer saw itself as having an inordinate appetite for drugs; rather, other nations allowed—perhaps, encouraged—their people to send drugs to undermine the United States. The American appetite for drugs was quite normal, possibly, better than normal. Other nations wanted to keep their drug production for the revenue or because they did not see the ethical issues involved.

The disengagement of the United States from the crusade it had started and promoted with such moral fervor detracted from any global plan to curb production, manufacture and consumption. More importantly, the civil war in China, which had begun in 1911 and soon led to the overthrow of the Manchu dynasty, fragmented one of the world's largest producers and consumers of opium. A central Chinese government did not recover control until the 1950s.

World War Two totally distracted the combatants from the narcotics issue. Then the war's conclusion in 1945 was quickly followed by new alignments of former enemies and allies splitting into two armed camps. During this "Cold War," which lasted until the early 1990s, great power rivalry dominated the narcotics issue. One striking example of this powerful influence is the question of opium production and heroin manufacture in the People's Republic of China (PRC).

In the early 1950s the United States accused the PRC of exporting heroin to obtain cash and undermine its enemies. The Soviet Union denounced this slander against the Chinese people. But when a split occurred between the USSR and the PRC in the 1960s, the Soviet Union began a campaign against the "Maoists" who, it claimed, were doing just what the United States had claimed. The United States, however, now defended the PRC and asserted the Soviets were slandering the Chinese people. Clearly, the chief factor in this prolonged international debate was not the "facts" of the case, but Cold War maneuvers between the two superpowers.

Eight decades of international crises have created complex issues. Necessarily basing control on sovereign nations has also meant that those sovereign nations can dissemble, postpone and ignore pleas for effective control. Then, also, major players in the drug field have been preoccupied with worries much greater than that of narcotics. The lack of confident statistical reports and the ingenuity of smugglers have further hindered evaluation of drug control policies.

Policymakers also face the difficult question of what is effective treatment for drug abuse. Treatment programs report varying degrees of success, but there is no treatment that has the success of penicillin against pneumonia. Treatments also have their vogue at one time or another. Acupuncture, for example, has had a vogue at times as a remedy for addiction, but has been dismissed at other times as an ineffective superstition.

Framing a policy for the globe is particularly difficult if the goal is imposition of a single standard. The American confidence in a strict anti-drug position meets the reality of countries in different stages of development and also varying cultural attitudes toward the use of drugs including alcohol. Small countries may lack resources to mount a vigorous anti-drug enforcement campaign or may feel the need to profit from laundering drug money. How these complexities can be taken into account and yet allow formulation of a comprehensive and effective anti-drug policy is a knot that has yet to be fully unravelled.

Internationally we are witnessing trends which exert strong influence on an attempt to achieve a global consensus on international drug control policy. Of central importance is the resurgence of nationalism as in the former Yugoslavia and the former Soviet Union. But we also see large movements of consolidation aiming to erase national boundaries, boundaries that earlier in this century appeared unmovable. The consolidation of Europe under the European Economic Community may be considered part of this lifting of ancient boundaries and an assumption of much broader geographical responsibilities. The North American Free Trade Agreement may be cited as another example.

Beyond voluntary movements to remove or reduce national borders, we may be entering a period of unprecedented international coalition-building and co-operation. We now hear of a "right to intervene" in sovereign nations under certain "humanitarian" circumstances. Sending troops to Somalia and the Gulf region and protecting the Kurds in Northern Iraq represent responses by the United Nations to moral and economic issues considered serious enough to justify military operations. This new role for the UN—one envisioned for the League of Nations but unfulfilled—represents a transnational, global response that is unusual. Is it possible that the narcotics problem, quintessentially an international problem of supply, demand and money laundering, will rise to the level which will elicit from the UN Security Council a "right to intervene"?

The fact that all five permanent members of the Security Council are open in their admission of domestic narcotic problems and frustrated by the inability of individual states to control their borders and narco-traffickers is an ominous sign portending concerted action that will be unprecedented in the nearly century-long struggle against drugs. Should, however, such unprecedented action be taken by the UN or regional coalitions the danger exists that other motives may animate intervention; just as the anti-narcotic efforts in the past have been multi-determined.

The window of opportunity does not assure reasonable cooperation; it only makes it possible. People alive today grew up in a world in which global cooperation against narcotics was always blocked by one or another massive obstacle. This circumstance may constrain our thinking and hobble policy by causing us to overlook new opportunities. Recent events suggest that this rare moment may be seized to revitalize the global anti-drug campaign—or may be merely passed over with attention directed elsewhere.

2

U.S. Narcotics Foreign Policy in the Twentieth Century: An Analytical Overview

William O. Walker III

By early 1992 President George Bush and Secretary of State James A. Baker III had brought a semblance of order to U.S. drug policy. The White House had effectively defused drug control as the volatile political issue that it had been since perhaps 1969. More than any other administration since the inception of the world antidrug movement more than eighty years previous, the Bush administration endeavored to work closely with nations that produce and transship drugs. Whether bilaterally, regionally, or internationally, it sought to promote drug control in ways that in part broke with past practice. A recognition of the mutuality of the threat from drugs in the Western Hemisphere informed drug foreign policy since September 1989 when the Andean Strategy was announced. Success in the current phase of the war against drugs has remained limited, however, which ultimately brings into question the basic assumptions behind U.S. policy. Nevertheless, what the administration attempted to accomplish together with other nations had some historical precedent. What was different this time, though, was the way in which it pursued its goals. Bush, Baker, and others in Washington concerned with drug policy realized at the least that the United States alone could not effectively control the international flow of illicit drugs.

This essay examines how U.S. drug policy has evolved since the early years of the world antinarcotics movement. In brief, drug foreign policy has resulted from deliberations at both the national and international levels and has usually demonstrated little concern for existing conditions in producer states. In theory, that drawback is currently less true than ever before; in practice, awareness of the obstacles to control at the source is not quite so apparent.

As we learn more about the development of drug policy, it becomes increasingly appropriate to think of it in terms familiar to scholars, foreign policy analysts, and policymakers as well. That is, there exists something of a grand strategy; the point of U.S. drug policy has been to reduce the global flow of illegal opiates, cocaine, and marijuana. This supply-side approach to drugs has as its ultimate goal the maintenance of an antidrug regime, the contours of which have historically been set by the United States. Success in this endeavor means control at the source, that is, a dramatic lessening of the production of raw drug materials. Despite the nearly complete failure to reach this primary objective at any time in the course of the antidrug effort, no alternative strategy has been articulated that will conceivably replace the supply-side approach in the foreseeable future. Such has been the practical effect of U.S. influence over the movement.

Along with control at the source, U.S. officials pursued the interdiction of drugs in transit as a primary strategy. Yet as early as the mid-1930s, the limits of interdiction were manifest to drug control officials. In fact, rarely have they claimed more than a 10 or 15 percent rate of success for interdiction. Nevertheless, since at least 1969 the government has increasingly relied upon interdiction as a fundamental part of its antidrug strategy. As we shall see, the high visibility of interdiction efforts, successful or not, has been used to cast the blame for the lack of control at the source upon producer nations. The premise underlying this development suggests that producer states lack the political will to control drugs.

More recently, the United States has endeavored in a more concerted fashion than ever to impede the extensive laundering of drug money around the world. The revelations during 1991 about the drug-related activities of the Bank of Credit and Commerce International, however, dealt only with the tip of the laundering iceberg.[1]

It is perhaps symptomatic of the limitations of this aspect of antidrug strategy that the removal of General Manuel Antonio Noriega from power in December 1990 by means of Operation Just Cause actually served to insure the subsequent success of laundering activities in Panama.[2] Because of the relatively recent concern with money laundering as part of antidrug efforts and the patent failure of most efforts to prevent laundering, the issue will receive only limited attention in this essay.

The international antidrug movement and the formative U.S. role in it can be divided into five chronological periods. In the first two lasting until mid-1937, drug control was a foreign policy objective pursued essentially for its own sake. Then with the outbreak of the Sino-Japanese war, it became impossible to divorce control from larger security considerations—a situation that lasted until the defeat of Japan in August 1945. In the next period, from 1945 through 1969, U.S. drug control policy was essentially formulated in the shadow of security concerns arising out of the Cold War. Even the efforts to enhance international instruments of control ought to be seen in the context of greater policy concerns. Since Operation Intercept in 1969, however, drug control has made its greatest demands ever upon authorities in Washington to deal with the matter as a policy issue of the first priority.

The remainder of this essay will examine analytically these five periods. What were U.S. policy objectives and options at any given time? What basic assumptions underlay the choices policymakers made? How did policy outcomes influence subsequent drug control efforts? To what extent did events external to drug control influence the pattern of attempts at control? And, finally, did policymakers learn from earlier efforts to extend drug control and, if they did, were those lessons apparent in the subsequent evolution of drug policy? To the extent possible the presentation in the following sections will address this set of questions. Such a structure allows for comparison over time and therefore makes possible a well-informed assessment of the recent direction of U.S. drug policy.

The Early Years

International calls for drug control arose out of concern over a deteriorating situation in Asia, particularly in China, in the second half of the nineteenth century. As imports of opium from India to China continued apace, calls for curtailment of the trade emanated both from within the Middle Kingdom and from anti-opium societies in Great Britain. The remarkably easy victory of the Western powers in the Opium Wars at mid-century, however, had served largely to enhance the economic importance of opium for imperial Britain and directly influenced the nascent production of opium poppies throughout North and Southwest China. Domestic demand outstripped India's ability to supply the requirements of smokers. The very social fabric of China was being torn apart in a cloud of opium smoke.[3]

In Asia outside of China, opium smoking had long been an integral part of the culture of the resident Chinese population. To be sure, smoking was relatively contained within the Chinese community, but strong sentiment existed for ever more stringent controls. A system of taxation and dispensation, better known as the opium-farm system, catered to the demands of opium smokers in places like Java and Singapore. These lucrative enterprises, in reality little more than opium monopolies, were widely accepted as a fundamental part of the political economy of the region.[4]

Despite earlier disapproving of the participation of its nationals in the opium carrying trade to China, the government of the United States took no official notice of opium smoking until the time of the Spanish-American War. The acquisition of the Philippine Islands changed all that. Led by missionaries like Episcopal Bishop Charles H. Brent, who managed to capture the attention of President Theodore Roosevelt, the United States soon determined that its colony should rapidly free itself from the vice of opium smoking.[5]

Understandably, that task was far more easily identified than accomplished. And although the United States had to settle for the gradual elimination of opium smoking in the Philippines, at no time did concerned private citizens or public officials seriously think that opium smoking should have a place in the American empire. Similarly, the aftermath of the ill-fated Boxer Uprising in China exposed to Westerners the profound weaknesses of the Manchu Dynasty, which included an inability to curb opium smoking, and convinced U.S. authorities that China had to be delivered from the scourge of opium. The alternative was a China permanently weakened by the poppy, and in such a condition the dynasty could hardly survive. The implications for U.S. economic and political interests in East Asia were more grave than most policymakers and entrepreneurs wished to contemplate. Nothing less than the fate of the Open Door policy was at stake.[6]

This sense of foreboding about the very future of Western influence in Asia helped to prepare the way for the initial international anti-opium gathering at Shanghai in 1909. There opium, essentially in the form of smoking, was identified as a political and social problem of great magnitude. And despite contemporaneous Sino-British efforts to bring an end to the Indian opium trade, the conferees at Shanghai were careful not to make any binding arrangements about the trade's fate throughout East Asia. That more was not done at the meeting formally to assess the propriety of opium as a commercial commodity resulted from: its continuing, though declining, economic importance; a reluctance on the part of Asian governments outside of China to challenge the cultural and physiological hunger of their overseas Chinese populations for opium; and the uncertainty whether opium prohibition could take hold in China itself. Led by Brent and Dr. Hamilton Wright, a student of tropical diseases in the Far East, the U.S. delegation at Shanghai advocated curbs on opium production, thereby indirectly blaming Great Britain for China's debilitating troubles with opium.[7]

The British, whose approach to the opium question reflected a mixture of pragmatism, expediency, and cultural disdain, in turn found the United States to be obstructionist at the first Hague Opium Conference in 1911–1912. Dismissing the negotiating skills of Dr. Wright and denouncing

Washington's influence over China, which earnestly sought to "divert attention from [its] own shortcomings,"[8] the British helped to frame a formal convention intended to reduce the illicit traffic in raw and prepared opium. Despite wanting a more comprehensive agreement that included morphine and cocaine, U.S. representatives realized that such an accord was premature and therefore settled for what they could get. The subsequent outbreak of the Great War scuttled plans to build upon the Hague Convention in a systematic way.

Indeed, events other than the war outran the slow pace of policy planning in Washington. Specifically, just as the opium trade out of India neared an end, the emergence of warlord rule in China revived domestic poppy production on a grand scale. And it soon became clear that advocacy of strict opium control was a luxury that only states not in thrall to the drug economy could afford. Not only did opium virtually dominate China's political economy, but vast quantities of illicit morphine also poured into Manchuria, which had increasingly fallen under Japan's economic influence. In the Western Hemisphere, Bolivia and Peru resisted Washington's attempts to broaden the Hague Convention to include control over cocaine, which meant foreign intrusion into their traditional coca economies.

These setbacks for the global antidrug effort significantly affected policymaking in the United States. Until 1931 officials in Washington would keep themselves essentially estranged from the movement. Although a different reaction to events is fairly easy to imagine, the longer that the international scene remained unsettled, the more likely it was that domestic politics would influence relations between the United States and the movement. Hence, passage by Congress of the Harrison Narcotics Act in 1914 and two Supreme Court interpretations in 1919 of the law as a restrictive drug control measure worked to limit flexibility in the international arena. That is, the evolution of drug control as a law enforcement issue rather than a matter of public health took the issue out of the hands of humanitarian reformers like Brent and Wright and turned it over to the impersonal efficiency of the federal bureaucracy.[9]

Also, refusal by the United States to become a member of the League of Nations militated against the implementation of a drug policy responsive to the actual course of events. On their own terms and with considerable circumspection, U.S. authorities attended all the meetings of the League's Advisory Committee on Traffic in Opium and Other Dangerous Drugs, or Opium Advisory Committee (OAC), and participated at the Geneva Opium Conferences of 1924–1925. By the time the First Geneva Conference opened, it was apparent that the United States would accept no outcome of the deliberations other than its program of strict control at the source. Support for such an uncompromising agenda was virtually unanimous in the Department of State and in Congress, which had appropriated funds for U.S. attendance at the conference. At the head of the delegation was Representative Stephen G. Porter (R-PA), an avowed opponent of the OAC who had once told Secretary of State Charles Evans Hughes that "an effective remedy [to world drug problems] cannot be secured by compromise."[10] Accordingly, regret but not surprise accompanied U.S. withdrawal from Geneva in February 1925 before the work of the second conference was completed.[11]

The British rightly blamed Washington's untimely departure on conditions in China where overproduction of opium preordained to failure the First Geneva Conference, which considered the issue of opium smoking. In theory, the United States had the right to oppose the perpetuation of opium monopolies in their uniquely Asian form, but doing so made for ineffective policy. And although the second conference, which dealt more broadly with the production and manufacturing of narcotics, may not have met exacting U.S. standards, it was a notable advance over the vague agreements reached more than a decade earlier at The Hague. But distinctions such as these hardly mattered in Washington where until 1931 cooperation with the OAC would remain *pro forma* at best.

In reality, the United States deliberately attempted after the debacle at Geneva to undermine the work of the international antidrug movement. At the time of the Havana meeting of Pan-American states in 1928, which promised to be a querulous affair because of general opposition to U.S. hegemony in the hemisphere, policymakers considered asking governments in Latin America to sabotage the Second Geneva Opium Convention by refusing to sign it. Because the number of ratifications necessary to put the convention into effect was at hand, the idea was dropped, but it did signify the extent to which the United States would go to express its displeasure with the work of the OAC.[12] To a lesser extent, the United States also tried to circumvent the OAC in North China, where appeals to officials in Japan to clean up the morphine trade were intended to put forward a regional solution to the problem. Success in the effort, however, depended upon the dubious ability of civilian authorities in Tokyo to implement a conciliatory foreign policy toward China. The consolidation of power by Chiang Kai-shek's Kuomintang following the Northern Expedition from 1926 to 1928 made that development all the more unlikely.[13]

The Limits of Narcotics Foreign Policy

By the late 1920s, then, the United States had effectively isolated itself from the international antidrug movement. The irony was that U.S. officials hoped to force a restructuring upon the movement along the lines Porter had attempted to dictate at Geneva. Single-minded pursuit of control at the source blinded policymakers in more than one way. To be sure, they had tried and failed to expose the contradictions in Great Britain's approach to drug control; gradualism and dispensing monopolies, the basis of the so-called British system, had more resilience than authorities in Washington were prepared to admit.[14] Also, a regionalist approach to control, whether in Latin America or East Asia, could not exist independent of other foreign policy issues. That is, Japanese militarism and opposition to U.S. dominance in the Americas were certain to affect the course of antidrug activity. Furthermore, Washington's supply-side response to the international illicit traffic in drugs overlooked the economic and cultural obstacles that producer states had to overcome in order to put any antidrug convention into effect. Warnings of this sort were not new. Whether from Bolivia, China, or Persia, they resounded forcefully from producer states even before there existed a credible global movement for control, but were all but lost in the halcyon early days of the OAC.[15]

Washington's decision in late 1928 to abandon unilateralism and reach an accommodation with the OAC reflected a tactical, not a strategic, adjustment of operating assumptions. Rejecting the contrary perspective not only of Congressman Porter but also of Assistant Secretary of State Nelson Trusler Johnson and John Kenneth Caldwell, a narcotics expert in the Department of State's Division of Far Eastern Affairs, Undersecretary of State J. Reuben Clark discreetly worked to have a U.S. citizen named to the new Permanent Central Opium Board (PCOB). The PCOB was charged under the Geneva Opium Convention of 1925 with gathering statistics relating to all drug requirements for medical and scientific purposes and with tracking drug imports and exports. Herbert L. May, who had worked closely with the Opium Research Committee of the Foreign Policy Association in New York, became one of the original members of the PCOB.[16]

Seeing how counterproductive a policy of unilateralism had been, Caldwell reversed his earlier position and began looking for ways to mend relations between the United States and the OAC. Caldwell probably did so because he saw conditions deteriorating rapidly in Manchuria and North China and because he found the mercurial Porter a hindrance to effective policymaking. Desirous of bringing the United States back into the antidrug movement, the OAC assisted Caldwell in September 1929 by calling for a conference to be held to consider restricting the manufacture of drugs. Of immense benefit, too, to Caldwell's efforts was a scandal in the Narcotic Division of the Prohibition Unit in the Treasury Department, the agency in charge of U.S. domestic drug policy. Porter quickly introduced a bill to create a Federal Bureau of Narcotics (FBN) in the Treasury Department. On 14 June 1930, President Herbert Hoover signed the bill into law—less than two weeks before the congressman's untimely death.[17]

Heading the FBN was Harry J. Anslinger of Pennsylvania. A former State Department consul who had served as secretary of the interdepartmental Federal Narcotics Control Board, he soon earned a reputation for his uncompromising stand on drugs. Addicts, he once said, were "criminals first and addicts afterwards."[18] All things being equal, Anslinger might not have avidly supported the transformation of U.S. foreign drug policy that was underway when he took office. But among the many talents of the commissioner of narcotics, who would serve from 1930 until retiring in 1962, was a genius for bureaucratic legerdemain. He would do virtually anything to sustain the mission of his small, poorly funded bureau. In one important respect, that task was not difficult; Anslinger found a kindred spirit in Stuart J. Fuller, who had rejoined the State Department in 1930 to replace Caldwell as the chief narcotics officer. By the time Fuller's death ended their association in mid-1941, the two men had succeeded in bringing the world drug control movement under the influence of the United States.[19]

In short order, they expunged from U.S. drug foreign policy the intransigence of Porter and others who doubted the need for Washington's role in the movement. Having ended their nation's isolation from Geneva, they then placed the United States in the position of being able to dominate, if not actually dictate, the agenda of the OAC. This development owed itself not only to the force of Anslinger's personality and to Fuller's diplomatic skills, both of which were considerable, but also to drug-related events that simultaneously were taking place in East Asia. Far more than events elsewhere, what transpired between Japan and China affected the course of international drug control.

By 1930 the presence in abundance of manufactured drugs in North China greatly alarmed authorities in Geneva. Until the late 1910s, the place of origin of these drugs had been either Great Britain, the United States, or Japan, but soon thereafter the two Western powers had abandoned the trade—which then became increasingly uncontrollable. And as the imperial intention of Japan's Kwantung Army manifested itself in numerous problematic ways, including the commerce in manufactured narcotics, the League of Nations and its OAC could not help but take notice. Thus it was that the League prepared to convene a manufacturing limitation conference. By not deciding upon a final agenda in advance of the gathering, the League assured U.S. participation at the meeting. Caldwell, who would term the conference "an advantageous opportunity,"[20] convinced his superiors at the State Department that he ought to represent the United States at pre-conference planning sessions at Geneva.[21]

Caldwell's hard work quickly paid substantial dividends. Secretary of State Henry L. Stimson advised the U.S. delegation, which included Anslinger, not to oppose a broadly supported plan even if it did not insist upon immediate control at the source; limiting drug manufacturing would suffice in the short run. This goal, as expressed in the manufacturing limitation convention, would be reached by making estimates of drug needs submitted to the PCOB binding on the nations providing them. Moreover, the PCOB could place an embargo on nations that failed to live up to the agreement.[22]

U.S. participation at Geneva was a step of major symbolic and practical importance. In the first place, it indicated that the heyday of unilateralism was coming to a close and that U.S. officials were prepared to involve their nation more fully in the international drug control movement. Additionally, Washington's positive response to events at Geneva from the fall of 1929 onward predisposed officials to work more closely with the League on other, related matters. For example, policymakers welcomed the visit of a League commission of inquiry on opium smoking to the Philippine Islands and other locales throughout Asia outside of China proper. Along with the British, who favored an active American role internationally, U.S. officials discounted the efforts of Japanese authorities in the Kwantung Leased Territory to portray opium conditions as somehow less troubling than they actually were by conducting a highly visible antiopium campaign during the League visit.[23]

Spurred by the pessimistic findings of the commission of inquiry and also by the encouraging results of the manufacturing limitation conference, the Council of the League sponsored at Bangkok in November 1931 a Conference for the Suppression of Opium Smoking. The meeting—called to deal with the demand side of the drug issue—accomplished little of substance, in part because of the refusal of China to participate, but did result in a partial meeting of the minds in Washington and London about the implications of the Asian situation. Given events in Manchuria at the time, a virtual Anglo-American rapprochement on the issue of drug control was met with enthusiasm at Whitehall. At both the Department of State and the Federal Bureau of Narcotics, policymakers realized that the move away from unilateralism could not help but serve their policy and bureaucratic interests. In that sense, without abandoning their traditional goal of control at the source, U.S. officials had shrewdly made a tactical switch that would enable them more effectively to achieve their goal, or so they were hoping. In retrospect, the lessons that Caldwell, Fuller, and Anslinger learned from working with the League and its Opium Advisory Committee in the early 1930s served them and their successors well for nearly four decades.[24]

Although that conclusion held true at the international level, cognitive dissonance would have beset policymakers had they solely focused their attention at the time on actual events in drug producing and trafficking countries. In other words, U.S. officials were easily able to hold essentially contradictory positions on how to respond to drug-related developments because their tactics became increasingly flexible. In neither Latin America nor Asia could progress be found in efforts to control drugs at the source, let alone through interdiction. If those basic objectives were not formally incorporated into existing global antidrug conventions, they nevertheless were central to the conduct of bilateral relations over drugs. On that basis, however, U.S. antidrug diplomacy in the 1930s must be judged a failure. The remarkable irony was that failure hardly mattered, but only because of the importance of Washington's reconciliation with and subsequent leadership of the international movement at Geneva.

The process of developing a global drug control regime in the 1930s kept policymakers from re-evaluating the basic premises guiding antinarcotics policy. They were too busy convincing themselves that their counterparts in most other nations were prepared to adopt a drug control program similar to their own. It remains highly unlikely, however, that a reconsideration of the direction of drug policy would have taken place under any circumstances, but the policy priorities of U.S. officials made its absence a certainty. That state of affairs was unfortunate because events that authorities could not have hoped to control under any circumstances were scarcely conducive to control at the source.

Where, it is worth asking, did a U.S.-style antidrug program actually take shape during the 1930s? Legislatively, countries as different as Nationalist China and Mexico adopted controls on drugs that were somewhat similar to those of the United States. Despite, for example, the existence of numerous antidrug laws in Mexico, the government there did not really believe that drugs constituted a serious societal problem. Mexico's representative had proclaimed at the manufacturing limitation conference: "There [is] no problem of narcotic drugs in Mexico. Mexico produce[s] no raw material, [does] not manufacture narcotic drugs, [and does] not export them."[25] Not only did such assertions minimize the stark reality of production, consumption, and trafficking in Mexico, they were also more indicative of the official position on control than was the extensive corpus of antidrug legislation.

Chiang Kai-shek's China more than matched the disingenuity of Mexico. Prodded by the International Anti-Opium Association in Peiking, and by other concerned groups and many individuals, Nationalist leaders participated in at least one major anti-opium conference, advocated strict vigilance in the struggle against opium, and supported the issuance of decrees intended to rid China of the scourge of opium by 1940. What actually occurred was far different. Poor farmers were forced, often in times of extreme famine, to plant poppies instead of rice or other grains. Such was the grim legacy of a decade of warlord rule in China following the death of Yuan Shih-kai in 1916. The Kuomintang not only suborned such a practice by regional warlords in service to its own power and authority, it also made certain that proceeds from the sale to Chinese masses of smoking opium would fill party coffers. Shrewdly, Chiang Kai-shek denounced the opium-related depredations of the Kwantung Army throughout North China even as he profited from his people's dependence on the drug.[26]

To be sure, some U.S. diplomats such as Ambassador Nelson T. Johnson found the generalissimo's actions wholly transparent but ultimately absolved him of responsibility for them, arguing that he "must accept [the situation] as he finds it."[27] Not all U.S. representatives in China accepted in comparably sanguine terms the tactics of the Kuomintang. Even those stationed in North China could not unequivocally condemn Japanese involvement with the commerce in opiates; there were simply too many independent entrepreneurs involved in the business. Nonetheless, the Chinese held a comparative advantage over the Japanese when the United States and Great Britain assessed the opium situation in China. Japan's imperial ambition, couched in either economic or military terms, virtually guaranteed such a reaction.

Indicative, too, of the futility of U.S. drug policy goals was the chaotic situation in Honduras in the early and mid-1930s. Manufactured drugs largely of European origin were being smuggled through Honduras to the United States where they were either sold or exchanged for guns. The guns, it seems, were intended to be used in an effort to overthrow the Honduran government. By 1935 a prominent Honduran drug control official had been murdered, which induced the Ministry of Foreign Affairs to ask the FBN for antinarcotics assistance. Although Anslinger and Fuller did not respond positively to the request, they did monitor as closely as possible throughout the remainder of the decade drug smuggling operations based in Honduras. This activity evidently took place without even the tacit approval of the Honduran government. That the drug issue did not cause a significant rift in Honduran-U.S. relations testifies to the security imperatives that underlay the functioning of the Good Neighbor Policy by the late 1930s. All the same, officials in Washington became increasingly reluctant to impute good faith to Honduras over its drug control record. As we shall see, they came to doubt even more strongly Tokyo's professed commitment to the global antidrug effort.[28]

The Mexican, Sino-Japanese, and Honduran examples represent the kinds of problems confronting U.S. drug control officials in the 1930s. They dealt with these challenges to their policies by employing a device psychologists term "defensive avoidance." In the case of Mexico, Fuller initially minimized the disparity in antidrug activity across the border by pointing to instances of smuggling on both sides of the Rio Grande. Only in 1939 would U.S. officials resort to the exceptional step of helping to force from office the chief Mexican drug control official, Leopoldo Salazar Viniegra. Although his replacement, José Siurob, did not alter Salazar's controversial policies, including a dispensation scheme, U.S. officials preferred to have in power a man in whom they placed considerable trust. When Siurob finally suspended the most troubling portions of Mexico's drug control regulations, Anslinger and his colleagues congratulated themselves on their victory.[29]

Significant for present purposes is how U.S. policymakers had been able, at the expense of Mexican sovereignty, to ignore the problems largely created by their strict emphasis on control at the source. In another important way, officials in Washington minimized the differences in drug control philosophies between the two countries. In 1930 and 1932, the two nations had signed agreements for the exchange of information about mutual narcotics problems. Although U.S. officials were not convinced that the accords were as useful as they might be, a perspective somewhat at odds with that in Mexico, Anslinger and Fuller could point to the arrangement as an indication of Mexico's good intentions in the effort to control drugs. Doing so accordingly made Salazar Viniegra seem to be the exception rather than the rule whenever U.S. officials wondered about the legitimacy of Mexican antidrug actions. The perception that the government of Mexico acted with good intentions informed U.S.-Mexican relations over drugs, with one notable exception in the late 1940s, until Nixon's Operation Intercept in 1969.

As previously suggested, the depredations of Japanese forces in North China and beyond through the mid-1930s enabled the State Department and the FBN to view the dubious opium control efforts of the Kuomintang in a similarly favorable light. And, to some extent, Chiang Kai-shek's government did attempt to reduce the amount of opium under cultivation as conflict with Japan became more of a certainty. Pressure from the Chinese Communist Party (CCP), anti-opium reformers, and elements within the Kuomintang combined to force Chiang to rationalize the nationwide commerce in smoking opium. By the spring of 1937 the numerous opium-related actions of both the Kuomintang and Japanese forces were coming under increasing scrutiny at Geneva. Although Fuller and Anslinger were inclined to impute good faith to Chiang's opium control efforts, at the same time they warned the Chinese representatives to the League that progress against opium was long overdue. The documentary record indicates that U.S. and British officials were prepared to make representations to China about the traffic in opium but refrained from doing so in the aftermath of the onset of the Sino-Japanese War in July 1937.[30]

Drugs and Global War

The Pacific War, as it has also been called, essentially compelled Washington to accept Chinese good faith so far as opium control was concerned. The brutal rape of Nanking in December and the rapid advance of Japanese forces out of North China and along the China coast focussed Washington's attention on the use of opium as a weapon of war. Despite considerable evidence from Anglo-American diplomats throughout Manchuria and North China that civilian administrators were trying with limited success to control the business in opiates, U.S. authorities concluded that Tokyo had no intention of living up to the anti-opium agreements it had previously signed. The presumption of Japanese perfidy extended virtual *carte blanche* to the Kuomintang's opium control policy—even though the facts indicated that such a dispensation was not warranted.

The supply-side narcotics control programs of the United States possessed a large degree of ethnocentrism and xenophobia. The major prevailing assumption behind U.S. policy held that the nation's drug problems were fundamentally foreign in origin. As such, the advent of global conflict in the late 1930s presented U.S. policymakers with an opportunity and a challenge. In the first place, war in Europe and Asia slowed the world's illicit narcotics traffic, thus allowing Anslinger, Fuller, and George A. Morlock, who succeeded Fuller at the Department of State in 1941 upon Fuller's death, to strengthen U.S. domination of the global drug control movement by moving the operations of the Permanent Central Opium Board and the Drug Supervisory Body to the United States. By the end of the Second World War, U.S. officials were well positioned to set the agenda of the Commission on Narcotic Drugs (CND) in the newly created United Nations (UN). And in the first three decades of its existence the CND essentially accepted U.S. antinarcotics objectives as its own.[31]

The challenge posed by global war was not so easily met by Anslinger and his colleagues. At issue was the very future of drug control officials as prominent policymakers in Washington. What role would drug policy bureaucrats have in the conduct of U.S. security policy? During the immediate prewar years and the war itself, the FBN and the narcotics section of the Department of State helped to maintain the security of the West against the Axis powers. On the most basic level, the FBN commissioner was responsible for meeting Allied needs for medicinal drugs. He did so, under a directive issued through the War Production Board, by working with the Defense Supplies Corporation and the Board of Economic Warfare. So long as the primary opium producing nations outside of China neither fell to Germany or Japan nor adopted a neutral position in the war, Anslinger's task was an easy one.[32]

In the Americas, however, Argentina and Chile were believed to be producing opiates for Germany. There existed some fear, too, that opium from Peru and Mexico might find its way to the Axis. In the case of Argentina, Anslinger threatened unspecified reprisals against one major firm, Hoffmann-LaRoche Inc., if the shipments in question continued. Peru's role in the Allied war effort was secured by the sale of cocaine for medicinal needs through the Lend-Lease program. And the U.S. government may have paid informants as much as $10,000 per year for information about drug production in Mexico.[33]

Moreover, the inexorable spread of Japanese influence into the best poppy growing regions of Burma offered to the Japanese government a major source of opium for medical needs. Anslinger et al. did manage to keep a similar situation from coming about in the Near East in Iran and Turkey by buying large quantities of opium from those two suppliers. In the case of Iran, Anslinger had the occasion in the early Cold War to reward the Iranian government for its wartime loyalty to the Allied cause by not pressing the young Shah over the production of illicit opium, much of which found its way to the black market in Indochina. Such diplomatic largess was repaid following the Shah's ascension to the Peacock throne in the wake of the coup of 1953 against Mossadeq's regime when Iran became a reliable ally at the CND in the global struggle against drugs.[34]

Drugs, Security, and the Cold War

Neither providing the Allies with a source of narcotics during the war nor overseeing the maintenance of the global anti-opium apparatus was the most important action Anslinger undertook to guarantee the relevance of his bureau to U.S. global security interests. He interpreted President Franklin D. Roosevelt's vague anticolonial sentiments regarding Southeast Asia as a clarion call to eliminate opium smoking from the former colonial possessions of France, Great Britain, and the Netherlands. Just as Anslinger and Fuller had argued that Chinese affinity for opium had eased the way of Japanese forces into South China, they warned that continued opium smoking would render former colonies more susceptible to internal decay and, as a result, to foreign subversion.[35]

Evidence for this dubious hypothesis came in the form of FBN and State Department allegations that Communists in China were, like the Japanese before them, prepared to ply their enemies with opium in order to suit their ideological ends. With the coming to power of the Chinese Communist Party in October 1949 and the CCP's subsequent exclusion of

Western influence from China, Anslinger's allegations about drug-related subversion of the West and Japan from Peiking could not be disproved. Moreover, having an adversary who was presumably willing to use narcotics as a weapon of war strongly reinforced the traditional supply-side strategy of U.S. drug control officials. Yet as I indicate in *Opium and Foreign Policy*, the CCP had learned a vital lesson by observing the actions of imperial Japan: A people drugged with opium do not make good subjects.

In the aftermath of its successful seizure of power, the CCP could not afford to tolerate the presence of opiates in China. The social and economic costs would have been unacceptable; the possibility that party members would be corrupted was too great a risk to take, especially after having called for the extirpation of opium from China for many years. This conclusion does not argue that no opium-related abuses took place. No doubt some did; yet the documentary record in the United States and Great Britain is remarkably free of any reliable evidence that would sustain such a charge. Anslinger did, however, interpret one attempt by the CCP to obtain foreign currency through the sale of opium seized from Japanese forces as evidence of Communist Chinese willingness to profit from the illicit commerce at the expense of the West.[36]

In the immediate aftermath of the war, Anslinger was not so preoccupied with the FBN's role in the national security state that he ignored the opportunity to further his country's supply-side agenda at the United Nations. Two examples demonstrate his remarkable attention to virtually all drug-related matters and at the same time reveal his apparent inability to learn from past experience about the limits of policies based upon control at the source. In short, Anslinger used his considerable bureaucratic skills to bolster basic assumptions about foreign responsibility that had long informed U.S. drug policy.

The end of the war witnessed both a gradual rise in drug use and addiction in the United States and the revival of an active, illicit drug trade from Mexico. Not satisfied with the dilatory response of the Mexican government to quiet diplomatic overtures, Anslinger took Mexico to task in 1947 at the second meeting of the CND for what he saw as laxity in its antidrug activity. The public rebuke evidently had the desired effect because officials in Mexico City promised to strengthen their antidrug operations at home and soon became more involved in the work of the CND.[37]

U.S. drug control authorities also feared that prosperity after the war might stimulate the international cocaine trade. Hoping to circumscribe such a development, they supported the sending of a mission to Bolivia and Peru, the purpose of which was to evaluate the place of coca in Andean society. Wartime developments led U.S. officials to believe that Peru might be willing to consider strictly controlling coca leaf production, but that hope proved to be ephemeral. The Commission of Inquiry on the

Coca Leaf recalled the integral place of coca in the Andes and concluded that only either improved socioeconomic conditions in producing regions or stronger government will could effect the desired results. Important for present purposes is that nothing about the commission's findings persuaded U.S. officials to question their belief that Andean authorities were more or less favorably disposed toward a U.S.-style coca control program.[38] That basic assumption would not be seriously challenged, as we shall soon see, until the 1960s.

Instances like those involving Mexico and Bolivia and Peru were not unimportant to U.S. officials in the early Cold War, but they do not adequately show the intersection of security policy and drug control activities. It was in Asia that such a nexus was most readily discernible. The political economy of East Asia and Southeast Asia in the first half of the twentieth century is only fully understood when the once opaque role of opium is taken into account. Fortunately, recent scholarship has clarified the place of opium in the making of modern Asia. Although discussed earlier, Communist China's centrality to the issue deserves some elaboration.

Traffic in heroin destined for Western markets resumed as the Second World War came to an end. Despite indications that the source of opium came partially from those areas of China controlled by the Kuomintang, Anslinger and his State Department colleagues were loath to blame their Chinese friends for the reappearance of the trade. For some months before the CCP seized power in October 1949 and for years thereafter, policymakers in Washington blamed Mao Zedong's forces for orchestrating the world heroin business. The less Western observers had access to China, the stronger the allegations became against the CCP. Occasional doubters, whether in London or Washington, were drowned out by the mass of unverifiable information emanating from the FBN and Foggy Bottom. The CND became an especially important vehicle for disseminating the anti-China message.

From the vantage point provided by recent scholarship, it is hard not to conclude that a purposeful campaign of disinformation was taking place. Available evidence indicates that to a limited extent some elements in the CCP sought to exchange opiates for hard currency; there is no reliable indication, however, of a plan to demoralize the West with heroin—as Anslinger and a few others were charging. Instead, it seems more likely that the head of the FBN, in making his numerous allegations against the CCP, actually sought to help hide anti-Chinese covert operations by Kuomintang forces operating out of the Golden Triangle.[39] The objectives of U.S. security policy in Asia, although in theory clearly separate from drug control policy, had taken precedence over the pursuit of control at the source. And Anslinger readily accommodated himself and the FBN to those larger goals.

In effect, beginning around 1950 drug officials decided to suborn drug trafficking out of Asia in the name of anticommunism. Doing so set a precedent that has not entirely been supplanted to the present. At the time, however, both the bureaucratic goal of the FBN to contribute to the development of the national security state and the actual imperatives of security policy at the height of the early Cold War render the actions of Anslinger explicable, if not defensible.

Nowhere did involvement of the FBN with security policy have greater long-term consequences than in Indochina. Supporting and ultimately following the French into Vietnam meant accepting the drug-related interests of several clients—both in Indochina and the general Southeast Asia region. If the emperor Bao Dai and the mandarins of Saigon enriched themselves by participating in the opiate trade—and they did—then U.S. policymakers—who knew that the emperor enjoyed opium's profits—had to tolerate the commerce in heroin to the West as the price of attempting to save Indochina from communism.

In doing so, Washington was ironically following the French lead. After some indecision, France had agreed by the late 1940s to eliminate the longstanding opium smoking monopoly in Vietnam. This threat to their livelihood moved Saigon's opium merchants to involve themselves ever more deeply in an illicit opium business emanating from the Persian Gulf. As Ho Chi Minh's forces proved difficult to subdue, French officials began clandestinely to work with elements in the opiate trade in order to keep the Viet Minh at bay. What U.S. officials knew about these operations is still not certain, but it is clear that they established similar links in the 1950s and after to key participants—growers, traders, and corrupt politicians—in the Southeast Asian opium business as one means of fighting the spread of communism. Central Intelligence Agency (CIA) "security assets" were easier to enroll in the fight than they were to control.[40]

Forging a close relationship between drug control policy and national security had a number of unanticipated consequences. To be sure, the federal drug bureaucracy has increasingly been able since 1950 to designate narcotics control as a security matter. By 1986, as we shall see, drug control and U.S. national security were formally linked, at least rhetorically. In the near term, though, joining drug control policy and security policy made the conduct of foreign policy far more problematic than it otherwise might have been. Waging the Cold War in Indochina meant bringing much of Southeast Asia into the campaigns against communism. As we have seen, the United States supported the presence in the Golden Triangle of forces loyal to Chiang Kai-shek, despite the strong opposition of the government of Burma. Burmese neutrality was seen for some time in

Washington in the 1950s as an obstacle to the containment of communism. In Thailand the logic of Cold War policy fashioned dubious linkages with unscrupulous leaders like General Phao Sriyanon, whose personal and political fortunes depended upon the trade in opium. Throughout Indochina numerous local participants in the opium business, whether in the hills or the cities, offered their allegiance to the United States and its allies in Saigon. In return, their dependence upon the opium trade as a source of income remained undisturbed, and probably increased.

At length, the heroin trade out of Southeast Asia boomed. And in Indochina itself, the appearance of U.S. advisors in the 1950s and U.S. combat forces a decade later sparked a resurgence of the regional drug trade. Thus, the 1953 UN Opium Conference, which adopted comprehensive controls on opium, must be judged an exercise in futility as it pertained to Southeast Asia.[41] It seems fair to observe that the rising levels of drug usage and addiction in the West by 1960 and after partly resulted from the suborning of the drug business in the name of national security. If the impetus behind drug usage and dependence should be seen in its social as well as its physiological context, then U.S. drug control officials must bear some of the responsibility for the rise in use and abuse. The convergence of narcotics policy and security interests in the early Cold War made drugs available to untold numbers of U.S. citizens. Another important, long-term legacy of the drug and security policy nexus was the willingness of authorities to ignore the drug-related actions of CIA assets, such as the contras in Nicaragua and General Noriega in Panama, until they became expendable.

A drug policy bureaucracy that, in effect, set aside its own objectives in the name of security had lost a sense of proportion where drug control was concerned. Objectively, the illicit drug traffic constituted a serious foreign policy problem, not a dire threat to the nation's well-being. Yet the historical efforts of Anslinger and others to propagate a supply-side strategy finally rendered drug policy hostage to other, more important foreign and security policy interests. In this way the linkage between drugs and security was cemented. To perpetuate the influence of the FBN, drug control authorities accepted a subordinate place at the policymaking table.

In the 1960s several important developments marked U.S. drug control policy. As a lasting testimony to Harry J. Anslinger's tenure as narcotics commissioner, which came to a close in 1962, nations from around the world signed and ultimately ratified the 1961 Single Convention on Narcotic Drugs, thus placing under one instrument nearly all prior international antidrug accords.[42] In effect, a consensus had been reached favoring a supply-side approach to drug control. Thereafter, control would be a matter of international as well as national security.

The practical effect for Washington of the Single Convention was to place increasing emphasis upon bilateral relations. And in that process frustration became the order of the day. Drugs from Southeast Asia continued to flood the West. Latin America became a greater source than ever before for cocaine, marihuana, and heroin. Demand for drugs by recreational and heavy consumers seemed to rise exponentially. Organizational changes did little to curb demand; the Anslinger-less FBN, mired in scandal, became in 1968 the Bureau of Narcotics and Dangerous Drugs (BNDD). But the BNDD had no Anslinger to dominate the policymaking process.

Chaos did not necessarily reign supreme. The decade of the 1960s had begun with an appeal from Mexico to the administration of President Dwight D. Eisenhower for antidrug assistance. By 1964 the Agency For International Development (AID) in the State Department had devised a program that previewed the future of U.S. antidrug assistance programs. Included in the aid package were funds for crop eradication and weapons to combat the illicit traffic out of Mexico. Throughout Lyndon Johnson's presidency, officials tried but failed because of their unilateral nature to formalize trans-border antidrug operations with Mexico.[43]

In the Andes an Inter-American Consultative Group on Coca Leaf Problems met at Lima in 1964 but achieved meager results. Bolivia would not even sign the Single Convention until 1975; and Peru, although a signatory power, declared that reduction of the coca crop could not be considered for perhaps twenty-five years. Complicating the already sensitive relations between Washington and Lima was the creation of a national coca monopoly in 1969.[44]

Notwithstanding these several setbacks in the cause of drug control, the earlier linkage of drugs and security offered a new way to promote drug control. A variant of supply-side tactics, the road to drug control would emphasize law enforcement as part of a general foreign aid package. U.S. policymakers in the 1960s worried that the "revolution of rising expectations" in the Third World, which encompassed most drug producing countries, could not easily be controlled. They nevertheless sought to do so by tying together development and security assistance as provided to local law enforcement programs by AID, part of which was intended to be used for narcotics control. It is not clear from available data whether the drug control performance of producer states improved, but that is doubtful given the extensive funding that Washington made available in the 1970s and after. Almost imperceptibly, drug control had disappeared by the late 1960s as an autonomous foreign policy issue. Starting in 1969 the association between drugs and security would grow increasingly close.[45]

The Failure of Strategy

The more that U.S. drug officials equated their activities with security policy, the less relevant became one of the basic assumptions behind U.S. drug control. Since Anslinger and Fuller first attempted in 1930 to fashion a global antidrug regime, the United States acted as if producer and transit countries, with a few notable exceptions, shared America's goals. That assumption changed entirely by 1969, transformed by the security imperative attending drug policy in the 1960s. The event most symbolic of the dramatic change in U.S. thinking was Operation Intercept at the Mexican border. In subjecting all traffic at the border to great delays in order to restrict the flow of drugs north from Mexico, the administration of President Richard M. Nixon did two things. First, it made interdiction as important as control at the source. Second, and more significant, it served notice that the production of drugs threatened U.S. security and demonstrated a lack of political will by the country of origin in the fight against drugs. From 1969 on U.S. policymakers, whether in the executive branch or Congress, have assumed the existence of an adversarial relationship with a majority of producer states.[46]

In a major exception to this general rule, Turkey and the United States worked out an arrangement in 1972 that persuaded the Turkish government briefly to halt state-regulated production of opium poppies. A considerable amount of Turkey's crop had found its way into the heroin trade destined for Western Europe and the United States. In severing the French Connection, the Nixon administration temporarily muted congressional and public criticism of federal drug policy without disturbing the linkage between drug control and security policy.[47]

Despite the administration's Turkish success, congressional committees took an increasing interest in the making of U.S. drug policy. As early as 1971, the House Foreign Affairs Committee expressed grave concern about the extent of abuse of Southeast Asian heroin by U.S. servicemen returning from Indochina. One committee report held, in line with traditional U.S. policy, that "the problem must be attacked at the source."[48] What differed was the manner of attack that Congress had under consideration: a pre-emptive buy of the Southeast Asian heroin supply. Officials in the executive branch rejected such a proposal at least twice by mid-decade. Notwithstanding the unknown costs that annual pre-emptive buys would have entailed, the idea found scant favor in the White House because it threatened to raise drug control as an issue on its own merits and thus undermine the drug-security relationship.[49]

Even as the assault on executive policymaking prerogatives was being defeated on one front, the drug-security nexus was being reinforced on another. The patience of the United States for the apparent inability of Latin American states to control production and trafficking was wearing thin. As that happened, the pre-1969 diplomacy of persuasion inexorably gave way to the politics of pressure. Following Operation Intercept, both the United States and Mexico endeavored to put the best possible face on a contentious situation by hastily devising what they termed "Operation Cooperation." Soon thereafter, authorities in Mexico City initiated *La Campaña Permanente*, in which Mexican resources and assistance from the Drug Enforcement Administration (DEA), one of the successsor agencies to the FBN, were used to curtail opium poppy growth and heroin production.[50]

So far as can be ascertained, Mexico's drug control record in the late 1970s was a relatively good one. Yet, as the United States and Mexico tried to find common ground against drugs, political developments in Washington made that task much more difficult. The House Select Committee on Narcotics Abuse and Control (HSC) came into existence in 1976. Headed by activist congressmen dedicated to crop eradication who increasingly hoped to militarize the antidrug fight, the HSC looked beyond promise and began to assess performance in Latin America's drug control record. Again, Mexico caught the eye of drug control advocates in the United States. It is clear that President José López Portillo had in his government officials who were profiting from drug production and trafficking. What López Portillo knew about that situation remains unclear; in any event, by the time Ronald Reagan's presidency began in January 1981, members of Congress and some administration officials, although few then in DEA headquarters, were doubting Mexico's good faith regarding drug control. Ironically, Mexicans had their own doubts about the U.S. antidrug commitment because of strict legal prohibitions against the spraying of paraquat on domestic marijuana. But the realities of power in U.S.-Mexican relations made that concern irrelevant in the bilateral relationship.[51]

Mexico, of course, was not the only country subjected to close scrutiny by drug control proponents in the United States. Colombia called attention to itself both when it considered a plan to legalize and tax the marijuana trade and after the boom in the cocaine industry became apparent. Also, Peru and Bolivia were heavily criticized in Washington for failure to enforce the coca controls envisioned by the 1961 Single Convention. Bolivia especially fell out of favor with Washington during and after the year-long hold on power by General Luis García Meza as a result of what has accurately been termed a "cocaine coup." To U.S. authorities, Bolivia seemed little more than a nation in thrall to the coca leaf and, hence, cocaine. Throughout the Andes, it seemed as though the so-called kings of cocaine were constructing a powerful, albeit decentralized empire.[52]

Viewed from the perspective of official Washington, it is not surprising that pressure instead of persuasion increasingly characterized U.S. drug policy by the 1980s. The United States purposefully set out to transform drug control policies and operations in Latin America at that time; this effort took place on a number of levels. The HSC more than any other congressional committee held to account Latin Americans, and indeed the Reagan administration, for the integrity of their antidrug activities. It essentially arrogated to itself the role of watchdog over drug policy. With no particular mandate, save the presumed interests and fears of an ill-defined constituency, the HSC held hearings, conducted study missions, and released reports about the state of drug control in the hemisphere.[53] In so doing, the committee resembled somewhat the House Foreign Affairs Committee in the 1920s, then operating under the leadership of Stephen G. Porter. Porter, as we have seen, isolated the United States from the work of the League of Nations Opium Advisory Committee by withdrawing the U.S. delegation from an opium conference in 1925 when other nations in attendance refused to accept without reservations the principle of control at the source.

Not only, in the 1980s, did the HSC rally support throughout Congress for a foreign policy promoting extensive eradication of crops in the Andes and in Mexico, it also called for a dramatic improvement in the rate of drug interdiction, thereby directly criticizing the antidrug efforts of the Reagan administration. In that regard, committee leaders encouraged a militarization of the so-called war on drugs over the consistent opposition of Secretary Casper Weinberger's Department of Defense. By the end of the decade, though, it seemed as if selective low intensity warfare had taken its place, as needed, next to control at the source and interdiction as a basic component of U.S. antidrug strategy. Low intensity conflict as a significant part of U.S. strategy was unveiled when proposed U.S. assistance to Peru and Colombia in the aftermath of the drug summit held at Cartagena, Colombia, in February 1990 emphasized law enforcement assistance and military aid against drug production and trafficking.[54]

Also desirous of pressuring Latin American leaders to do more to control drugs were the three agencies most responsible for drug law enforcement: DEA, Customs, and the Coast Guard. DEA agents had operated abroad at the invitation of host governments virtually since the agency's creation in 1973. In the strictest sense, their mission was to gather information and to assist in the training of local antidrug forces, such as the mobile units (UMOPAR) created in the early 1980s in Bolivia and Peru. Nowhere was the DEA presence more controversial than in Mexico, where in early 1985 agent Enrique Camarena Salazar and his Mexican pilot were abducted, tortured, and killed. The case remained unsettled to the satisfaction of the DEA for some time despite the arrest and successful prosecution of many of those allegedly responsible for the crime.[55] Demonstrating how negatively the Camarena case affected U.S.-Mexican relations was the publication in *Proceso* in April 1990 of the names of DEA agents operating in Mexico.

Whereas DEA agents in the field wanted the Camarena issue to be resolved even if it impaired U.S.-Mexican relations, officials at DEA headquarters could never afford to be so uncompromising. Were the agency to withdraw its agents from too many areas of operation abroad, and there have occurred several instances of such retrenchment in South America and Southeast Asia, the very future of the agency might be in jeopardy. Thus, top officials at DEA did not make settlement of the Camarena dispute a test case for future cordial relations with Mexico.

There existed until President George Bush visited Mexico in November 1990, however, something of a carrot-and-stick approach. The U.S. Customs Agency, at least until Commissioner William von Raab resigned in July 1989, could not be outdone in its vehement denunciation of Mexico's antidrug record. So flamboyant and strident was von Raab that he found little difficulty in making public his feelings about Mexico whenever the spirit moved him. As for the Coast Guard, it has long had an important role to play so far as drug interdiction is concerned. Throughout the 1980s it carried out its mission, armed with increasingly sophisticated technology if only to keep up with the remarkable capabilities of large-scale narcotraffickers. Just the same, the adaptability and ingenuity of the traffickers placed a great strain on the resources of the Coast Guard, which ultimately moved Coast Guard officials to advocate putting greater diplomatic pressure than before on producer and trafficking nations.[56]

Sentiments for a much tougher policy in response to Latin America's drug control record were regularly voiced in Congress after 1985. The rhetoric of prominent members of the Senate Foreign Relations Committee and also the House Foreign Affairs Committee, to name but two of the committees most involved with narcotic foreign policy, demonstrated to what extent the politics of pressure eclipsed the diplomacy of persuasion. Senator Jesse Helms (R-NC) and Representative Larry Smith (D-FL) denounced the administration of Mexico's Miguel de la Madrid Hurtado as though it actively sponsored drug trafficking to the United States as a matter of policy. And although neither Helms nor Smith had any special expertise about the drug issue, they did have an eye for an attractive political issue and they made the most of it.

Helms, Smith, and likeminded others in Congress doubtless seemed like something of a rogue elephant to Department of State officials in charge of drug policy. Indeed, the requirement that the president of the United States certify the antidrug record of sovereign states in Latin America placed the department on the defensive in the bureaucratic battle to define the contours of U.S. policy. Nevertheless, the printed record in the 1980s of testimony before Congress by the several assistant secretaries of state for international narcotics matters does not show a bureau that found the politics of pressure disagreeable. As such, it is conceivable that the national interest certification accorded Mexico in 1988, for example, was intended by the White House to elicit calls from Congress to pressure Mexico about drugs.[57]

Whether or not that was true, narcotic foreign policy became highly politicized under President Reagan. Fidel Castro's Cuba and the Sandinista leadership in Nicaragua were charged with sponsoring the transport of drugs, especially cocaine, to the United States, yet the Reagan administration all but ignored drug trafficking by anti-Castro Cubans and the Nicaraguan contras. Such distortion of the facts, if not outright deception, had historical precedent, as we have seen, in Anslinger's allegations about Communist China's involvement with the opiate trade. And Mexico, whose foreign policy interests in Central America and the Caribbean were often at odds with those of the United States, had to pay the price for its dissenting positions.

Pressure for Latin America to adopt U.S.-style drug control programs can also be seen in the handling of economic development programs funded by AID. So limited was U.S. and international help for crop substitution and alternative development strategies that few farmers in Bolivia or Peru, the countries for which this assistance was primarily proposed, could have been expected to turn away from coca for another crop—no matter how volatile the market price of coca leaves. The point is not that Bolivians or Peruvians were demanding dollar-for-dollar income replacement; they were not. Rather, coca farmers, as well as processors and small-time traffickers, sought a reliable source of income if they were going to ignore the market forces that made coca an attractive economic choice. As structured in the 1980s and early 1990s, though, the development strategies devised in the United States failed to address the basic concerns of those persons in the coca-cocaine business.[58] Indeed, aid programs were closely linked to effective crop destruction and, hence, were tied as well to presidential certification. It has not been the purpose of AID to address other than the visible symptoms of this vicious cycle. When viewed in that light, Bush's promises at Cartagena about development assistance for the Andes, as one component of the Andean Strategy announced in September 1989, must be judged as being somewhat disingenuous.

U.S. drug policy toward Latin America relied on the tactics of pressure rather than the diplomacy of persuasion in two other important respects since 1985. On 8 April 1986 President Reagan issued a national security decision directive to the effect that drug production and trafficking constituted a grave threat to the security of the hemisphere. It therefore followed that those nations under attack by the drug merchants, especially in the Andes, ought to defend themselves individually or in concert. In practice, this meant a greater emphasis on control at the source and even more vigorous efforts in source countries to interdict illegal drugs. The United States would provide advice, training, and equipment, and the war against drugs would be waged, first, in Latin America and, second, in international waters.

This strategy largely ignored, however, competing security objectives that could have compromised U.S. antidrug objectives. Panama's General Noriega, for example, was arguably the Reagan administration's most vital security asset in Central America, despite his well-deserved reputation for double-dealing. Noriega was deemed indispensable to the administration and remained so as long as William Casey headed the CIA.[59] And the administration chose to overlook the involvement of several Honduran military officials in the drug trade because Honduras willingly served as a sanctuary for the contras. Such contradictions in security priorities were not lost on those nations, notably Colombia, that were asked to serve in the front line of the drug war.[60]

In addition, considerable U.S. pressure against producer, processing, and transit countries accompanied the militarization of drug strategy. Going far beyond an upgrading of the mission of the Coast Guard, the United States virtually insisted that the battle be taken to the source countries. To be sure, aid for some military operations came after being requested by Latin American governments. Yet it seems reasonable to ask how much of a choice Bolivia had in March of 1986 when what became Operation Blast Furnace was being proposed.[61] It is unlikely, too, that Colombia had many options other than a war with the Medellín cartel after the assassination of presidential candidate Luis Carlos Galán in August 1989. The Bush White House partially viewed the response to the killing as a test of the political will of the government of Virgilio Barco Vargas.[62] (Indeed, when Barco's successor, Cesar Gaviria, sought to design a Colombian response to the violence of the Medellín cartel, Bob Martinez, head of the Office of National Drug Control Policy, proclaimed that Colombia was on trial before the world.)

An unwillingness to strike directly at illicit production and trafficking would have jeopardized U.S. aid programs. With this implicit threat at the ready, the United States—in early 1987 even before the Galán murder—had fashioned a more extensive antidrug strategy for the Andes, Operation Snowcap. But Snowcap, slow in getting under way, soon ran into difficulty, especially in Peru where the Maoist Sendero Luminoso controlled coca-growing areas in the Upper Huallaga Valley. Proposals late in the decade to send U.S. Special Forces into the Andes were too controversial for Lima to accept openly, but by mid-1991 President Alberto K. Fujimori had agreed to their limited use.[63]

The evolution of a more aggressive antidrug strategy by the 1980s inevitably led to greater expectations among policymakers in Washington. Controlling drugs moved into the highest rank of foreign policy priorities, at least rhetorically. Yet both crop eradication programs and drug interdiction campaigns, despite several spectacular, singular achievements, did not significantly impede the global flow of drugs—as the annual Department of State International Narcotics Control Strategy Report attests.[64]

Policymakers traditionally had argued that an activist drug control strategy abroad would reduce consumption at home. Not until Congress passed the 1988 Anti-Drug Abuse Act would they seriously begin to address the issue of demand, and then did so essentially as part of a law enforcement approach. Accordingly, demand reduction strategies largely existed as a by-product of other antinarcotics objectives.[65] In effect, authorities were betting that demand for popular drugs, in this case cocaine more than heroin, would decline—as it always previously had. What they assumed, however, to be a cyclical theory of demand may in reality have been more of a spiral with absolute usage steadily on the rise.

Drug control strategy was also intended to deter newcomers from entering the business at all stages, from production to sale on the street. A tougher approach in the Chapare of Bolivia, in the Upper Huallaga Valley of Peru, or even in the Caribbean would produce the desired result of lowering consumption on the streets of New York, to cite but one example. Likewise, a strategy that emphasized strict and certain law enforcement might compel lesser players to get out of the game. Had policymakers paid closer attention to what they read in the analyses of Peter Reuter and his colleagues at the RAND Corporation, they would not have been so sanguine about the prospects for success of a strategy based upon deterrence and compellence. The risk factor for would-be entrepreneurs pondering whether to enter the drug business was almost statistically insignificant. And the rewards, although of remarkably disparate magnitudes at different levels of the trade, were sufficient to sustain the promise of unaccustomed wealth.[66]

Also anticipated as a result of drug strategy in the 1980s, particularly after Reagan issued his national security directive, was the apprehension of major traffickers. A number of seizures of important figures did take place, especially in Mexico and Gaviria's Colombia, but they did not appreciably affect the structure or functioning of the drug trade out of South America or Mexico, let alone in the United States. (Likewise, the fate of the heroin trade out of Southeast Asia scarcely depended upon the continued participation of its two most notorious, recent leaders: Lo Hsing-han and Khun Sa.[67])

One related outcome of the focus on major traffickers in Latin America was to be a reduction in money laundering. Hence, the seizure of Noriega and the arrest of top officials of several major banks held out the promise of greater success, yet that hope was leavened by the realization that the laundering of money remains a serious problem in Panama—a country whose government after 1990 owed its very existence to the United States.

Another expected result of the battle against drugs was an increase in the price of drugs so that the economic incentive to consume would diminish. Again, U.S. strategists would do well to heed the analyses prepared at the RAND Corporation. For street prices appreciably to rise, the rate of interdiction would have to be far greater than it has ever been. Even if as much as 30 percent of illegal cocaine is seized, and few experts claim that seizures come close to that figure, the available supply would probably keep prices down and profits for traffickers acceptably high. Not even the vigorous pursuit of the longtime strategy of interdiction presents a serious threat to the major trafficking networks.

Finally, for a brief period of time as the Cold War waned, policymakers looked to the war on drugs to provide U.S. forces with a contemporary military mission, however limited. After the Department of Defense under Secretary Dick Cheney overcame its reluctance to get involved in the drug war in Latin America and the Caribbean, commitments in the form of advice, training, and limited operations proliferated on a unilateral and bilateral basis. Yet the war remained a low intensity conflict for both practical political and diplomatic reasons. As a result, the war on drugs was deemed a losing budgetary and doctrinal proposition for the U.S. military and evoked demands for little more than a minimal expenditure of resources.

The unanticipated consequences of the Reagan-Bush drug war in Latin America were no more salutary. Inter-American relations have been strained by the politics of pressure. Palpable tension at the San Antonio drug summit in February 1992, dubbed Cartagena II, challenged the facade of a common front against drugs.[68] Only the terrible indebtedness of producer nations and their need for economic assistance from Washington, no matter what that amount turns out to be, prevented greater deterioration in relations with the United States. Partially responsible for this situation were the militarization of drug control strategy and the mandated process of certification—both of which arguably constituted an implicit threat to the sovereignty of producer, processing, and trafficking nations. At the least, certification was demeaning to producer nations in that it assumed a lack of will to take action against drugs—as though the drug issue existed apart from other vital issues of the moment.

It seemed, too, that defining the drug business as a threat to national security contributed to the realization of that very condition in the Andes.

The institutional integrity of Bolivia, Colombia, and Peru was somewhat weaker around 1990 than before. Perhaps the economic troubles confronting those countries would have undermined national political and social institutions even without the compounding factor of the illicit coca business and the cocaine trade. Yet pressure from the United States to wage war against the cocaine barons, in the name of national security, has made more difficult the governing process. If drug abuse is a visible symptom of grave societal ills in the United States, in Latin America the drug business stood as one of the basic causes of institutional decay.[69]

Conclusion

The complex policy choices facing U.S. authorities in the wake of the 1992 San Antonio meeting would be rendered far more problematic were narcotic foreign policy to remain based upon the politics of pressure and adversarial relationships. President Bush and Secretary Baker, however, did have other traditions to draw upon even were they not going to reconsider the historic operating assumptions underlying U.S. strategy. They could, if they chose, adopt an internationalism approach similar to that which marked U.S. policy in the early 1930s. Immediately after the 1990 summit at Cartagena, Baker seemed about to do just that. At Cartagena, the UN, and a subsequent world cocaine meeting in London, Baker acknowledged that illicit drug traffic should be dealt with on a multilateral basis and that the United States clearly needed to address the issue of domestic demand for drugs. Also indicating this belief had been Washington's support for the 1988 UN Convention Against Illicit Traffic in Narcotic Drugs and Psychotropic Substances. Yet, as always, multilateralism could only accomplish so much. The rationale for revising U.S. drug strategy would therefore have to reside elsewhere, perhaps in the U.S. experience with drug control in Asia since around 1980.[70]

Neither the politics of pressure nor the diplomacy of persuasion meant much in the Asian context. Drug-related events there unfolded without regard for Western interests. At the same time, U.S. authorities were right to view the situation, whether in Southeast Asia or in Southwest Asia, as basically inseparable from regional security concerns. In that light, the presence of DEA advisers in China, Thailand, Laos, and even Myanmar (Burma) became explicable. That is, at any given moment the control of opium production and trafficking could assist the political, and hence security, goals of local ruling elites. Whenever their interests and those of the United States coincided, as they did in the late 1970s in Thailand and in Laos and China a decade later, limited progress was evident in the war against drugs. Yet wherever chaos attended the political scene, as was the case in Myanmar or in Afghanistan, efforts to advance the cause of drug control accomplished little.[71]

The central point here is that antidrug programs in Asia existed as simply one of several foreign policy interests for the United States. If expectations are low regarding what can be achieved in the short term, policymakers have nevertheless begun to understand the historical complexity of the Asian situation. As Assistant Secretary of State Dominick L. DeCarlo explained in 1982 to a subcommittee of the Senate Foreign Relations Committee: "The opium growing areas of all three countries of the Golden Triangle are remote, trackless, and rugged, [and are] inhabited by ethnically distinctive tribal people who have grown opium for decades as their major cash crop."[72]

When comparable understanding accompanies U.S. drug control strategy elsewhere, particularly in Latin America, U.S. officials may be better able to appreciate the great complexity of the drug situation, both abroad and at home. Should that day come, then policymakers might comprehend the shortcomings of a supply-side approach and in so doing finally learn the lessons that producing countries have been trying for decades to teach them.

Notes

1. "The Dirtiest Bank of All," *Time*, 29 July 1991, pp. 42–47.

2. U.S. Department of State, Bureau of International Narcotics Matters, *International Narcotics Control Strategy Report, March 1991*, 171.

3. Jonathan Spence, "Opium Smoking in Ch'ing China," in ed. Frederic Wakeman, Jr., and Carolyn Grant, *Conflict and Control in Late Imperial China* (Berkeley and Los Angeles: University of California Press, 1975), 144–72.

4. James R. Rush, *Opium to Java: Revenue Farming and Chinese Enterprise in Colonial Java, 1860–1910* (Ithaca: Cornell University Press, 1990); Carl A. Trocki, *Opium and Empire: Chinese Society in Colonial Singapore, 1800–1910* (Ithaca: Cornell University Press, 1990).

5. Alexander C. Zabriskie, *Bishop Brent: Crusader for Christian Unity* (Philadelphia: The Westminster Press, 1948).

6. William O. Walker III, *Opium and Foreign Policy: The Anglo-American Search for Order in Asia, 1912–1954* (Chapel Hill: University of North Carolina Press, 1991), 13–19.

7. Arnold H. Taylor, *American Diplomacy and the Narcotics Traffic, 1900–1939: A Study in International Humanitarian Reform* (Durham: Duke University Press, 1969), 47–82.

8. Great Britain, Foreign Office, *The Opium Trade, 1910–1941*, FO 415: Correspondence Respecting Opium, 6 vols. (Wilmington, DE: Scholarly Resources, 1974), 2: V, January–June 1912, no. 81.

9. David F. Musto, *The American Disease: Origins of Narcotic Control*, expanded ed. (New York: Oxford University Press, 1987), 54–68, 121–50.

10. U.S. Congress, House of Representatives, Document No. 380, *The Traffic in Habit-Forming Narcotic Drugs: Hearings before the Committee on Foreign Affairs*, 68 Cong., 1 sess., on H.J. Res. 195 "Authorizing an Appropriation for the Participation of the United States in Two International Conferences for the Control of Habit-Forming Narcotic Drugs," 21 February 1924 (Washington, D.C.: Government Printing Office, 1924), 21 for Porter to Hughes, 12 February 1923.

11. Taylor, *American Diplomacy*, 171–209.

12. William O. Walker III, *Drug Control in the Americas*, rev. ed. (Albuquerque: University of New Mexico Press, 1989), 55–56, 60.

13. Walker, *Opium and Foreign Policy*, 42–46.

14. Terry M. Parssinen, *Secret Passions, Secret Remedies: Narcotic Drugs in British Society, 1820–1930* (Philadelphia: ISHI, 1983), 183–200; Arnold S. Trebach, *The Heroin Solution* (New Haven: Yale University Press, 1982), 85–117.

15. Walker, *Drug Control in the Americas*, 50–51.

16. Taylor, *American Diplomacy*, 222–23.

17. Musto, *The American Disease*, 206–9.

18. League of Nations, Advisory Committee on Traffic in Opium and Other Dangerous Drugs, *Report to the Council on the Work of the Twenty-Fourth Session, Held at Geneva, 15 May to 12 June 1939* C.202.M.131.1939.XI. (Geneva: League of Nations, 1939), 47–48, 63.

19. On Anslinger see John C. McWilliams, *The Protectors: Harry J. Anslinger and the Federal Bureau of Narcotics, 1930–1962* (Newark: University of Delaware Press, 1990); on Anslinger and Fuller see Walker, *Drug Control in the Americas*, passim; idem, *Opium and Foreign Policy*, passim.

20. Memorandum by Caldwell to Johnson, 8 October 1929, Record Group 59, General Records of the Department of State, decimal file 511.4A6/1.5, National Archives, Washington, D.C.

21. Walker, *Drug Control in the Americas*, 61–63; idem, *Opium and Foreign Policy*, 56.

22. Taylor, *American Diplomacy*, 233–67.

23. Ibid., 271–79.

24. Walker, *Opium and Foreign Policy*, 55–56.

25. League of Nations, *Records of the Conference for the Limitation of the Manufacture of Narcotic Drugs, Held at Geneva, 27 May to 13 July 1931*, "Volume I: Plenary Meetings, Text of the Debates," C.509.M.214.1931.XI. (Geneva: League of Nations, 1931), 39.

26. Walker, *Opium and Foreign Policy*, 62–82.

27. Johnson to Stanley K. Hornbeck, 31 May 1934, Nelson T. Johnson Papers, General Correspondence, Box 23, Manuscript Division, Library of Congress, Washington, D.C.

28. Walker, *Drug Control in the Americas*, 86–92, 140–51.

29. Ibid., 119–33.

30. Walker, *Opium and Foreign Policy*, 83–105.

31. Douglas Clark Kinder and William O. Walker III, "Stable Force in a Storm: Harry J. Anslinger and United States Narcotic Foreign Policy, 1930–1962," *Journal of American History*, 72 (March 1986): 922.

32. Ibid., 919–21.

33. Walker, *Drug Control in the Americas*, 153–61.
34. Kinder and Walker, "Stable Force in a Storm," 920–21, 923 n. 45.
35. Walker, *Opium and Foreign Policy*, 153–58.
36. Ibid., 168–75, 186–88.
37. Walker, *Drug Control in the Americas*, 177–79.
38. Ibid., 190.
39. Alfred W. McCoy, *The Politics of Heroin: CIA Complicity in the Global Drug Trade* (Brooklyn: Lawrence Hill, 1991), 163–75; Walker, *Opium and Foreign Policy*, 195–98, 200–13.
40. McCoy, *The Politics of Heroin*, 131–61.
41. George A. Morlock, "Recent Developments in the International Control of Narcotics," *Department of State Bulletin*, 13 September 1954, pp. 366–71.
42. Taylor, *American Diplomacy*, 336.
43. See Mexico, Country File, National Security File, Lyndon Baines Johnson Library, University of Texas, Austin, Texas.
44. Walker, *Drug Control in the Americas*, 197.
45. D. Michael Shafer, *Deadly Paradigms: The Failure of U.S. Counterinsurgency Policy* (Princeton: Princeton University Press, 1988), 79–103; Michael T. Klare, *Supplying Repression: U.S. Support for Authoritarian Regimes Abroad* (Washington, D.C.: Institute for Policy Studies, 1977), 7–25.
46. Richard B. Craig, "Operación Intercepción: una política de presión internacional," *Foro Internacional*, 22 (October–December 1981): 203–30.
47. Edward Jay Epstein, *Agency of Fear: Opiates and Political Power in America* (New York: G. P. Putnam's Sons, 1977), 86–95.
48. U.S. Congress, House of Representatives, *Report of A Special Study Mission*, "The World Heroin Problem," 92 Cong., 1 sess., 27 May 1971 (Washington, D.C.: Government Office, 1971), 1.
49. McCoy, *The Politics of Heroin*, 429.
50. Richard B. Craig, "La Campaña Permanente: Mexico's Antidrug Campaign," *Journal of Interamerican Studies and World Affairs*, 20 (May 1978): 107–31.
51. Walker, *Drug Control in the Americas*, 193–95.
52. Ibid., 195–201; Rensselaer W. Lee III, *White Labyrinth: Cocaine and Political Power* (New Brunswick, NJ: Transaction Publishers, 1989), 119–20; Guy Gugliotta and Jeff Leen, *Kings of Cocaine: Inside the Medellín Cartel—an Astonishing True Story of Murder, Money, and International Corruption* (New York: Simon and Schuster, 1989).
53. Walker, *Drug Control in the Americas*, 193 ff.
54. U.S. General Accounting Office, *The Drug War: U.S. Programs in Peru Face Serious Obstacles*, GAO/NSIAD-92-36, October 1991; idem, *Drug War: Observations on Counternarcotics Aid to Colombia*, GAO/NSIAD-91-296, September 1991.
55. Elaine Shannon, *Desperados: Latin Drug Lords, U.S. Lawmen, and the War America Can't Win* (New York: Viking, 1988).
56. On the U.S. military and the drug war see Bruce Michael Bagley, *Myths of Militarization: The Role of the Military in the War on Drugs in the Americas* (Coral Gables, FL: University of Miami North-South Center, 1991); Donald Mabry, "The U.S. Military and the War on Drugs in Latin America," *Journal of Interamerican Studies and World Affairs*, 30 (Summer/Fall 1988): 53–76.

57. William O. Walker III, "After Camarena: U.S. Drug Control Policy and Mexico," Unpublished Paper: Latin American Studies Association XV International Congress, Miami, Florida, December 1989.

58. Jaime Malamud-Goti, *Smoke and Mirrors: The Paradox of the Drug Wars* (Boulder: Westview Press, 1992); U.S. Department of State, Office of Inspector General, *Report of Audit: Drug Control Activities in Bolivia*, 2–CI–001, October 1991; and Kevin Healy, "Political Ascent of Bolivia's Peasant Coca Leaf Farmers," *Journal of Interamerican Studies and World Affairs*, 33 (Spring 1991): 87–121.

59. John Dinges, *Our Man in Panama: How General Noriega Used the U.S.—and Made Millions in Drugs and Arms* (New York: Random House, 1990).

60. Bruce Michael Bagley, "Dateline Drug Wars: Colombia: The Wrong Strategy," *Foreign Policy*, no. 77 (Winter 1989–90): 154–71.

61. Michael H. Abbott, "The Army and the Drug War: Politics or National Security," *Parameters*, 18 (December 1988): 95–112; Lt. Col. Sewall H. Menzel, U.S. Army, Ret., "Operation Blast Furnace," *Army*, 39 (November 1989): 24–32.

62. Bagley, "Colombia: The Wrong Strategy."

63. U.S. Congress, House of Representatives, *Thirteenth Report by the Committee on Government Operations*, "Stopping the Flood of Cocaine with Operation Snowcap: Is It Working?," 101 Cong., 2 sess., 14 August 1990 (Washington, D.C.: Government Printing Office, 1990).

64. See the Department of State's *International Narcotics Control Strategy Report*. The report is issued each year on 1 March, with an update in the fall.

65. Raphael Francis Perl, "The US Congress, International Drug Policy, and the Anti-Drug Abuse Act of 1988," *Journal of Interamerican Studies and World Affairs*, 30 (Summer/Fall 1988): 19–51.

66. Peter Reuter, Gordon Crawford, Jonathan Cave, *Sealing the Borders: The Effects of Increased Military Participation in Drug Interdiction*, R-3594-USDP (Santa Monica: The RAND Corporation, January 1988); Peter Reuter, *Quantity Illusions and Paradoxes of Drug Interdiction: Federal Intervention into Vice Policy*, N-2929-USDP (Santa Monica: The RAND Corporation, April 1989).

67. McCoy, *The Politics of Heroin*, 387–435.

68. *Washington Post*, 28 February 1992, p. A2; ibid., 3 March 1992, p. A13.

69. "Colombia Cracks Up," *NACLA Report on the Americas*, 23 (April 1990): 12–40; Peter R. Andreas, Eva C. Berman, Morris J. Blachman, and Kenneth E. Sharpe, "Dead-End Drug Wars," *Foreign Policy*, no. 85 (Winter 1991–92): 106–28.

70. On the UN and London meetings see *New York Times*, 21 February 1990, p. A3; ibid., 23 February 1990, p. A5; UN General Assembly, Seventeenth Special Session, *Adoption of a Political Declaration and a Global Programme of Action* (draft report) A/S-17/AC.1/L.3, 22 February 1990; and *Washington Post*, 12 April 1990, p. A34.

71. U.S. Congress, House of Representatives, *Hearing before the Committee on Foreign Affairs*, "Narcotics Review in Southeast/Southwest Asia, the Middle East, and Africa," 100 Cong., 2 sess., 15 March 1988 (Washington, D.C.: Government Printing Office, 1988); U.S. General Accounting Office, *Drug Control: U.S. Supported Efforts in Burma, Pakistan, and Thailand*, GAO/NSIAD-88-94, February 1988;

idem, *Drug Control: Enforcement Efforts in Burma Are Not Effective*, GAO/NSIAD-89–197, September 1989.

72. U.S. Congress, Senate, *Hearing before the Subcommittee on East Asian and Pacific Affairs of the Committee on Foreign Relations*, "Southeast Asian Drug Trade," 97 Cong., 2 sess., 6 May 1982 (Washington, D.C.: Government Printing Office, 1982), 8.

3

U.S. Foreign Policy and International Narcotics Control: Challenges and Opportunities in the 1990s and Beyond

Melvyn Levitsky

The United States faces a number of threats to its security and well-being in the post–Cold War era. Among the most insidious of these threats is the international narcotics trade. Perhaps more so than any other post–Cold War issue, the narcotics trade has the potential to inflict staggering economic and social costs on the United States while simultaneously undermining the political and economic stability of many of our foreign allies and other countries. In this regard, drugs pose as great a risk to our national security as terrorism, environmental degradation, or nuclear proliferation. The challenge for U.S. foreign policy is how to respond to this threat in harmony with our other interests; what course to pursue today to secure our tomorrow.

Against this backdrop, narcotics control has emerged in recent years as an increasingly central issue in the formulation and implementation of American foreign policy. The need to control drug production and trafficking now underlies much of our relations with Latin America and Asia, is playing an increasingly important role in our African and European initiatives, and looms as a major issue in our relations with the newly independent CIS states. Our goal is to reduce the flow of drugs to the United States by demonstrating to the international community that we have a common interest in stopping this menace and by working with the producer and transit countries to strengthen their political will and ability to fight it.

Our initiatives are beginning to pay off. With the inauguration of our comprehensive counternarcotics strategy in 1989, U.S. efforts have become more focused, international narcotic control cooperation has increased, and production and trafficking are down on several fronts. In short, we have taken the offensive and prospects for further advances are good if we can sustain the effort.

Narcotics as a Foreign Policy Issue

Rapidly expanding narcotics production and trafficking during the 1970s and 1980s established the international drug trade as one of the most dangerous and costly threats to U.S. national interests. Although the clandestine nature of the drug trade hides its full effects, the social, economic, and political costs that we can measure are sobering. At the trade's zenith in the late 1980s, it was estimated that over 23 million Americans were using illegal drugs; by 1988, according to a recent study, about 41,000 babies were born addicted to drugs; and in 1990, about 6,000 Americans died from using cocaine and heroin. As a leading cause for high student dropout rates and a barrier that prevents students from reentering school, drug abuse is seriously undermining our educational system. Drug abuse also saps our economic vitality, costing an estimated $58.3 billion in lost productivity in 1988. In addition, public health and criminal justice experts believe that the rising murder and violent crime rates in our cities are closely linked to growing competition among lawless, drug-dealing gangs and to violent, paranoid behavior caused by the use of crack cocaine and other drugs. The major international drug syndicates are meanwhile profiting handsomely from this decay; according to the Office of National Drug Control Policy, the U.S. drug market may generate approximately $40 billion in untaxed underground retail sales, much of which flows into the accounts of these powerful organizations.

By the mid-1980s, the sheer magnitude of the international challenge was staggering. Virtually all of the cocaine and heroin—the most addictive and violence-provoking drugs—and much of the marijuana we consumed came from abroad. By 1989, cocaine use in the United States had helped to fuel a four-fold increase in coca production in the Andes. The threat that coca cultivation could expand into Ecuador, Venezuela, Brazil, and other neighboring countries increased. Colombian-based networks grew to dominate the trade, flying raw materials produced in Bolivia and Peru to cocaine-processing laboratories scattered throughout Colombia. They completed the chain by establishing a web of air and maritime smuggling operations that spread through neighboring countries, the Caribbean, Central America, and Mexico to their own distributors in the United States. Such an infrastructure enabled them to produce and deliver tons of cocaine at a time, shipments that grossed the networks tens of millions of dollars per transaction and billions of dollars per year.

With access to more than enough coca to supply the U.S. market, cocaine traffickers aggressively began to expand their trade to Europe, Asia, and other world markets. Even though Colombian traffickers are in the forefront of this effort, other traffickers have moved to capitalize on this opportunity. For instance, recent signs of increased cocaine refining in Bolivia and Peru and the growing number of Brazilians, Venezuelans, and other South American cocaine smugglers arrested in Europe may reflect efforts by traffickers in these countries to circumvent Colombians and forge their own distribution networks.

In this regard, cocaine traffickers were starting to repeat a pattern that had already occurred in the heroin trade. Over the past decade, heroin traffickers developed new sources, markets, and routes as they shifted their operations to counter enforcement pressures and to capitalize on destabilizing political developments elsewhere in the world. As a result, the United States faced an increasingly large and fragmented threat. Production exploded. Last year we estimated that some 226,000 hectares of opium poppies were cultivated in no less than ten key countries, with most of the production concentrated in politically sensitive areas beyond the reach of central authorities such as in Burma and Afghanistan. Worldwide illicit opium production went from an estimated 1,500 tons in 1982 to over 3,800 tons last year, enough to supply the U.S. heroin market several times over. We believe Burma alone produced 60 percent of this opium, some 2,350 tons. Trafficking routes spread to Africa, the central Asian states, China, and other areas once thought to be immune to the problem, causing interdiction and investigation resources to be spread increasingly thin. What is especially disturbing, however, is that more and more people in the producing areas fell victim to drugs to the point that the largest heroin markets became the producing countries themselves, magnifying social and health problems in countries already facing serious challenges to their ability to deliver social services and health care.

More is at stake, however, than stopping trafficking. The accumulated power and wealth of the transnational drug industry erodes the democratic foundations of key drug-producing and transit countries and jeopardizes our relations with them. Further, it increases the threat to democracy-building efforts by corrupting the individuals and institutions essential to moving this process forward. The very sovereignty of some states is at risk as drug interests acquire control of vast swaths of territory and turn them into bases of operations. Such was the pattern in Burma, where opium-producing warlord armies virtually controlled the northeastern Shan states. A similar situation prevails in Pakistan where drug and tribal interests combine to exclude Islamabad's authority over large parts of the North-West Frontier Province. And in Peru, traffickers and insurgents in the Huallaga Valley—the world's largest coca-growing area—challenge government authority at every turn.

Without effective controls, there is no limit to how high drug figures can rise in the government. In the early 1970s, for example, we suspended our relations with Bolivia when a cabal of military officers took control of the government primarily to further trafficking operations. More recently in Panama, General Noriega enriched himself on the drug trade at the expense of the Panamanian people. We recently saw a similar situation in Bolivia where known drug figures were slated for top police and security positions. U.S. and international pressure stopped these appointments before they could give traffickers high level access to influence narcotics or other important national policies. The threat, however, is generally more indirect.

Corruption and intimidation, the traffickers' favored techniques, are powerful tools in advancing their interests while they erode effective response. As enforcement efforts have intensified, traffickers have shifted their sights from low-level police and judicial officials to a campaign aimed at crippling narcotics control policies at the top. Weak judiciaries became key targets. In several Andean countries, for example, traffickers have exerted enormous pressure on high-ranking justice officials, jurists, and congressmen in an attempt to weaken, abolish, or prevent the enactment of antidrug laws. For a time, they virtually paralyzed the judicial system in Colombia through an assassination campaign that killed a Minister of Justice, several Supreme Court judges, a retired National Police Commander, scores of lesser officials, and close family members of high-ranking executive officials.

At the same time, the traffickers' associations with guerrilla and terrorist organizations further raise the security stakes and complicate narcotics control options. The trafficker-insurgent relationships that have emerged in Colombia, Peru, Guatemala, and elsewhere create a symbiotic relationship with the guerrillas providing protection in exchange for the revenues that they extort from drug producers.

The traffickers' vast wealth meanwhile gives them an enormous capacity to influence the media, business, banking, and other key commercial and social institutions in their favor. To the extent that traffickers can make it appear that public support is on their side, they improve their chances of engineering bloodless coups against the government's counternarcotics policy-makers. Accordingly, traffickers in some countries have sought to acquire control of newspapers and radio stations which they use to attack government drug control efforts, condemn U.S. policy, and promote the myth that narcotics production and trafficking are economically beneficial at home.

On this score, the traffickers' propaganda is dead wrong. Increasingly, research shows that trafficking is a net drain on the economies of drug-producing and transit countries. On the macro level, the inflow of drug dollars exacerbates inflation and overvalues domestic currencies, thereby raising labor and land costs and undercutting efforts to expand licit exports. Traffickers generally do not invest their wealth in innovative or productive endeavors and the extent to which they invest in legitimate industries, their corrupt, crass, and violent business practices erode the social, moral, and ethical values of these firms. Moreover, the concentration of wealth in their hands impedes income distribution efforts and enlarges the underground economy, causing a greater share of economic activity to be conducted outside the taxable reach of the government. This, in turn, undermines the government's credibility by damaging its ability to sustain social support systems. Drug production also exacts a high cost on the environment as rain forests are slashed and burned to make room for drug crops and millions of gallons of chemical wastes are discarded into the rivers in areas of drug refining.

Developing a Strategy

In 1988 several important breakthroughs occurred that have put us on a course reversing the dangerous and costly production, trafficking, and abuse trends of earlier decades. Domestically, the passage of the Anti-Drug Abuse Act of 1988 established the Office of National Drug Control Policy—the Drug Czar—and mandated the development of a comprehensive, integrated, national drug control strategy. At the same time, the United Nations completed the UN Convention Against Illicit Traffic in Narcotic Drugs and Psychotropic Substances, an agreement that set the stage for unprecedented international cooperation to pursue increasingly complex international counternarcotics tactics. These complementary developments reflected the mounting intolerance of the drug menace by the American public, its policy makers, and the international community generally, and paved the way for fundamental changes in how we were going to attack the international drug trade.

The Office of National Drug Control Policy has the overall responsibility for formulating and coordinating the federal government's drug control policy. It moved immediately to assess the counternarcotics threat and in 1989—with involvement of the entire drug control community—published the first National Drug Control Strategy, which it has updated annually. The strategy is comprehensive, addressing supply, demand, and treatment, its top priority being to reduce the availability of cocaine to the United States. Cocaine affects more people, causes more crime, generates more illegal income, and leads to more deaths and injuries than any other illicit drug. This, plus the fact that the vast majority of world production is intended for the American market, made cocaine our most pressing concern.

The second and simultaneous priority has been to reduce heroin supplies. Here the challenge is considerably different. The United States consumes only a small portion of the world's total output, which comes from nearly a dozen widely scattered countries. In addition, most of the production occurs outside the effective reach of central governments in areas dominated by well-armed, semiautonomous ethnic or tribal groups.

To translate these priorities into action, we have implemented four sub-strategies—Andean, Potential Source and Transit Countries, Mexican, and Heroin. While each sub-strategy is tailored to respond to unique challenges, collectively they seek to achieve progress across three broad fronts.

First, the sub-strategies seek to attack the major organizations by creating an international political and legal environment that is hostile to narcotics trafficking. In many countries this means working to pass conspiracy, asset forfeiture, and other laws and then develop the institutions needed to prosecute the leading traffickers who manage and finance the trade. In an industry where the raw materials are so abundant and the labor and capital so inexpensive relative to the profits, quality leadership is its least expendable asset. Yet this leadership has generally been overlooked by past control tactics that have focused on interdiction and crop suppression. The leaders have been able to rebound from these operations usually by expanding and deepening their corrupt ties to the political, legal, and security institutions. The way to break this chain is for governments to target, investigate, and convict the drug leaders and in so doing send a message to other would-be kingpins that if they venture into this business, they are likely to pay with their freedom.

Second, the strategies seek to increase the costs of operations to international traffickers through interdiction and other enforcement actions to attack the drug infrastructure. These measures are most effective when they can erode traffickers' profits and weaken their organizations, raise drug prices and lower demand, and create financial barriers that prevent new organizations from entering the trade. In this regard, the strategies emphasize improved detection and monitoring to locate drug shipments, caches, and processing centers and enhanced capabilities of response forces to attack these targets. Because the traffickers have the advantage of being unpredictable—their operations are not constrained by national boundaries or timetables—the keys to success are intelligence, training, and mobility. Other tactics that require broad international cooperation also play a role on this front. For instance, we pursue a variety of international agreements to control chemical supplies and money laundering in a bid to deny traffickers vital ingredients needed to process illicit drugs and the profits from their labors. At the same time, all of these efforts generate information and evidence that support the first objective of dismantling the industry's leadership and eventually their organizations.

Finally, the strategies aim at reducing and eventually eliminating the cultivation of illegal drugs. Based on the simple axiom that if there were no drug crops there would be no cocaine, heroin, or marijuana trades, crop control has been a key element of our international counternarcotics efforts from the beginning. This goal involves not only efforts to curtail production in traditional areas that supply the U.S. market, but to prevent cultivation from spreading to new areas as well. Successful programs in Turkey, Mexico, Pakistan, Thailand, Bolivia, and Colombia at various times in the past have shown that this tactic can work provided growers can find alternative livelihoods and that governments have the will and ability to enforce production bans. Crop substitution or rural development schemes without the enforcement deterrent simply will not work, and this latter condition almost always requires governments to have political control over the growing areas. Consequently, crop control efforts are not the work of a few months; they take time to effect a substantial change.

The National Strategy emphasizes bilateral and multilateral initiatives, although the United States can pursue some objectives unilaterally, such as intensified interdiction operations on the high seas or in international air space. In the past, the effectiveness of multilateral efforts has been limited by the international community's reluctance to engage in the antidrug struggle, an attitude that tended to dismiss narcotics as largely a consumer country, principally U.S., problem. The 1988 UN Convention, however, underscored the growing international awareness that no country was immune to the drug threat and provided an effective tool for fostering innovative international control measures.

In addition to providing for many of the legal measures the United States had adopted with other nations—such as criminalizing the cultivation, production, transport, and sale of drugs—the Convention set the stage for an international anti-drug cartel, capable of responding to the threat on all fronts. For instance, the Convention outlaws money laundering and requires the states to enact laws empowering the courts to obtain financial and commercial records and the government to confiscate properties derived from drug offenses. It also includes provisions to prevent the diversion of key chemicals into illicit channels and establishes a mechanism to facilitate extraditions between countries even if they are not bound by a formal extradition treaty.

The treaty has provided significant opportunities for countries that are reluctant, or not equipped, to take aggressive police actions to work in less conspicuous, but no less vital, arenas. This is most evident in the chemical control and money laundering areas. The United States and 26 other major chemical manufacturing nations have formed the Chemical Action Task Force to make recommendations concerning chemicals for inclusion in the Convention and the implementation of its provisions. Based on work by the Task Force, the UN recently agreed to add ten new chemicals to its list. The effectiveness of the chemical control instrument was highlighted by the promulgation of tighter chemical sale and control regulations in the United States in 1988. Until then, cocaine traffickers relied almost entirely on U.S. chemical suppliers, but they have since switched primarily to European and other sources to avoid the record keeping and other scrutiny that inhibits diversion and could lead to their arrest and prosecution.

Similar efforts to internationalize the attack on money laundering are also underway. Here the problem is complicated by the number of countries that can serve as money laundering centers and the many ways drug funds can be exchanged, but the strategic concept is the same: to focus the international community on the point where narcotics transactions must leave the underground and surface in legitimate financial arenas. The Financial Action Task Force (FATF) is at the forefront of several international organizations working on this priority. The FATF representatives—from the United States and 25 other countries that are the major financial centers of the world—are working on recommendations concerning bank and non-bank regulations, reporting requirements, and other measures to facilitate controlling and investigating traffickers' assets. Noteworthy progress has already been achieved by many countries who have taken the first step to draft anti-money laundering legislation, and by others, such as Thailand, who have enacted such laws.

Mobilizing the international community behind the chemical and money control approaches has the potential for achieving large payoffs with relatively little expense. Such efforts, however, will take time to gel. They will require a lengthy legislative process by several countries followed by institution-building and training to equip them to handle complex legal and administrative procedures. Moreover, effective chemical and money controls will require significantly enhanced intelligence collection and analysis to distinguish illegal from legal transactions and to identify the principal drug interests behind them.

The Actors

Among the National Strategy's first accomplishments was to focus and coordinate the roles of the "supply reduction" agencies by developing implementation plans that assigned goals and objectives to each sub-strategy. These implementation plans address specific program elements, such as the need to support intelligence, river control, air interdiction, and administration of justice. They relate resource requirements to program priorities and also establish timelines for accomplishing goals and objectives. Moreover, the plans incorporate measures of effectiveness—some numerical and some qualitative—that enable us to chart progress, redirect resources, and shift course once the goals are reached.

The National Strategy has established a mechanism to coordinate and maximize the actions of the counternarcotics agencies. On the broadest level, each is invited to make contributions to the National Strategy and comment on its drafts so that by the time the report is published, major policy and operational roles have been formed. Within this context, there are a series of routine boards, meetings, and working groups to develop guidance and assign responsibilities for implementing the strategies and responding to ad hoc contingencies. At the highest levels, either the National Security Council or ONDCP chairs these sessions. A mirror image exists in the embassies where the country narcotics team, headed by the designated narcotics coordinator—usually the Deputy Chief of Mission—develops the mission's counternarcotics plan, assigns responsibilities, and coordinates operations, always under the authority of the U.S. Ambassador, the representative of the President.

The State Department, particularly its Bureau of International Narcotics Matters (INM), is at the forefront of policy planning and implementation efforts. The Anti-Drug Abuse Act of 1988 gives the Secretary of State responsibility for coordinating all assistance provided by the United States Government to support international efforts to combat narcotics production and trafficking. In this regard, the Department's major objective is to promote greater foreign government cooperation, commitment, and action to narcotics control objectives through diplomatic, foreign assistance, and other initiatives.

At the center of this process is the Presidential certification of foreign international narcotics control cooperation. According to the Foreign Assistance Act, the President must identify the key narcotics producing and trafficking countries—based on production and smuggling values determined by Congress—review their efforts, and then decide whether they should be certified as having fully cooperated with the United States in narcotics control or as having taken adequate steps on their own against narcotics production and trafficking. The Department of State is responsible for drafting the report and making recommendations to the President which he reviews and sends to Congress. While the certification legislation tends to restrict the Administration's policy options, the threat of decertification—in which a country could lose most assistance from the United States and have the United States vote against its requests for aid from multilateral developmental institutions—has spurred countries to greater antidrug actions than they might otherwise have taken.

Most of the Department's efforts, however, are channeled into a positive approach, which builds the political will and institutions that will enable foreign governments to initiate and expand counternarcotics efforts. INM has been the main apparatus in this effort—directly administering programs in 14 key drug producing and trafficking countries where we maintain stable relations, and funding limited counternarcotics agreements in some 36 other countries. Ranging from about $1 million to over $20 million each, INM's country programs generally include law enforcement and judicial enhancement, public awareness, demand reduction, and, where applicable, crop-suppression components. The programs are carefully tailored to each country's drug role. They are designed first to demonstrate that we and the host nation share a common security interest in fighting the drug trade and then proceed, through a series of agreements, to train, equip, and build their antidrug institutions to the point that the host nations can sustain their own counternarcotics operations. Cooperation in stemming drug abuse is also often a feature of these agreements.

Under the National Strategy, the overall focus of INM's programs emphasizes supporting tougher law enforcement efforts reflected in more interdiction operations and criminal investigations targeted at the kingpins' organizations. In many countries, this has required a substantial investment in training, equipment—such as helicopters—and logistics to improve the quality of the police while simultaneously working on less visible fronts to strengthen judicial systems with the laws, procedures, prosecutors, courts, and other tools necessary to prosecute major drug figures. If host governments decide to use the military in counternarcotics, INM can provide training and certain equipment to support these units also.

The Strategy, drawing extensively on contributions from the Departments of State and Defense, also sets conditions for the disbursement of economic (ESF) and military (FMF) security assistance to key drug producing and transit countries. Although not focused against specific drug objectives, these funds are nevertheless an integral part of our overall efforts to strengthen the economic, political, and social resistance of the Andean countries to the cocaine trade. For instance, the Economic Support Fund (ESF), administered by the Agency for International Development, is an all grant program that promotes economic reform and development through balance of payments and other forms of support. In this regard, ESF programs in Colombia, Bolivia, and Peru seek to erode the economic attractiveness of drug trafficking by providing payments to supplant illicit currency inflows, generate jobs and income, finance productive imports, and foster economic stabilization. FMF is a largely grant program that can be used to enhance the counternarcotics capabilities of security forces belonging to U.S. friends and allies. Recent FMF grants have enabled Colombia, Bolivia, Peru, Ecuador, Jamaica, the Dominican Republic, and other cocaine producing and transit countries to finance the acquisition of U.S. military articles, services, and training relevant to drug control objectives. Both ESF and FMF assistance are conditioned on a country's drug control performance, adherence to sound economic policies, and respect for human rights. In fiscal year 1991, the U.S. Government disbursed about $186 million in ESF and $112 million in FMF assistance for counternarcotics purposes.

The Departments of Justice, Defense, and Treasury, AID, and other agencies also have major roles in the international strategy. Justice is most prominently represented by the Drug Enforcement Administration (DEA), which has some 300 agents and personnel assigned to 50 U.S. embassies. They have a major liaison, training, and advisory role to play. Since 1970, DEA, with INM funds, has trained more than 22,000 foreign police officials. Although DEA does not unilaterally conduct investigations overseas, it cooperates with its foreign counterparts to develop evidence and pursue leads in support of investigations at home and abroad. DEA has become increasingly involved—especially in the Andes—in designing major counternarcotics campaigns for host nation authorities. DEA is also a primary collector of foreign narcotics intelligence. The FBI and Marshalls Service are other Justice Department agencies that provide specialized support in the areas of money laundering and fugitives while the Department's Criminal Division manages extraditions to the United States and supports the State Department in negotiating mutual legal assistance and extradition treaties.

Once narcotics trafficking became clearly defined as a national security threat, the Department of Defense assumed an increasingly pivotal foreign counternarcotics role. Prevented by law from having a direct law enforcement mission, DoD has been designated the lead agency for detection and monitoring of aerial and maritime transit of illegal drugs into the United States. This has brought a substantial amount of surveillance, communications, and command and control assets to bear on the effort, enhancing intelligence and interdiction capabilities. DoD also trains foreign military forces for counternarcotics missions and has limited authority to transfer surplus military equipment to foreign governments for counternarcotics purposes.

The U.S. Treasury is engaged in both traditional and innovative enforcement efforts. Treasury has been designated by Congress as the lead agency for negotiating international agreements on money laundering cooperation; it analyzes financial transaction reports and passes this information to enforcement and other agencies. Its Customs Service is one of the agencies with authority to investigate international money laundering. The U.S. Customs Service is meanwhile expanding its historical role of intercepting contraband at ports of entry to farther reaching operations. For instance, Customs employs a sophisticated electronic detection network which supports efforts to monitor, track, and apprehend drug-laden aircraft well before they cross the U.S. border. Customs also conducts an extensive international training program funded by INM. Since 1973, it has provided expert training in areas ranging from money laundering to sniffer dogs for over 12,000 participants from 114 countries.

The U.S. Coast Guard, the principal maritime law enforcement agency for the United States, rounds out the group of agencies that focus primarily on interdiction. It employs aircraft and cutters in a broad array of strategies against smugglers and participates in joint agency and joint nation interdiction operations. It works overseas to help develop riverine programs to control drugs and chemicals that move on inland waterways, and, with INM funds, conducts an extensive program of classroom and on-site training.

Through its responsibility to design and implement assistance programs worldwide, the Agency for International Development (AID) is responsible for the expanded assistance program proposed by the Andean Strategy. In this regard, AID is to help coca-producing countries diversify their economies away from coca dependency and towards open, outward market economies. It seeks to accomplish this through various rural development and crop reduction programs as well as balance of payment support initiatives, all of which are tied to progress in drug control. AID also supports institution building and public awareness efforts through various programs to improve the administration of justice and to reduce and treat drug abuse.

The United States Information Agency also has a major role in the public awareness dimension of our strategy. Through its contacts with opinion makers and other elites, the USIA has been instrumental in making key drug producing and transit countries aware of how severely they are affected by the drug trade. In many countries, USIA's teleconferences and other media tools are the primary information conduits for generating public support for U.S. counternarcotics policy.

Finally, the end of the Cold War has also freed-up additional intelligence community resources to target against the drug threat. The creation of the CIA's Counternarcotics Center in 1989 reflects the community's expanded counternarcotics role and commitment to developing better strategic assessments for policymakers and more timely and focused intelligence to support tactical operations.

Turning Process into Progress

After nearly three years, it is fair to ask if our international narcotics control strategy is up to the task—if our policies in the Andes and elsewhere are producing the results we want at slowing the trade and restoring political, social, and economic stability to the countries most at risk. As we make our judgments, however, we must keep in mind the scope of the threat and that it did not emerge overnight and, therefore, will not be solved so quickly either. Indeed, combatting the drug trade is more like fighting a disease than a war: it can crop up anywhere, anytime; often becomes visible only after the damage is done; and can even infect the very agents tasked with stopping it. Despite these caveats, there are encouraging signs that our efforts are succeeding.

A number of quantitative and qualitative indicators highlight our progress in the last few years. Indeed, many of the operational and policy breakthroughs we have made were unimaginable just a few years ago. In terms of boosting political will, from which all other initiatives must flow, our Andean strategy has produced impressive gains. This was underscored in the 1990 Cartagena Antidrug Summit, involving the presidents of Colombia, Bolivia, Peru, and the United States, and in the expanded Summit this year in San Antonio which Mexico, Venezuela, and Ecuador also attended. Both of these sessions produced commitments to cooperate in such areas as enhanced training, information sharing, chemical and money laundering controls, and demand reduction. We also agreed on the need for alternative economic development to wean producers away from coca cultivation and on the importance of international assistance and trade and development in the region.

The overall improved political will to fight the drug trade is being reflected in a broad spectrum of result-producing initiatives. Crop eradication and suppression programs combined with alternative development, for instance, are reducing the range of coca and opium production even in the face of serious political and security challenges.

- Coca cultivation in the Andes peaked in 1989 and has since declined some 4 percent.
- Opium production is in overall decline in Mexico, Thailand, Laos, and Pakistan—countries where INM has long administered crop control programs.
- Colombia, meanwhile, is moving rapidly to get ahead of its burgeoning opium crop; in less than a year the government has eradicated some 5,000 hectares of poppies, but cultivation continues to expand as traffickers feverishly replant fields and extend cultivation to additional areas.

There have also been important advances in interdiction and other enforcement tactics. Last year, interdiction efforts in Colombia, Mexico, and Central America netted a record 180 tons of cocaine; the worldwide effort may have topped 300 tons. While we do not have all the data needed to evaluate the full effects of these operations, the pressure is hurting the traffickers. Each ton seized represents wasted efforts and eats into their profits. In addition, the losses are forcing them to adopt countermeasures they would prefer to avoid such as shifting to alternate and more costly routes and seeking more efficient but expensive processing techniques.

The destruction, confiscation, and control of key assets is similarly raising trafficking costs. Traffickers have had to take millions of dollars out of their profits to rebuild a smuggling infrastructure heavily damaged by intensified laboratory raids, aircraft, boat, and chemical seizures, property confiscations, and other enforcement operations in the Andes.

Even with mounting interdiction and eradication successes, the war on drugs is not likely to succeed until the highest level traffickers—those who constitute the trade's greatest political threat—are prevented from operating with impunity. Progress along these lines is measured more by the quality than the quantity of effort and is discernible in such signs as a government's increasing willingness to view the narcotics trade as a national security threat, strengthen its overall judicial system, respond to corruption, and enter into—and uphold commitments made under—international narcotics control agreements.

Nowhere are such accomplishments more visible than in Colombia. President Gaviria is leading a major overhaul of the Constitution and legal system so that Colombia, for the first time, will have the capacity to deal swiftly and effectively with major drug criminals. Since 1989, the police have conducted major operations in Medellín and Cali—the headquarters of the world's most powerful cocaine syndicates—where they have seized assets and documents, and have arrested some key traffickers who are now in prison and awaiting trial. The fact that several internationally notorious kingpins surrendered in 1991 rather than flee Colombia indicates that Colombian traffickers no longer feel that they can operate safely outside their borders; they, in effect, have become prisoners in their own country. Even though cocaine capo Pablo Escobar escaped from prison in 1992, his death in 1993, prior to capture by government authorities, sent a strong message to Colombia's traffickers that they are not secure. Expert advice and financial assistance from the United States have helped to secure these gains, but ultimately they reflect the courageous efforts of the Colombian government and people who have had to confront violent trafficker resistance at nearly every turn.

Colombia is not alone in making progress on this front. Ecuador recently launched a major campaign to apprehend the leadership of one of South America's most notorious cocaine trafficking syndicates, and is now in the process of bringing them to trial. With the encouragement and help of the United States, Pakistan and Thailand have strengthened their drug laws and many other countries are also pushing to get conspiracy, asset forfeiture, and judicial reform statutes passed by their legislatures. Once in place, these measures will greatly expand opportunities to share intelligence, seek indictment and extraditions, control and regulate the movement of chemicals, money, and cargo, and take other steps to identify, target, and prosecute the most important drug figures.

Outlook: Challenges and Opportunities Ahead

The progress we have finally been able to achieve against the drug trade is due largely to the implementation of a national strategy that focuses our limited assets on the most vulnerable and vital drug targets, to the increased resources we have been able to bring to bear on the threat, and to the enhanced international commitment to narcotics control. When compared to the overall size of the international drug challenge, however, this progress constitutes just a beginning. The tasks ahead remain formidable. Major obstacles remain in getting our antinarcotics allies fully committed to the struggle, traffickers are sure to counter antidrug operations by adjusting routes, methods, and operations, and the changes in the new world order are likely to create both challenges and opportunities for our future antidrug policy.

Despite the growing international commitment to narcotics control, the lack of resources and competing political priorities will limit cooperation from many of the frontline producing and transit countries. Many of these countries, such as Peru and Bolivia, are among the poorest in the world, and at a time when productivity is falling and debt service is rising, they simply do not have the resources to press the drug fight on all fronts, even with assistance. Even if they recognize the national security threat posed by narcotics trafficking, competition from similarly dire economic, political, or social challenges drains attention and resources. The need to respond to a natural disaster, an energy crisis, or a rapidly developing political challenge, for instance, can setback considerably efforts to build and sustain counternarcotics momentum. Thus, it is important that we keep our relations with these countries directed at long-term goals aimed at building institutions and focused on the most critical elements of the drug trade while working to foster the economic and political base that will eventually allow them to sustain a greater share of the effort.

Changing trafficking patterns will complicate our effort to reach this plateau. The history of the drug trade is largely one of traffickers shifting production areas, routes, and methods to avoid pressure in one area or to capitalize on opportunities in another. Countries that have had little experience with the drug problem can find themselves quickly becoming victims of the trade with few resources and skills to combat it. Currently, cocaine traffickers are engaged in this very process, a sign that our pressure over the past two years is having an effect. As we have intensified efforts to thwart their smuggling operations through the Bahamas and Mexico, for example, they have moved increasingly into Central America and the eastern Caribbean, moves that have raised their operating costs but also spread interdiction and enforcement resources even thinner. They meanwhile continue to press for new outlets through neighboring countries as reflected by the increased volume of cocaine seized in Venezuela, Brazil, Ecuador, and elsewhere.

Two other areas of concern could also play into the hands of the international cocaine and heroin traffickers. First are the predictions, and some preliminary indications, that as the United States makes progress against cocaine, it will move towards a greater heroin problem. Past trends show that a period of stimulant—cocaine—abuse is historically followed by a period of depressant—opiate—abuse. Some observers, pointing to evidence of greater heroin availability reflected in increased heroin purity and lower prices on the streets, assert that this trend is already underway.

Colombian drug traffickers appear to be positioning themselves for such a development. In less that two years they have planted thousands of hectares of poppies in a major effort to produce opium. Even though the full extent of this problem is not known, Bogota—with substantial assistance from the United States—has responded quickly with a manual and herbicidal eradication campaign that has destroyed thousands of hectares of poppies. The immediacy and intensity of the response underscores how high the stakes in this challenge are. For Colombia, if the traffickers succeed in getting a foothold on the heroin trade, they could gain additional wealth and power that offset the losses they have recently suffered on the cocaine front. Colombian opium production, meanwhile, poses a potentially significant threat to the United States even though it makes a relatively insignificant addition to the already overwhelming world supply. Unlike production in Asia, which serves a vast regional and international market, we would expect virtually all of Colombia's output to be targeted at the United States and distributed by efficient, brutal, and well-entrenched organizations. Consequently, if this problem takes root in Colombia it could dramatically increase heroin availability in the United States and foster greater use and addiction.

U.S. counterdrug policy must also be poised to meet the new challenges arising out of the profound political, economic, and social changes occurring in Europe and Asia. The disintegration of authoritarian rule in East Europe and Central Asia creates potentially vast marketing and smuggling opportunities for international heroin and cocaine traffickers alike. Greater personal freedom will likely facilitate experimentation with drug use—the first step toward building a drug market—while efforts to develop free-market economies with more open borders, greater commerce, and less regulation will make smuggling easier. New markets here would not only add to the wealth of the heroin and cocaine traffickers, boosting their ability to withstand trafficking setbacks elsewhere, they could create room for other criminal organizations, heretofore locked out of the trade by limited opportunities and tight competition, to enter the arena. The effect will be to further fragment the industry and confront authorities with more trafficking targets. In addition, government policies designed to earn foreign exchange could abet drug interests in other ways. For instance, traffickers would likely take advantage of any liberalized banking, investment, or chemical processing regulations to turn these areas into important money laundering centers or chemical suppliers. Meanwhile in East Asia, rapid economic growth has produced an increasingly cosmopolitan and wealthy class of consumers, ripe targets for the cocaine trade. The expanding commercial trade between this region and the rest of the world, including drug source areas, is creating new smuggling routes and methods. It is also adding to the commercial cargo trade, one of the fastest growing and most challenging smuggling problems.

While we must brace for this worst case scenario, the new world order also offers a number of new policy opportunities. For instance, it increases the prospects for gaining access to key drug producing areas that have long been outside our area of influence. In this regard, we are looking forward to working with Afghanistan—the world's second largest opium producer and a major heroin source—for the first time since the late 1970s. This is a necessary first step for eventually bringing the drug trade in this country under control. The changing international political landscape could also accelerate the opening of Burma, Laos, Iran, and Lebanon, countries that have functioned as virtual drug-producing safe havens in large part because of our lack of access and oversight. Meanwhile, the East European and Central Asian states have an enforcement infrastructure that can be turned to focus on international narcotics syndicates rather than the political enemies they have historically targeted. The security forces, for instance, are trained in investigative and intelligence techniques, have the wherewithal to conduct surveillance, and know how to develop and exploit files—prerequisites to tackling the major organizations. Finally, we will be looking for narcotics control advantages flowing from the planned political and economic integration of Western Europe. Here we would hope that the removal of internal borders would promote greater sharing of intelligence and other enforcement assets across the continent, counterbalancing whatever drug control leverage will be lost owing to reduced customs controls. In addition, we would look to a united Europe to develop a more generous, consistent, and results-oriented approach to counternarcotics assistance for producing and transit countries.

Congress will continue to be a critical partner in the development and implementation of foreign counternarcotics policy. It must continue to recognize that our foreign policy efforts are an integral part of our overall strategy and are essential to achieving lasting progress against this menace. It must also legislate and appropriate in a way that allows us to operate in a dynamic environment. The Executive branch must have the flexibility to adjust to changing threats and to switch tactics when we find better ways of achieving our goals. Congress should also try to keep the level of funding commensurate with the nature of the threat. The counternarcotics community does not seek an extraordinarily large amount of money to fight the battle—the amount that was budgeted for foreign supply reduction efforts in 1992 was approximately $4 billion. In fact, the absorptive capacity of many countries—their ability to use the assistance we can provide—is a natural constraint on how much money we can pump into this effort. Our budgetary goal—and what the National Strategy has helped accomplish—is to focus our limited funds on where they can be most effective. To do this, the Executive Branch needs the support and positive involvement of Congress.

These points underscore the fact that the stakes are simply too high for us to back away from the international narcotics control challenge. To do so would have a disastrous effect on the gains we have achieved and the progress that is within our grasp. Worldwide counternarcotics efforts are at their highest plateau ever and, more important, are focused on the most critical elements of the trade—the kingpins, their finances, their major processing and transshipment centers, even their corrupt contacts in government. Such targeting dramatically underscores the courageous reversal in the commitment of some Latin American, Asian, and other leaders to fight the trade. We cannot win without their support. They cannot win without the advice and assistance they need from us to build the institutions that will ultimately defeat the trade. If we were to back away now, we would leave many of the leaders who have accepted, or are planning to accept, the narcotics control challenge dangerously exposed.

Narcotics control will remain an important foreign policy priority for the United States in the decade ahead. The Department of State and other members of the foreign policy community intend to meet the challenge by continuing to develop and implement forward leaning programs to strengthen international political, economic, and social resistance to the drug trade. With our National Strategy in place and producing results, and with the emergence, for the first time, of an international antinarcotics cartel of producer, transit, and consumer countries, the prospects for expanded progress are good. Indeed, the pursuit of these initiatives promises to make the next decade one that further reduces the international drug threat.

4

International Drug Policy and the U.S. Congress

Raphael F. Perl

The U.S. Congress has greater influence over foreign policy than its counterpart organizations in other nations. This influence extends to the formulation of international narcotics control policy, in which the Congress has chosen to take an active and often leading role. The formal international narcotics policy making role of the Congress is embodied in legislation (including appropriation of funds) and oversight. Congress exercises informal influence on the drafting and conduct of international narcotics policy through oversight and investigative hearings, consultation, informal advice, public education, and legislative prodding.

The congressional role in making foreign "narcopolicy" is notably affected by a congressional committee structure that permits numerous committees to exercise jurisdiction over narcotics-related issues. The result has been widespread congressional involvement in the making of narcotics policy and some fragmentation of such policy as congressional action compartmentalizes itself within the jurisdictional domains of committees.

The U.S. Congress has consistently expanded its role in shaping foreign policy since the early 1970's and drug policy is no exception to this trend. Congress increasingly played an active—and arguably leading—role in the foreign narcopolicy in the 1980's; continued to play a major role in international drug policy in the early 1990's; and can be expected to remain a major player in the foreign drug policy arena through the beginning of the twenty-first century.

Congressional involvement in evaluating and shaping foreign drug policy in the 1990's may be viewed in a historical context of four phases of congressional activity beginning in the 1980's. Phase I ended a few months prior to enactment of the 1986 Anti-Drug Abuse Act.[1] This phase was characterized by relatively limited congressional activity and focus. During this period, drugs were not a top priority for the Congress and no comprehensive "omnibus" legislation was enacted. Phase II began in 1986, included enactment of the 1986 Drug Act, and continued until early 1988. This period was characterized by a focus on foreign supply reduction. Sharp questioning of past policy began as it became evident that past international drug policies were not successful in stemming the flood of drugs into the United States, and the public put intense pressure on Congress to produce results.

Phase III, which began in early 1988 and ran through mid-1990, resulted in the 1988 Anti-Drug Abuse Act.[2] Congress sought to re-evaluate policy—while maintaining a drug policy leadership role—by requiring the executive branch to submit to Congress a coordinated and consolidated anti-drug strategy to serve as the basis of congressional scrutiny and oversight. During this period, the position popularly referred to as "drug czar" was created, a new national drug control strategy was promulgated by the executive branch, and the Andean Drug Initiative was begun. This period also reflects an emerging recognition of the economic and social context within which the drug trade operates. For example, the International Narcotics Control Act of 1989[3] included provisions linking economic and trade policy to international drug policy and expressed the sense of Congress that trade policy should be coordinated with narcotics control objectives.

Phase IV began after the Cartagena Drug Summit in mid-1990 and continues to be in effect in mid-1993. Phase IV is characterized by decreasing congressional and public interest in international narcotics control, but increased congressional frustration over the lack of concretely demonstrable "results" indicative of progress and success. During this period Congress passed the International Narcotics Control Act of 1992.[4] The Act established interim procedures for fiscal years 1993 and 1994 for the executive branch to ease, simplify and consolidate standards and procedures for certifying to Congress which major drug producing or transit countries are eligible to receive United States foreign assistance.

These patterns of legislative activity reflected initially limited public awareness of the seriousness of the drug problem (Phase I); heavy public pressure for immediate congressional action and solutions (Phase II); and increasing public and congressional disillusionment with executive branch policies (Phases III and IV).

Policymakers have clearly noted a decline in public perception of the ranking of the drug issue among U.S. problems. In September 1990, public alarm over the drug issue peaked with 54 percent of adults polled responding that drugs were the most important problem facing the United States. By January 1992, this figure had decreased to a mere 4 percent.[5]

This decline in public interest coincided with a period of increasing budgetary constraints on the foreign aid account and increasing public demands to spend money on the home front. Congress has responded by voicing increasing skepticism as to whether or not current international drug control initiatives are succeeding and whether, indeed, they can succeed.

Areas of major congressional concern and scrutiny during the four phases discussed above include: (1) overall soundness of strategy, (2) effectiveness of U.S. drug policy leadership, (3) adequacy of resources, (4) need for international and host nation cooperation, (5) danger of a single issue foreign policy, and (6) measurement of effectiveness. An area of enhanced congressional concern throughout the mid-1990's and beyond is likely to be the danger drug trafficking organizations pose to national security.

Congressional International Narcotics Control Role as Part of an Expanded Foreign Policy Role

The U.S. Constitution divides the foreign policy powers between the executive and legislative branches in such a way that each branch shares in the process and plays an important but usually different role.[6] The question of who makes foreign policy, however, is not clearly defined. Congress may sometimes delegate functions to the executive, and at other times claim those functions for itself. What is clear, however, is that while the executive branch executes foreign policy the two branches constantly interact and influence each other.[7]

Since the early 1970's, Congress has generally asserted and expanded its role in foreign policy. These endeavors have been based primarily on the constitutional powers to declare war, to regulate foreign commerce, and the power to make appropriations—the "power of the purse." Three noteworthy examples of such efforts include passage of (1) the War Powers Resolution, (2) amendments in 1976 to the Arms Export Control Act, and (3) amendments in 1975 to the Foreign Assistance Act. These measures contain provisions designed to assure Congress an active role in (1) the deployment of troops, (2) the sale of arms to foreign entities, and (3) the determination of human rights standards of conduct required for foreign nations to receive U.S. foreign assistance.[8]

The role of Congress in the formation of international narcotics policy cannot be viewed in a vacuum, but instead should be viewed within a general context of a domestic concern over drug abuse and an ongoing— and in recent decades accelerated—tug-of-war between the executive and legislative branch over foreign policy. Because narcotics control issues have often been hot political items, Congress inevitably has become involved in the formulation of foreign narcopolicy.

Congressional Role Shaped and Limited by Legislative Organizational Structure

The problem of international narcotics control is a multifaceted one. It may be approached as a foreign relations problem, as a family and health problem, as a public education problem, as a law enforcement problem, as a defense and national security problem, as a problem in judicial rules and practices, as an allocation of resources problem, as a regional, and/or border problem, as an agricultural and foreign trade problem,[9] as a banking problem, as an intelligence problem, as a science and research problem, and as a terrorism-connected problem.

Congress confronts national problems through a flexible system of standing committees, select committees, special caucuses, working groups and task forces. Generally, the committees jurisdictionally reflect the complex map of executive branch agencies which they fund and oversee. Currently a total of 53 House committees and subcommittees in the House and 21 in the Senate exercise jurisdiction over the many policy aspects of U.S. national drug policy.[10]

In addition, Congress draws upon a staff of foreign relations, law, science, economics, and other policy specialists at the Congressional Research Service; a budget policy staff through the Congressional Budget Office; a technical advisory staff through the Office of Technology Assessment, and a large investigative and oversight staff through the General Accounting Office, which also maintains offices overseas. Thus, in the foreign policy field, Congress has equipped itself with substantial resources beyond those generally, but not specifically, available to it from the press, universities, and the executive branch.

These offices listed in the above paragraph continually provide Congress with reports, recommendations, and information relating to international narcotics control. These reports are required to be non-partisan, balanced and objective in nature, to assure Congress the benefits of often-competing perspectives.

Many in Congress have argued that the executive branch structure for formulating and implementing international narcotics control policy is inadequate because the complex labyrinth of federal agencies with often overlapping drug related jurisdictions promotes fragmented policies. Proponents of this view have often called for reorganization of the executive branch drug policy structure under more centralized leadership—the so-called "drug czar" concept.[11]

The issue of centralization of executive-branch drug policy making raises a question whether congressional organization is adequate for a successful war on drugs. During 1993, 74 House committees and subcommittees had jurisdiction over writing or overseeing some provisions of drug control legislation.[12] As the jurisdictional responsibilities of congressional committees tend to reflect the labyrinth of federal agencies involved in international narcotics policy formulation and implementation, the argument can be made that the decentralized congressional assignment of responsibility for drug policy produces a fragmented congressional approach to the problem. On occasion, party leaders employ formal and informal means, such as the multiple referral of measures, to promote policy integration when numerous committees address the same topic. In the main, however, just as no executive branch agency has full responsibility for drug (or trade, or environmental or education, etc.) policy, no congressional committee has overall centralized responsibility for drug policy formulation and/or oversight.[13]

One option for Congress would be to consider formation of a joint committee on narcotics with key members from both Houses appointed to the Committee. A precedent for such a committee would be the Joint Committee on Atomic Energy formed in 1946 in response to legislation calling for the development of new national policies for the newly dawned atomic age. The Committee was vested with exclusive legislative jurisdiction over all aspects of the nation's developing nuclear program, both civilian and military. Thus, all bills, resolutions, or other matters relating to the development, use, or control of atomic energy were required by law to be referred to the Joint Committee. In addition, the Committee was assigned "watchdog" responsibility over the then newly created Atomic Energy Commission which was required by law to keep the Joint Committee fully and currently informed with respect to the Commission's activities. The coordinative attractions of this model are attractive. The major downside factor is that drug trafficking control is an enterprise with few similarities to Atomic Energy production and technology control where the U.S. Government had a near monopoly.

Another congressional option might be to create one permanent narcotics committee with broad jurisdictional responsibilities in each House of Congress. For instance, a select committee on narcotics (modeled after each chamber's intelligence panels) with legislative authority might be established in both the House and Senate. Such an option, however, clearly implies transfer of legislative jurisdiction from several powerful standing committees—a prospect that bodes ill for centralization of congressional narcopolicy.

The Congressional Role in
International Narcotics Control Legislation

The role of Congress in shaping international narcotics policy can be divided into two major components. One is legislation; the other oversight. Congress may initiate new foreign narcopolicy by using legislation to establish new programs, to condition and limit spending, to set new objectives and guidelines, and to authorize and direct the executive branch to undertake specified activities. Most noteworthy of such legislative initiatives are the international narcotics control provisions of the Anti-Drug Abuse Acts of 1986 and 1988, as amended by the International Narcotics Control Act of 1992, which relate to the imposition of sanctions against uncooperative major illicit drug producing and/or transit countries.[14] These provisions represent a major reversal of policy roles previously played by the Congress and the President in the decision to deny assistance to certain drug producing or drug transit countries. Under previous legislation, the initiative to make the initial determination that certain countries would not be eligible for foreign assistance rested with the President. Under the new laws, Congress has taken that initiative and made the determination that certain categories of countries will not receive aid, while the President's role has been reduced to enforcing the terms of, or seeking exceptions to, this congressional determination.[15]

The Anti-Drug Abuse Acts of 1986 and 1988, as modified by the 1992 International Narcotics Control Act, link cooperation on international narcotics control issues by major illicit drug producing or transit countries with their eligibility for U.S. foreign aid, and under certain circumstances, U.S. trade benefits.[16] This process, commonly referred to as "certification," requires the President to withhold 50 percent of U.S. foreign assistance at the start of each fiscal year (October 1) pending a determination of certification on, or after, March 1.

On the first day of March each year, the President sends to the Congress a list of major illicit drug producing and/or transit countries he certifies as eligible to receive full U.S. assistance. Congress then has 45 days of continuous session to evaluate the President's determinations of certification, and to enact country specific resolutions of disapproval, should it so choose.[17]

A determination of certification may be justified on grounds: that U.S. "national interest" precludes imposition of sanctions and that, therefore, aid should be disbursed. However, other criteria which are indicative of differing levels of narcotics control cooperation with the United States generally form the basis for a presidential determination of certification. The law provides for a "more generic" standard of narcotics cooperation to be applied by the President for fiscal years 1993 and 1994 and then reverts to more specific criteria which allow a president less flexibility in justifying determinations of certification to Congress.

The standard applied for certification of major illicit drug producing or transit countries for fiscal years 1993 and 1994 requires that "the country has cooperated fully with the United States, or has taken adequate steps on its own, to achieve full compliance with the goals and objectives established by the United Nations Convention Against Illicit Traffic in Narcotic Drugs and Psychotropic Substances." For subsequent years, full "cooperation" and "adequate" steps are not linked to the broad generic goals of the UN Anti-Drug Trafficking Convention, but rather to more specific criteria indicative of law enforcement cooperation. Thus, for 1995 and subsequent fiscal years (absent changes in the law) countries must cooperate fully or take adequate steps on their own: (1) in satisfying goals agreed to in a bi-lateral narcotics agreement; (2) in preventing illicit drugs from being sold in the United States, transported to the United States, or sold to U.S. Government personnel or their dependents; (3) in preventing and punishing drug-related money laundering; and (4) in preventing and punishing drug-related bribery and public corruption.[18]

If a President does not issue a determination of certification for a major drug producing or transit country, or if the Congress disapproves his determination for a specific country, some sanctions must be imposed. The President is required to withhold 50 percent of U.S. assistance allocated each fiscal year to the non-certified country. Moreover, the President is also required to instruct the U.S. Executive Director of each multilateral development bank to vote against loans or other use of bank funds by the non-certified country.

To date, Congress has not decertified any country certified by the President as eligible to receive foreign assistance under the above provisions. However, a resolution to decertify Panama was passed in 1987 and one to decertify Mexico passed in 1988.[19] Also, in 1988, the Senate passed a resolution to place Haiti on the list of major illicit drug producing and/or trafficking countries, thereby making Haiti subject to certification requirements.[20]

Congressional Role in International Narcotics Control Oversight

Congress not only passes laws and funds programs, but also attempts to ensure that they are properly implemented. Congress monitors and influences foreign narcopolicy by regular oversight of executive branch implementation of international narcotics control policy. Important mechanisms for exercising this oversight function are hearings and investigations. These frequently result in published hearing transcripts and reports. The number of published congressional hearings, reports and documents related to international narcotics control issues has seen dramatic increases and declines over the past ten years. According to a computerized data bank maintained by the General Accounting Office, 20 such items were published by the Congress in 1979, and 46 were published in 1987, but just 25 in the first ten months of 1992.

Central roles in congressional oversight of international narcotics control policy are played by the Senate Foreign Relations Committee and the House Foreign Affairs Committee. These two committees oversee the Department of State and other foreign affairs agencies. In addition, the House Select Committee on Narcotics Abuse and Control, the Senate Caucus on International Narcotics Control, and the House and Senate Appropriations Committees regularly oversee U.S. international narcotics policy.

A representative sampling of congressional hearings from the Second Session of the 100th Congress on international narcotics control and related issues reveals a primary focus on gathering factual data, although emphasis on strategy is also present.[21] Hearings in the 102nd Congress tended to be more strategy oriented.[22]

Hearings offer both the Administration and committees the opportunity to make their viewpoints known and to hear recognized authorities outside their respective organizations. They also afford committees the opportunity to submit in-depth written follow-up questions. Hearings may also serve to function as the congressional equivalent of an executive branch press conference, drawing the public's attention to ineffective executive branch policies and marshalling public support for proposed legislative reform and/or changes in administration policy.

In addition to hearings, regularly used congressional oversight mechanisms include notification requirements and reporting requirements. Notification requirements require an executive official (usually the President) to report to Congress upon the occurrence of a specified event. Reporting requirements usually require the submission to Congress of specific information within the framework of a formal report. Reports may be *one-time* reports, or *periodic* reports. Research performed by the Congressional Research Service of the Library of Congress in March 1986 identified 19 reporting/notification requirements relating to international narcotics control issues. Similar research in September 1988 revealed that the number of such requirements in law had risen from 19 to 34, an increase of almost 79 percent in only 2 1/2 years. By September 1992, this number had reached 44.[23]

Key notification requirements in the area of international narcotics control are those relating to the certification process, i.e., determining which major illicit drug producing or transit countries should be exempt from congressionally mandated sanctions.[24] The law, by requiring that Congress be given the President's list of exempt countries (and the reason for their exemption) before such exemptions become effective, affords Congress the opportunity to monitor and explore the basis and rationale of a president's certification determinations.

The central periodic reporting oversight requirement in international narcotics control requires annual submission (on March 1) by the Department of State to the Congress of its International Narcotics Control Strategy Report (INCSR). This report is critical in the certification process, as the President will normally base his determinations of certification on the information contained therein. The INCSR and its September Mid-Year Update[25] are prepared by the Department of State's Bureau of International Narcotics Matters and are the most widely read and useful reports provided by the Administration on international narcotics control. Information required by additional periodic reports is often included in the INCSR.

An example of an oversight report requirement triggered by a specified event is one stating that records on use of aircraft provided to a foreign country for narcotics control pursuant to the international provisions of the Anti-Drug Abuse Act of 1986 be made available to Congress upon request.[26] An example of a one-time oversight report requirement is a provision of a 1986 law mandating that the Secretary of State shall report to the Congress by February 8, 1986, on the advisability of encouraging the establishment of a Latin American Regional Narcotics Organization. This report was received by the Congress on July 30, 1986.[27]

Records maintained by the Congressional Research Service indicate that in October 1992, a total of 44 reporting and notification requirements in the area of international narcotics control assisted the Congress in varying degrees in the performance of its oversight functions.[28] These requirements may serve as a trigger for congressional action such as the requirement giving Congress 45 days to override a presidential determination of certification after receiving notification of such determination from the President. It is worth noting that such reporting requirements often serve as compromises between those in Congress who would prohibit the President from undertaking certain activities (such as granting any assistance to certain illicit drug producing or transit countries) and those in Congress who would support leaving the President a free hand in such determinations. Finally, by requiring submission of a study (such as the INCSR) and data which might not otherwise be available, Congress can influence the policy of the executive branch, and sometimes that of other nations by sensitizing public officials to areas of congressional concern.

Congressional Role as an Informal Role

Members of Congress often influence international narcotics control policy by providing advice to both the executive branch and representatives of foreign governments through informal contacts. Informal contacts with foreign officials are facilitated by congressional participation in such groups as the Interparliamentary Union, the European Parliament, the Canada-U.S. Interparliamentary Group, the Andean Parliament, Mexico–United States Interparliamentary Conferences, and by visits of congressional delegations to countries considered by the United States to be major illicit drug producing or transit nations.

The certification process also facilitates the exercise of such informal channels of influence. Such activity swings into high gear shortly before March 1 of each year (the release date of the State Department's International Narcotics Control Strategy Report, and the President's determinations of certification for major illicit drug producing and transit countries). During this period, Department of State officials carefully assess the sense of the Congress on the issue of Presidential certification of specific countries and attempt to reach informal agreement on countries to be granted or denied certification and on the justification to be cited for such determinations.

Issues of Congressional Concern

Congress has demonstrated ongoing concern over six aspects of U.S. international narcotics control policy. These issues involve: (1) overall soundness of strategy, (2) effectiveness of U.S. drug policy leadership, (3) adequacy of resources, (4) need for international and host nation cooperation, (5) danger of a single issue foreign policy, and (6) measurement of effectiveness. Focus on these issues is likely to intensify in the mid- and late 1990's as is focus on a seventh issue, the rise of drug trafficking as a national security threat.

Soundness of Strategy

Interdiction/law enforcement activity and economic diversification are cornerstones of current international narcotics control strategy. Such policies aim at reducing the supply of drugs to the U.S. market and account for approximately 30 percent of the $12.7 billion federal anti-drug control budget for fiscal year 1993. Proponents of such policies point to massive seizures of drugs, traffickers and money and maintain that providing economic alternatives to growers, and raising risks and costs to refiners, traffickers, and consumers will reduce the supply and use of illicit drugs in the U.S. marketplace.

Critics, on the other hand, see drug production as expanding, and see interdiction as costly and able to seize only a small percentage of illicit drugs entering the United States. They suggest that assuming a best case scenario, one in which illicit drug supplies to the United States were severely curtailed, users would simply pay more for their drugs or switch to synthetic or U.S.-grown substitutes. For such analysts, interdiction is seen as useful only to stabilize the flow of illicit drugs to the United States in order to buy time to implement domestic prevention and treatment programs.

Current U.S. international narcotics control policy is thus based on two basic assumptions: (1) it is possible to reduce the illicit supply of drugs to the United States; and (2) such reductions will favorably impact on illicit drug use in the United States. Individual Members of Congress and some influential congressional staff question the validity of both these assumptions and whether it is effective to allocate the lion's share of Federal antidrug funding to support programs aimed at reducing illicit drug supplies.[29]

Effectiveness of U.S. Drug Policy Leadership

Coordination and centralization of U.S. international drug policy has been—and will be—an ongoing area of concern for Congress. Since passage of the 1988 Anti-Drug Abuse Act, congressional attention has regularly focused on the effectiveness of the "drug czar's" office and whether it has sufficient authority to ensure effective implementation of its policies, programs, and priorities.

This controversy remains very much alive with critics repeatedly charging that the drug war in effect does not have a leader and cannot have a leader as the office of National Drug Control Policy was designed primarily as a policy coordinating body without actual command authority. Some go so far as to suggest that Congress should severely curtail funding for—or abolish—the office.

Supporters of the drug czar concept, on the other hand, maintain that the office has used its limited authority effectively: a national drug control strategy has been formulated; a diverse federal bureaucracy is on board to implement it; and resources have been more effectively employed to achieve desired results. Supporters of the drug czar office concept staunchly maintain that if even more is to be expected from the office, Congress should increase its authority and operating budget.

The White House, in February 1993, announced that it was: (1) substantially reducing the size of the drug czar's office, and (2) raising the status of its director to a cabinet level position. The overall effectiveness of such changes and whether the office in charge of national drug control policy will have sufficient authority to ensure desired implementation of its policies, programs and priorities will remain an issue of ongoing congressional concern.

Adequacy of Resources

Various sources suggest that the illicit drug trade generates, worldwide, in excess of $300 billion per year in gross total receipts to criminal organizations engaged in the trade. Given the scale of "enemy" resources, are U.S. counter-drug expenditures of under $15 billion per year sufficient to wage effective "battle"? A question regularly raised in Congress is: given this large discrepancy in available resources, would another billion dollars—or another 10 billion dollars—make a difference?

Demands on Congress to fund domestic programs and growing demands on the U.S. foreign aid program to revitalize the former Soviet Union and Eastern Europe, fund peacekeeping and humanitarian assistance operations, and respond to other emerging international threats will be taken into account by lawmakers when asked to fund international narcotics control programs.

Need for International and Host Nation Cooperation

U.S. foreign drug policy cannot be pursued in a vacuum. Essentially all elements of U.S. international narcotics control policy require international cooperation. U.S. strategy often assumes willing partners, but foreign nations are often willing to cooperate (if at all) in differing degrees for differing reasons. The degree to which foreign nations—particularly major illicit drug producing or transit countries—cooperate with the United States on narcotic control issues is a major foreign aid determinant factor for Congress. And increasingly individual Members of Congress would like to see more counter-drug cost burdensharing arrangements with other industrialized nations.

Danger of a Single-Issue Foreign Policy

Another area of concern for Congress is the degree to which concentration on drug related measures compromises other fundamental foreign policy goals such as stability, democracy, respect for human rights, the environment, and overcoming poverty. A particular concern has been that programs promoting host nation military involvement in counter-drug operations may promote policies that strengthen the power of the military at the expense of often fragile civilian democratic institutions.

Further, providing counter-narcotics training to law enforcement and military agencies in countries such as Peru is seen by many in Congress as problematic as such agencies often have dismal histories of human rights violations. Congress, in the International Narcotics Control Act of 1992,[30] exempted narcotics-related military assistance for fiscal years 1993 and 1994 from the provisions of the Foreign Assistance Act which prohibit military assistance to civilian law enforcement agencies. Programs providing such assistance, however, will be subject to enhanced congressional oversight as long as they are maintained.

Measurement of Effectiveness

A key concern for Congress is whether U.S. international drug policy is able to produce evidence demonstrating success. In times of severe budgetary constraints, Congress finds itself increasingly pressed to show results for programs and policies it has been funding over the last decade. Absent is a dramatic decease in worldwide production of illicit drugs, or a sustained decrease in U.S. domestic consumption; success is difficult to conceptualize. The other alternative, to measure success in terms of the consequences of no programs, reduced programs, or enhanced or modified international narcotics control programs, proves even more problematic.

Drug Trafficking as a National Security Threat

A final issue of increasing concern to Congress is the danger the international drug trade poses to international stability and U.S. national security interests. As the Soviet empire collapses and colonially established nations attempt to redefine themselves geographically with borders to accommodate indigenous ethnic groups, what is often a loss of centralized control provides fertile ground for massive breakdowns in law and order. A virulent growth of criminal organizations engaged in the illicit drug trade can easily follow, especially if financed from without. Increasingly, such organizations are of a scale and capability to threaten the national security of nations where they operate and subvert emerging democratic institutions. Moreover, opportunities for active expansion of their smuggling activities into the national security sensitive areas such as weapons proliferation remain virtually unlimited. A related problem arises as members of ruling elites use state protected channels to facilitate drug trafficking activities. The emergence of such "narcocracies" and the rising national security threat posed by them and growing criminal organizations engaged in the drug trade is likely to be the subject of extensive congressional interest in the coming decade.

Notes

1. The Anti-Drug Abuse Act of 1986 (P.L. 99-570) set the stage for congressional involvement in foreign anti-drug policy in the later 1980's and the 1990's. Prior to enactment of the 1986 Act, the President was charged with the responsibility of determining whether a major illicit drug transit or drug producing country should be denied foreign aid for lack of cooperation on narcotics issues.

The 1986 Anti-Drug Abuse Act, however, represented a major policy shift which assured Congress an active role in international narcotics policy. In the 1986 Act, Congress amended Section 481 of the Foreign Assistance and added new sections to the Trade Act of 1974 (P.L. 93-618) whereby *Congress* determined that aid would be suspended to all major illicit producing and transit countries and not restored unless the President made an exception, by "certifying" a country. The 1986 Act further gave Congress the right to override presidential determinations by joint resolution, in a process similar to the congressional role in disapproving major foreign arms sales.

These new provisions reversed the roles previously played by Congress and the President in the denial of assistance to certain drug producing or drug transit countries. Under previous legislation, the initiative rested with the President to make the initial determination that certain countries would not be eligible for foreign assistance. Under the 1986 law, Congress was to make the determination that certain categories of countries would not receive aid, reducing the President's role to enforcing the terms of, or seeking exceptions to, this congressional determination.

2. Anti-Drug Abuse Act of 1988, P.L. 100-690.
3. P.L. 101-231.
4. P.L. 102-583.
5. *New York Times* and CBS News nationwide survey, *New York Times*, July 28, 1992, p. A12.
6. Congress has the power to raise and support armies, provide and maintain a navy, declare war, lay and collect taxes and duties, pay debts, regulate foreign trade, to make all necessary and proper laws, and to make appropriations. See: U.S. Constitution, art. I, sec. 8. The President is Chief Executive and Commander in Chief of the Army and Navy and has the power to receive ambassadors and other public ministers. See: U.S. Constitution, art. II, sec. 1. Treaties and appointments of ambassadors and other public ministers are made by the President with the advice and consent of the Senate.
7. U.S. Library of Congress, Congressional Research Service, "Foreign Policy Roles of the President and the Congress." Report No. 93-20F (by) Ellen Collier. Washington, D.C. January 6, 1993. See also, Thomas M. Frank, and Edward Weisband, *Foreign Policy by Congress*, New York, Oxford University Press, 1979.
8. In 1973, Congress passed the War Powers Resolution which gives Congress a decision making role in the deployment of U.S. troops into hostilities by requiring consultation with Congress prior to deployment and by requiring congressional authorization for the ongoing deployment of forces after 60 to 90

days. (See P.L. 93-148, November 7, 1973.) Amendments to the Arms Export Control Act passed in 1976, gave Congress the power to prohibit an arms sale by passage of a joint resolution. [See sec. 36(c) of the Arms Export Control Act, P.L. 90-629 (82 Stat. 1320) as amended by sec. 211(a) of P.L. 94-329 (90 Stat. 740).] In addition Congress, since the mid-1970's has consistently used the power of the purse to set conditions on the disbursement of foreign aid, particularly to countries which engage in a consistent pattern of gross violations of internationally recognized human rights. See sec. 116 of the Foreign Assistance Act of 1961, P.L. 87-195 (75 Stat. 424) as amended by sec. 310 of P.L. 94-161 (89 Stat. 849), December 20, 1975.

9. Note that according to a 1988 study by the Congressional Research Service, narcotics products comprised more than half the value of our nation's agricultural imports.

10. See: U.S. Library of Congress, Congressional Research Service, "House and Senate Standing Committees and Subcommittees with Jurisdiction over National Drug Abuse Policy" (by) Carol Hardy, Washington, D.C., September 27, 1988. Report No. 88-634 GOV.

Important standing committees involved in international narcotics control issues include the Senate Foreign Relations Committee (and its Subcommittee on Terrorism, Narcotics, and International Operations), the House Foreign Affairs Committee (and its Task Force on International Narcotics Control), the Armed Services Committees, the House Ways and Means Committee, the Appropriations Committees, the Banking Committees, the Government Operations Committees, the Judiciary Committees, the Merchant Marine and Fisheries Committees, and the Agriculture Committees.

Major select Committees involved in international narcotics control issues include the Select Intelligence Committees. The Select Committee on Narcotics Abuse and Control was abolished in spring of 1993 in an effort to reduce the number of committees and subcommittees and overall costs of Congress. The Senate Caucus on International Narcotics Control, modeled after the Helsinki Commission, functions in many aspects as the Senate equivalent of the former House Select Committee on Narcotics Abuse and Control by holding hearings, issuing reports, enhancing public awareness and consensus building. Informal congressional groups, also actively involved in international narcotics control issues include the Senate and Congressional (House) Border Caucuses, the Senate Drug Enforcement Caucus, and the bicameral Congressional Crime Caucus.

11. See 100th Congress, 2d. Session, National Narcotics Leadership Act of 1987, S. 789 (Biden)/H.R. 2454 (Rangel/Gilman, Rodino). Modified provisions of the act were passed by the House as an amendment to the proposed Omnibus Drug Initiative Act of 1988 (H.R. 5210).

Congress, in the Anti-Drug Abuse Act of 1988, took a cut at addressing these concerns. The Act abolished the National Drug Policy Board and established an Office of National Drug Policy in the Executive Office of the President, headed by a cabinet-level Director of National Drug Control Policy, subject to confirmation by the Senate. The "drug czar" position, as enacted, was a compromise between those who favored creation of a position with strong centralized authority and those who favored a more loosely structured coordinating structure. The Director was to serve as the principal adviser to the National Security Council on drug control policy and attend and participate in meetings of the Council. Among the responsibilities of the Director are: (1) establishing policies, objectives, and priorities for the national drug control program; (2) promulgating annually a national drug control strategy; (3) coordinating and overseeing implementation of agency policies, objectives, and priorities; and (4) developing (with advice from individual agencies) a consolidated national drug control program budget proposal. In addition, individual agencies are required to provide the Director with the information needed for drug control.

12. Supra, note 10.

13. William J. Bennett was confirmed by the Senate for the first "drug czar" position on March 10, 1989.

14. Title II of P.L. 99–570, 100 Stat. 3207, sec. 2005 which amends section 481(h) of the Foreign Assistance Act of 1961, and sec. 2013 of P.L. 99–570 which *sub silentio* establishes special certification requirements for Mexico. These provisions were repeated and/or modified by the International Narcotics Control Act of 1992, P.L. 102–583, Section 6 of which repealed all sections of the 1986 Act except sections 2001, 2010, 2018 and 2029 and repealed all sections of the 1998 Act except sections 4001, 4306, 4308, 4309, 4501, 4702 and 4804. See also, Title IX which adds secs. 802 through 805 to the Trade Act of 1974. The latter provisions include discretionary trade and aviation sanctions against uncooperative major illicit trafficking and/or transit countries. See also Title IV, secs. 4407 and 4408 of the Anti-Drug Abuse Act of 1988 which were repealed by the 1992 International Narcotics Control Act.

15. For the text of Section 481(h) of the Foreign Assistance Act of 1961 prior to its amendment by P.L. 99–570, see U.S. Congress, Committee on Foreign Affairs, Committee of Foreign Relations, *Legislation on Foreign Relations through 1985*, edited by Raphael F. Perl. April 1986. Vol. I. pp. 110–111.

16. Note that some trade sanctions are automatically imposed pursuant to sections 802–805 of the Trade Act of 1974 (P.L. 93–618 as amended) if a major illicit drug producing or drug transit country is not certified under the Act, denial of a major quota is required. Discretionary sanctions include: (1) Denial of preferential tariff treatment to a country's exports under the Generalized System of Preferences (GSP) and the Caribbean Basin Economic Recovery Act; (2) Duty increases of up to 50 percent of value on a country's exports to the United States; (3) Curtailment of air transportation and traffic between the United States and the non-certified country; and (4) Withdrawal of U.S. participation in any pre-clearance customs arrangements with the non-certified country.

17. The International Narcotics Control Act of 1992, P.L. 102–583, reduces the 45 days of continuous session period to 45 calendar days.

18. The International Narcotics Control Act of 1992, P.L. 102–583, Sec. 5(a) which adds sections 490 and 490A to the Foreign Assistance Act of 1961.

19. See: 100th Congress, 1st session, S.J. Res. 91 and S.J. Res. 268 respectively.

20. 100th Congress, 2d Session, S.J. Res. 285. The issue of whether to require certification of Haiti points out a previous arguable shortcoming in the language of the law which did not clearly define (or require the executive branch to establish guidelines defining) a "major illicit drug transit country" in terms of the quantities of drugs which must transit a country for it to be thus classified. In addition, "transit" is not clearly defined. For example, if the destination of the drugs transiting a country were ultimately Europe or Cuba, and not the United States, should the country be placed on the list requiring certification?

21. Some representative titles from the second session of the 100th Congress include: (1) U.S. Foreign Policy and International Narcotics Control, U.S. Congress, House Select Committee on Narcotics Abuse and Control (two printed parts), March 16 and March 29, 1988, SNAC No. 100-2-2 and 100-2-3, (2) Worldwide Narcotics Review of the 1988 International Narcotics Control Strategy Report, U.S. Congress, Committee of Foreign Affairs, March 3, 1988, (3) Narcotics Review in South America, U.S. Congress Committee on Foreign Relations, March 17 and March 27, 1988, (4) Recent Developments in Colombia, U.S. Congress Committee on Foreign Relations, January 27, 1988, (5) Drugs and Money Laundering in Panama, U.S. Senate, Committee on Governmental Affairs, Permanent Subcommittee on Investigations, January 28, 1988, (6) Narcotics Review in Central America, U.S. Congress, House Committee on Foreign Affairs, March 10, 1988, (7) Bahamas and Puerto Rico Drug Interdiction Activities, U.S. Congress, Senate Committee on Appropriations, Special Hearing, Fiscal year 1989, S. HRG 100-693, (8) Narcotics Review in the Caribbean, U.S. Congress, House Committee on Foreign Affairs, March 9, 1988, and (9) Narcotics Review in Southeast/Southwest Asia, The Middle East and Africa, U.S. Congress House Committee on Foreign Affairs, March 15, 1988.

22. Examples from the 102nd Congress include: (1) Review of the Second Year of the National Drug Control Strategy, U.S. Senate, Committee on the Judiciary, September 6, 1991, S. HRG. 102-650, (2) Andean Drug Initiative, U.S. Senate, Committee on Foreign Relations, Subcommittee on Terrorism, Narcotics, and International Operations, February 20, 1992, S. HRG. 102-657, (3) Review of the 1992 International Narcotics Control Strategy Report, U.S. Congress, Committee on Foreign Affairs, Subcommittee on Western Hemisphere Affairs, March 3, 4, 11, and 12, 1992, and (4) The San Antonio Summit and the Andean Strategy. U.S. Congress, House Select Committee on Narcotics Abuse and Control, March 26, 1992, SCNAC-102-2-4.

23. For a discussion of Reporting Requirements, see also: U.S. Congress, House Committee on Foreign Affairs, Review of the President's Narcotics Control Legislative Request: Should Certification be repealed?, testimony of Honorable Melvyn Levitsky, May 2, 1992.

24. See P.L. 102-583, Section 5, which adds Sections 489 and 490A to the Foreign Assistance Act of 1961 in lieu of major substantive provisions of Section 481.

25. Note that the mid-year update requirement was suspended for fiscal years 1993 and 1994 and the reporting requirements for inclusion in the an-

nual report were modified for those years to simplify compilation of the annual report by the Department of State. See: P.L. 102–583, Section 5.

26. Section 485 of the Foreign Assistance Act of 1961.

27. See P.L. 99–83, sec. 615(b).

28. See also testimony of Honorable Melvyn Levitsky, supra, note 23.

29. See, for example, the House Appropriations Committee Report on the 1993 Foreign Operations Appropriations Bill, Report 102–585, 102D Congress 2d Session, Section on International Narcotics Control/Drug War.

30. P.L. 102–583, Sec. 7.

5

The Role of Law Enforcement

David L. Westrate

In the short span of two decades, the United States has experienced a serious deterioration of many of our most fundamental institutions and today we struggle to recover lost ground as a nation. The quality of our educational system has degenerated by most accounts. Our ability to compete in the international market place hit an all-time low and as we move into the 1990s we hear cries for protectionism and even isolationism.

During the 1980s and 1990s, the cocaine epidemic has raged through an uninformed middle and upper class. Crack cocaine emerged as the poor man's variety that has devastated the less fortunate, particularly of our inner cities.

In 1991, many U.S. cities set new records for murder. The nation's capitol is ravaged with fear and violence, with its former mayor sentenced to prison for cocaine abuse. Many believe that we have lost a generation of young males in the inner cities. Those who must solve these problems find that they have few viable options, and worse, diminished resources due to current economic conditions.

In September of 1975, the Domestic Council Drug Abuse Task Force submitted a white paper on drug abuse to President Ford. In this paper, cocaine was given a low rating for dependence liability, severity of personal consequence, size of the core problem, and a medium rating for social consequences. Concern for cocaine abuse was diminished even further in the Carter Administration, which is reflected in the historical record.

No one could possibly have known how wrong we were as we charged headlong into the 1980s flush with prosperity as a nation. Many citizens believed cocaine to be a harmless recreational substance. Efforts to decriminalize marijuana use in the 1970s were partially successful, and many in drug law enforcement believed that the decriminalization or legalization of cocaine was virtually inevitable. Life was fast, hopes high, and drug use was often glamorized in the media.

Some grudging progress is being made through prevention and education. The 1991 National Household Survey on Drug Abuse concluded that "current (in the past 30 days) illicit drug use among youth (12 to 17 years old) declined by more than half between 1985 and 1991, dropping from 14.9 percent to 6.8 percent." While there is hope on the horizon, those of us who confront this issue every day know how much more difficult it will be to project this progress into the inner city where the ingredients for prosperity do not exist. Today's reality is: the deterioration of the family structure; weapon detection systems in our schools; a high-school dropout rate of 12 percent; no jobs; no hope of jobs; and cities on the verge of bankruptcy. Many believe that our cities are on an inevitable path toward serious urban disorder, as our police forces struggle to re-establish their image in their communities. We must not underestimate the seriousness of this situation nor overestimate the progress that has been made or can be made. All of these and other familiar problems of American cities today are, in part, the end result of our inability to control the supply of illegal drugs or the demand for them. How ironic it is that those who advocated a tolerant approach to drug use must now realize that this tolerance most devastated those segments of our society that they have sought most to support. It is hoped that there are very few who do not understand the cruel reality of drug addiction and trafficking in the United States and the potential for the same experience in other nations.

It is unlikely that the framers of our Constitution would have expected the President of the United States to address the nation's "drug addiction" problem in his report to the people. Yet, on January 20, 1989, President Bush stated in his inaugural address: "This scourge will stop."

We can achieve his goal if we are realistic and relentless in addressing the source of illegal drugs, the demand for them, and perhaps, most importantly, the root causes of despair and addiction. Drug law enforcement plays a very important role in the effort. This is especially true in the international environment, the source of most of the drug types causing the majority of our problems. This chapter will highlight the progress we have made in international drug law enforcement and what the future may hold.

Establishing the Infrastructure and the Political Will to Act

The impact of cocaine in the past decade has pushed the drug issue to the highest levels of international policy and diplomacy. For the first time in history, the presidents of the United States, Bolivia, Colombia, and Peru met at Cartagena, Colombia, in February of 1990 exclusively on the drug crisis. A second meeting was held in February of 1992 at San Antonio, Texas, and seven nations' presidents participated.

In the 1990s we will continue to see the devastation of cocaine abuse migrate to Europe and the Pacific. The impact will most likely be felt in countries considered to be our closest allies in Western Europe, Japan, and Australia. Free societies, open borders, and populations with expendable incomes leave these countries most at risk.

A rising heroin trade will impact heavily on countries such as China, who are vulnerable to the traditional attack of this drug. The drug issue therefore will be on the world's political and diplomatic agenda into the twenty-first century.

By itself, drug law enforcement cannot be expected to solve the problem worldwide. It must be complemented by strong diplomatic initiatives, viable economic alternatives for drug-growing peasants, effective criminal justice systems in key countries, and expanded use of relatively new approaches, such as removing the profit of drug trafficking and controlling precursor and essential chemicals.

Drug law enforcement efforts will never be successful if constrained by national borders. To be successful, we must be able to mount a multinational attack on trafficking organizations in every nation in which they operate. There can be no safe haven for drug profits and no protection due to drug-related corruption. Experience has taught us a hard lesson—that real progress is not made until the political leadership of a nation perceives the threat of drugs to be real and of significant magnitude to warrant action when weighed against the other national and international interests of that country. This has been observed in developed and nondeveloped nations as well.

The ultimate objective of the United States drug law enforcement effort has been to create a worldwide capability and willingness to attack drug trafficking organizations with a system that is transparent to national borders. This effort must have available to it the most up-to-date laws and law enforcement techniques. Our progress toward this objective became clear to Jose Gonzolo Rodriguez-Gacha, a principal leader of the Medellín Cartel. Throughout the 1980s, he and his associates amassed hundreds of millions of cocaine dollars and protected the business with intimidation and killing of scores of Colombians. The victims included Colombian officials, judges, journalists, and, of course, presidential candidate, Louis Carlos Galan.

An intense law enforcement campaign was launched against Rodriguez-Gacha, which featured attacks against his financial empire. Action was taken in Luxembourg, United Kingdom, Switzerland, Austria, United States, Hong Kong, Panama, and Colombia. He could no longer trust his people and he developed a cash flow problem. As a result, he was forced to leave his protected area to personally direct a 600-kilo shipment. The Colombian National Police killed him and his son in a gun fight at the location of this shipment in December of 1989. In all, over $100 million was seized in these eight countries. Many of these law enforcement actions against his assets were accomplished on time-critical initial requests between law enforcement officials in these countries which have developed a working relationship strong enough to allow such informal action.

The lesson from the Rodriguez-Gacha case is that the international enforcement effort can work even when it involves a country like Colombia where these powerful figures enjoy such a high profile. There is in fact an ultimate breaking point in every country. The Rodriguez-Gacha case and hundreds like it did not just happen. Decades of institution building and working together have resulted in our ability to do the job internationally. The first United States drug law enforcement agents were dispatched to Paris, Rome, and Beirut in 1936. They were agents of the Federal Bureau of Narcotics of the U.S. Treasury Department. Their purpose was to extend the ability of our agents to pursue the criminal organizations to the ultimate source. For years, these attaches and others worked quietly from the back rooms of our embassies and consulates. Their mission and purpose, while important, was not on the diplomatic agenda.

Through training and case making, these agents began to build a worldwide network of expertise in drug law enforcement, which functions very well today. The Drug Enforcement Administration (DEA) now has attaches assigned in 50 nations. Almost 10 percent of DEA's total agent work force is assigned abroad.

Drug Liaison Officers (DLOs), foreign-counterpart equivalents of DEA country attaches, are now based in the United States and elsewhere. Eight DLOs from five nations—Australia, Canada, France, Germany, the United Kingdom—are assigned to their embassies in Washington, D.C. The same five nations, plus Italy, have twelve DLOs assigned to other cities in the United States—Honolulu, Los Angeles, Miami, and New York.

In Bangkok, the DLO presence is institutionalized in the Foreign Anti-Narcotics Community (FANC) organization, which seeks to coordinate the multinational effort there. DLOs from drug law enforcement agencies of 14 nations, plus the International Criminal Police Organization (INTERPOL) are assigned in Bangkok and participate in the FANC group.

Further deployment of attaches is now being realized in Latin America and Europe by countries other than the United States. Obviously, the deployment of these law enforcement officers is considered significant by each nation and the host country to their mutual investigative needs.

The objective of the deployment of DEA personnel overseas is based primarily on extending our effective reach beyond the limits of our borders. Any observer of illegal drug supply reduction efforts must conclude that supply reduction cannot be achieved only at home. To have true impact on the imported illicit drug supplies requires a global attack on the organizations, including the supporting infrastructures of finances, transportation, raw materials, chemicals, and corruption.

This comprehensive approach, however, is becoming a reality only in recent years. Many of the required actions are not controlled by law enforcement elements, especially within its traditional role.

Law enforcement agencies have expanded their role into nontraditional areas and perhaps most importantly have become a source of influence for change in terms of new legislation, new techniques, and more open sharing of intelligence. Law enforcement has also been one of the most important sources of information on the seriousness of the drug problem which is forcing an attitude change worldwide, particularly at the policy and political levels.

The deployment of DEA agents to 50 nations has not only extended our parochial investigative reach, but it has also created an informal network between these specific nations and others served by these DEA attaches. DEA, with its communications network and data base, has connected all of these national narcotics suppression authorities together. In effect, we have created a global narcotics investigative force. DEA's computerized data base of narcotics violators contains about three million records as of 1992—a third of which are not U.S. citizens. This system, known as the Narcotics and Dangerous Drugs Information System (NADDIS) is twenty years old and, because of the DEA's interaction with other nations, it represents a comprehensive base of trafficker information worldwide. As of this writing, DEA also has extensive interaction with China, the former Soviet Union, and other significant nations where we are not permanently represented. All of these cooperating nations benefit from this data through DEA offices, and DEA serves, in many cases, as the point of exchange of information and coordination between countries which have not developed the ability to interface on investigations between themselves. This unique structure is working extremely well considering the variations in laws, politics, economic strength, and political will reflected by those participating.

There is a unique and critical bond which holds this international drug law enforcement coalition together. It is nurtured by law enforcement professionals who work together in an area of specialization which is dangerous, intriguing, frustrating, and challenging. To be successful, the international team must, first, trust in one another and, second, have the tools to do the job. Trust has been built through training and working together every day on investigations year-in and year-out.

DEA predecessor agencies began a formal international law enforcement training program in the 1960s. Since that time, this effort has resulted in training over 35,000 students worldwide. The training effort is coordinated with the Bureau of International Narcotics Matters (INM) of the U.S. Department of State. INM also has provided the majority of the funding for these efforts over the years. The specific objectives of DEA's International Training Program are to upgrade drug law enforcement capabilities of foreign counterparts; to encourage and assist key countries in developing self-sufficient drug investigative training programs; to provide foreign officials with the motivation, as well as the necessary skills and knowledge required to initiate high level drug investigations; and to increase cooperation and communication between foreign police and DEA personnel and among foreign police stationed along international trafficking routes.

To achieve these aims in a comprehensive manner, a wide variety of training courses is provided. These include analytic investigative methods, clandestine laboratories, conspiracy law, demand reduction, diversion of drugs and chemicals, extradition and mutual legal assistance treaties, financial investigation techniques, forensic laboratory analysis, intelligence collection and analysis, methods of instruction, narco-terrorism, and supervision and management.

Many of the officers who attend these multinational training schools establish permanent relationships, and as they are progressively promoted up their respective chain of command, their cooperation with one another is sustained and strengthened. Other agencies, such as INTERPOL, also add to the fabric of international drug law enforcement in significant and complementary ways. The INTERPOL organization adds a layer of communication and intelligence exchange to all member nations, and INTERPOL is especially important to a large number of nations which do not otherwise have formal drug law enforcement liaison.

INTERPOL has some 158 member countries, each having a staffed National Central Bureau (NCB). The NCBs are linked by a modern telecommunications system whose hub is the secretariat general in Lyon, France, where, in 1991, over 300 INTERPOL personnel received or retransmitted approximately one million messages. It is estimated that 60 percent of this message traffic is drug related.

The United States participates fully in INTERPOL operations; a drug subdivision, consisting of 27 persons representing 18 nations, is headed by a DEA special agent on long-term assignment at Lyon. In Washington, D.C., there are just under 100 positions at the USNCB. Its data base, the INTERPOL Case Tracking System, contains records on more than 300,000 persons. In 1991, there were approximately 65,000 incoming requests to the USNCB from federal, state, and local law enforcement agencies or from other NCBs.

As operational and executive relationships matured, it was recognized that the operational aspects of the cocaine source problem could not be addressed without more aggressive multinational coordination at the executive level in law enforcement agencies from affected countries. In 1983, the DEA invited 13 countries to meet to discuss enhanced coordination. This initiative, known as the International Drug Enforcement Conference (IDEC), has provided a mechanism for planning and coordinating operations among chief executives of law enforcement agencies in cocaine-affected nations. President Bush addressed the IDEC membership in 1989 in Miami and stated that "I am honored to be here to talk to you ... the distinguished enforcement chiefs who have come (to Miami) from throughout the Americas—along with our friends and observers from Europe—to join forces in a new tradition of international cooperation. ... IDEC demonstrates that we will put aside national differences to do what must be done. ... And I commend (all) of you for having the foresight to establish this organization and for demonstrating the collective commitment to work together."

In the ninth IDEC Conference held in Cartagena, Colombia, in, April of 1991, DEA Administrator Robert C. Bonner opened his first conference and stated in part "Nowhere are successes of international cooperation better demonstrated than in the cooperative efforts of IDEC. When it comes to fighting drug traffickers, the nations of the world look to law enforcement for leadership, expertise, and commitment to translate anti-drug concepts and ideas into practical actions against these drug networks. IDEC provides that leadership, that expertise, and that commitment. ... Trafficking is not a problem to be solved independently, easily, or quickly. Eliminating the power of traffickers demands the strength and cooperation of all nations."

The work of IDEC has resulted in simultaneous enforcement actions over the years, enhanced coordination of all kinds, new legislation in several countries, implementation of chemical control initiatives, progress in financial investigations, and the exchange of good ideas at all levels. These operational leaders believe that much can be accomplished by simply deciding together what must be done and making it happen. No other group in international law enforcement has functioned like this and IDEC provides the mechanism to carry out the policy and initiatives that are needed. The potential of IDEC has been enhanced by the meetings of presidents at Cartagena, Colombia, and San Antonio, Texas, because the IDEC structure is one mechanism for implementing supply-side strategies and actions as directed by the presidents as a result of these meetings. DEA is now in the process of proposing the establishment of an IDEC-type conference for countries affected by the heroin trade.

The United Nations' executive leadership is also making a contribution to international drug law enforcement in a number of ways. For example, the Heads of Narcotic Law Enforcement Agencies, or HONLEA, exists within the UN structure as a specialized organization that meets annually. Established in 1974, the group was organized initially on a regional basis; Asia/Pacific was the first formed. Through presentations and discussions, the participating law enforcement executives establish cooperative relationships, are updated on current trafficking trends, and share information on new techniques and approaches.

The United Nations has also played a very significant role in the past decade in expanding certain concepts and tools in support of drug law enforcement. Beginning in the early 1980s, international experts began to develop the idea of a new United Nations convention which would bind signatory nations to use updated drug enforcement initiatives. In 1988, the Vienna Convention was completed and the 60 nations which are a party to it have agreed to new efforts in chemical control, asset removal, and controlled deliveries of drugs, among other initiatives. As the convention becomes ratified by more nations, we will see an increase in the ability of law enforcement authorities to work as one. This harmonization of activity in a wide range of countries, in addition to the traditionally affected nations, is critically important as drug abuse and trafficking spreads to the world at large. Europe is inundated with cocaine. Increased heroin production causes concern for potential new markets. Some believe that Africa represents the next area of significant drug cultivation. The new world order which promises openness of borders, expanded free trade, and a generally shrinking world is good. However, it also offers the opportunity for more rapid migration of crime, drug abuse, and trafficking.

The decade of the 1980s was a laboratory for experimentation in international drug law enforcement. More energy and new dimensions emerged, such as the military establishments entering the picture within their own countries, and other nations, in some cases. The position of trust and rapport enjoyed between DEA agents and our international colleagues has also been expanded. We are often allowed to take a very involved role in cases on foreign soil, such as working undercover. Officers from other nations have worked undercover in the United States as well, under DEA's umbrella.

This has become possible only because DEA has built a reputation of being a single-mission agency devoted exclusively to drug law enforcement. We have no political agenda nor are we involved in the national security intelligence agenda. As a result, we have been able to nurture the trust of our counterparts and thereby maximize our success in our area of specialization to the benefit of the United States.

As the traffic in illicit drugs becomes more complex, law enforcement must also become more sophisticated to meet the challenge. The structure for international cooperation between the United States and other nations is now largely in place; we have developed the trust and confidence to work together and therefore we have a solid foundation upon which to build.

Establishing the Tools of the Trade

Drug law enforcement is a specialty in many ways and has been the ground breaker for cooperation on other criminal violations as well. For example, many countries will cooperate on cases involving drug profits, but will not on tax matters. Nevertheless, the tools we need to do the job are now for the most part available.

Sharing Evidence

In the early days, joint investigations consisted mostly of the exchange of information with each country taking action within its boundaries consistent with their laws and procedures. This exchange was often done through the international letters rogatory system. The French Connection cases in the 1960s and 1970s are good examples of this.

In these cases and many like it, formal requests for information, investigations, and evidence were accomplished between judicial officials through this formal diplomatic process. While it was cumbersome, it was effective between nations with well-developed judicial systems. Many less-developed nations had no mechanism and oftentimes things were accomplished on an informal basis. With Mexico, for example, a method was developed which we referred to as JANUS prosecutions. Mexican prosecutors would travel to the United States to collect information, receive reports, and take sworn testimony. This material would be authenticated at a Mexican consulate or the embassy at Washington and used in Mexican prosecutions. While this concept with Mexico was valid, it was rarely used by Mexican prosecutors.

The letter rogatory system is cumbersome and today we have become more efficient in this exchange through establishing Mutual Legal Assistance Treaties (MLATs). Generally, these bilateral agreements allow the parties to obtain documentary evidence and other forms of assistance from one another, e.g., depositions and compulsory production of documents in the requesting country. Thus, in those countries with which the United States has entered into ratified MLATs, formal mechanisms now exist for obtaining information, for example, about criminal assets that have been transferred abroad by American traffickers. In addition, most recent MLATs explicitly address forfeiture issues, providing a means through which one country may request another to:

1. immobilize or freeze forfeitable assets;
2. initiate a forfeiture action against the property in question;
3. repatriate assets located abroad so that they can be forfeited here; or
4. enforce a forfeiture judgment issue by a court in the requesting country.

Notably, MLATs provide for execution of requests in accordance with the laws of the country to which the request is being made and is accomplished between the respective executive branches as compared to the respective judicial systems when using letters rogatory.

There is now an extensive practice of having narcotics officers from one nation testify in the court trials of another. This is often sensitive, especially when there are security and safety concerns for the officer who must testify in countries where violence and retaliation are endemic.

The Undercover Technique

The utilization of the undercover technique has become much more commonplace as a result of its extensive use in the United States and its obvious value in penetrating trafficking organizations. This technique was not available in many nations because of the "agent provocateur" restrictions in the legal systems based on the Napoleonic Code which formed the basis of law in many European countries. Under this legal doctrine, any undercover role for the police is illegal. By contrast, our laws prohibit the entrapment of a person into committing a crime which they are not predisposed to knowingly commit. But short of entrapment, U.S. authorities have a wide latitude to use undercover approaches.

Criminal investigations can be initiated in many ways, but in most cases are started on the basis of complaints from citizens. The investigation starts after the crime has been committed. A burglary detective who must start after the fact is at a great disadvantage compared to his colleague in undercover drug work who can, to a great extent, control the commission of the crime. The undercover drug agent can negotiate the circumstance of what will happen. This often gives the undercover drug officer the ability to set up details in such a way that the officer has the best possible advantage for his or her personal safety. How and where a delivery of drugs will take place, how the money will be paid, who will be present, testing the drug to be purchased, and counting the money, are some of the issues to be negotiated. The undercover officer can walk away at any time if the circumstances are not favorable.

The use of the most fundamental activity, the purchase of drugs, has been used extensively in the international environment for many years, where permitted. Even where it has been prohibited, often innovative approaches between enforcement agencies have allowed variations of such activity anyway. In the past decade, significant changes have occurred in undercover work and many nations now use it frequently, or at least view it as a necessary evil. As the drug problem exploded and authorities sought ways to combat it, the use of undercover work and conspiracy charges has become acceptable in many nations which would not use them before. The United States is clearly the most extensive user of the undercover technique and conspiracy prosecutions and aggressively promotes their use worldwide. There is no better evidence than the testimony of a sworn officer as to a direct conversation with a defendant. This often eliminates the need to call criminal informants whose credibility as witnesses may be questioned.

The undercover agent is often able to obtain audio and video recorded evidence of these activities for presentation in court. In fact, many juries in the United States today expect to hear or see the recordings of these events and feel shortchanged if they are not a part of the case.

Holland provides us with an example of the evolution of this activity in a country in which undercover activity was strictly forbidden. In Holland today, undercover cases are allowed by the prosecutor when certain criteria are met, and this new flexibility recognizes the need for law enforcement officers to be able to use this approach. France and Italy have also recently passed legislation which allows limited use of undercover roles as well.

During the 1980s, the use of the undercover technique has changed in many significant ways, which has had a profound impact on international cases. The first innovation was the establishment of the "reverse undercover case." In this situation, the agent reverses roles and becomes the supplier of the drugs instead of the traditional undercover role of purchaser. This was developed principally as a vehicle to seize trafficker assets or to involve a kingpin-level trafficker who would rarely meet with a new customer, as that new customer was always a possible undercover agent. In a reverse role, the agent offers large amounts of drugs for sale thereby attracting the criminal customer and his money. After negotiations, the trafficker is arrested on an attempt to distribute and a conspiracy charge and the money, vehicles, and other assets seized. This technique is subject to careful monitoring as government agents cannot be engaged in distribution of controlled lethal substances into the population, and strict control of these cases is maintained. State and local agencies have further enhanced this procedure by becoming distributors of retail-level crack cocaine, for example, as a means of arresting customers, seizing their money and assets used to facilitate the transaction thereby disrupting local drug markets.

As the expanded use of reverse undercover work proved successful in asset removal cases, other concepts were explored to utilize this approach in other ways to disrupt the major trafficking organizations. Major organizations or cartels need to acquire goods and services not readily available to them. In effect, they are willing to subcontract certain activities for a price. Transportation of drugs, the collection, movement, and laundering of money, the acquisition of a steady supply of quality precursor and essential chemicals, and the purchase of certain equipment, such as aircraft, boats, pill press machines, generators, microwave ovens, and the like, all provide new opportunities.

As an example, in the late 1970s DEA initiated a long-term undercover operation known as Operation GROUPER. In this case, a group of DEA agents provided an "off-load and transportation" service to major Colombian marijuana smugglers who were dominant at the time. In cooperation with the U.S. Coast Guard and U.S. Customs Service, seizures were made, but existence of the undercover operation was protected for over three years. The undercover operation ended successfully in March 1981 with indictment and arrests of the ringleaders of 14 major drug smuggling operations which accounted for 40 percent of the marijuana brought into the United States. The infiltration approach used by DEA in this investigation was the provision of off-loading services to maritime smugglers. Over $1 billion worth of drugs were seized: 1.2 million pounds of marijuana, 831 pounds of cocaine, and 3 million dosage units of quaaludes. In addition, DEA seized 30 vessels worth almost $10 million, plus 2 aircraft and arrested 122 persons in 7 states and Puerto Rico.

In the 1980s, major undercover efforts began to focus on money laundering and asset removal cases. In one example known as Operation SWORDFISH, DEA agents posed as investment consultants in a year-long investigation directed at U.S. and Colombian traffickers and money-launderers. Among 62 persons indicted in 1982 in the SWORDFISH sting were 4 bankers, 3 lawyers, and a doctor. DEA worked with a federal task force in South Florida, as well as with officials in the Cayman Islands, Colombia, Dominican Republic, Panama, Spain, and Switzerland. While focusing on the financial aspects of the trafficking, SWORDFISH tracked 9 tons of cocaine, 90 pounds of heroin, several tons of marijuana, and millions of doses of dangerous drugs. Forty-two U.S. and five foreign bank accounts were identified by the undercover investigators who moved over $19 million in drug funds for the traffickers. Many such sophisticated cases were made, including Operation PISCES, which was initiated in 1984. This major money-laundering case was focused in Miami, Los Angeles, and New York, and represented the largest effort of its kind. Almost 500 arrests were made and $80 million in assets seized during this three-year operation. Over $117 million were processed in 330 undercover financial transactions by the agents. In 1987, several very significant Colombian Cartel leaders were indicted as a result.

In early 1988, independent money laundering investigations were initiated by the Drug Enforcement Administration, U.S. Customs Service, the Internal Revenue Service, and the Federal Bureau of Investigation, both in Los Angeles and New York. The investigations revealed two international organizations composed of Armenians, Colombians, Argentinians, and other nationalities, who were laundering the proceeds from cocaine sales and possible Middle East heroin sales. The organizations functioned separately, but often worked in concert using similar methods. Both organizations used false gold sales and wholesale jewelry businesses as the cover for their laundering activities.

The money laundering centers were located in New York, Los Angeles, Houston, Miami and Fort Lauderdale, San Jose and San Francisco, and Atlanta. Documentation has shown that approximately $1.2 billion was laundered in drug profits by these organizations during a two-year period, with funds going to London, England, as well as Uruguay and Panama.

Varied investigative techniques were utilized throughout the investigation. In addition to an undercover penetration, various forms of surveillance, both physical and electronic, were established. Extensive analysis was conducted of bank records, currency transaction reports, and armored car shipping reports. All of these efforts provided evidence which outlined the scope, areas, and participants involved in the money laundering organizations.

During the next 13 months, leads from banking transactions and armored car records would lead to an international investigation that uncovered a massive criminal conspiracy that had little to do with the diamonds and precious stones that fill the Los Angeles jewelry district. The operation was called "La Mina" (the gold mine) by the Colombian drug bosses and code name Operation POLARCAP by the U.S. federal authorities.

At the center of the operation were the offices of Ropex and Andonian Brothers in Los Angeles and New York. The two businesses received millions of dollars a week from all over the country. In August 1988, federal judges in New York and Los Angeles authorized wire taps on the New York and the Los Angeles firms. Five months of high-tech surveillance yielded over 3,000 reels of video and audio tapes in five languages and two Armenian dialects. Hundreds of millions of dollars that were received in the two Los Angeles offices were moved electronically back to New York, then to Panama City and on to South America. It was used to pay operating expenses for coca paste, airplanes, political favors, payment to workers, etc.

In January 1989, the investigation was about to wind down. The court-authorized wiretap provided the investigators with the perfect excuse. On January 24, DEA agents intercepted a cryptic phone conversation: a huge currency shipment was about to leave New York destined for Los Angeles. The cryptic message was that the value of the shipment was "four kilos eight, six, nine." Presumably, a code for $4,869,000.00 was on its way from New York to Los Angeles. That night, New York investigators utilized a U.S. Customs Service dog trained to check for narcotics shipments. The Customs dog was taken to an armored car service cargo space at the airport where the dog alerted and tore into a 30-box shipment headed from the New York jewelry store to Los Angeles. Agents examined the boxes and found that they contained $4,869,000.00.

In February 1989, federal agents across the United States made arrests of subjects involved in these various related investigations. By the end of April 1989, there had been 112 defendants arrested in the United States and abroad. Charges placed against various defendants range from money laundering, conspiracy, aiding and abetting others in the sale and distribution of cocaine.

Drugs seized as a direct result of leads developed during the POLARCAP investigation were 16,124 kilograms of cocaine and 20,000 pounds of marijuana. Asset seizures of cash, real estate, domestic bank accounts, frozen foreign bank accounts, gold/jewelry and laundered trafficker funds totaled over $112 million. Operation POLARCAP was unique in a number of ways.

1. A number of bank accounts in Banco de Occidente in Panama which were used to launder funds in this investigation were also identified in a number of prior federal money laundering cases. An analysis of all of the involved investigations showed that Banco de Occidente had been instrumental in laundering over $412 million. This investigation resulted in the first indictment and conviction of a foreign financial institution for violations of U.S. money laws. Upon conviction, Banco de Occidente was ordered to pay the U.S. government $5 million as "substitute assets" for the drug proceeds which it laundered.
2. Of the $5 million forfeited from Banco de Occidente, $2 million was shared with the Governments of Canada and Switzerland for their assistance in this matter. This is the first such sharing of its kind, as authorized under the 1988 Omnibus Drug Initiative Legislation.
3. The 16 state and local departments which assisted the federal agen-

cies in these matters received approximately $40 million under the U.S. government's Asset Sharing Program.

Today's undercover operations have evolved into enormously complex and sensitive endeavors not imagined ten years ago.

The "Controlled Delivery" Technique

The use of the "controlled delivery" technique has similarly improved to a point where it is now very commonplace and a key to worldwide enforcement efforts. The undercover technique is often involved in these situations as well. In controlled deliveries, drugs are allowed to move from one country to a final destination in another, while controlled by law enforcement officers at each step of the way. This provides evidence for enforcement action at the source, as well as in the receiving country and in effect allows an attack on all elements of the illicit organization. This technique is used in one-kilo heroin cases from Southeast Asia or Southwest Asia, as well as multi-ton loads of cocaine or marijuana from Latin America. Often, such deliveries must transit other countries while en route and have raised many challenges of law and cooperation to be successful.

Even the parochial instinct to "make the big seizure in my country" for publicity value seems to have been set aside, for the overall good of the international case in most instances. The value of DEA agents stationed abroad has been ratified so often in these situations as the entire network can be activated to facilitate this type of investigation almost instantly and literally around the globe. Not only do these agents react simultaneously in many nations to seek permission for the movement of the controlled delivery of drugs, but often operational activities are required in each to conduct surveillance, support undercover agents, monitor telephone conversations, and the like. Controlled deliveries have now been expanded to nondrug commodities, such as money, chemicals, and equipment. Much like the simple undercover purchase of drugs has now evolved to a sophisticated, complex art form, the roots of today's complex controlled delivery lie in the hard work of the U.S. Customs Service officers who successfully moved a simple border seizure forward to the recipient. These early one-step exercises have evolved into today's world-class efforts often requiring the cooperation of multiple customs services, as well as police services around the world. U.S. Customs deserves much credit for the historical development of these activities in conjunction with their counterparts as well. Once again, law enforcement witnesses must testify in the courts of other countries in person or by legal instruments to be successful in controlled-delivery cases.

All controlled deliveries do not have a happy ending however. In March of 1988, the authorities of the People's Republic of China responded to encouragement to use the controlled-delivery technique. They had seized 10 pounds of heroin in a shipment of goldfish destined for San Francisco. Chinese officers and DEA agents carried the drugs to the United States via Hong Kong, and a number of arrests were made. Later, the Chinese agreed to produce a defendant incarcerated in China to assist in our prosecution in San Francisco. This type of cooperation had never been heard of before and the prospect of this level of joint effort was exciting. Unfortunately, a federal district court judge in San Francisco decided that the Chinese defendant/witness's request for political asylum had to be reviewed and he assigned an attorney to represent his interests. The witness had asserted that his statements given to the Chinese authorities had been coerced. The result was that we could not pursue the prosecution at that time and our Chinese colleagues went home completely disillusioned with our system of justice. This case is still in litigation and the incident continues to adversely affect the law enforcement relationship between the two countries. This matter illustrates how difficult it is to harmonize the laws and procedures of various nations.

Conspiracy Prosecutions

The use of conspiracy laws is perhaps the most significant investigative tool available to the drug law enforcement officers as it provides the means to prosecute the kingpin who is rarely involved in the actual handling of drugs, chemicals or cash. Further, the ability to include charges for criminal acts in foreign countries as part of a conspiracy case has done more to strengthen law enforcement's hand than perhaps any other single capability. When countries have and use conspiracy laws, the traffickers become truly vulnerable anywhere, given a viable judicial system. Twenty years ago, most countries had no conspiracy law or a weak statute at best. Those that did exist were often not effectively used. Thailand, a long-time holdout on the issue, has just passed a conspiracy statute and asset removal legislation—these are welcome developments.

Extradition/Expulsion

Perhaps the most successful joint efforts have involved the use of extradition or expulsion of a defendant from one country to another for trial where drug charges are pending. This truly destroys the protection of international boundaries behind which these international criminals have hidden for so many years. If there is no sanctuary, there is no safety. Extradition had been the only real concern for Colombia's cocaine cartel leaders as they have witnessed untouchables, such as Carlos Lehder of Colombia, Luis Arce Gomez of Bolivia, and Juan Matta Ballasteros of Honduras, brought to justice in the United States. The United States has extradited many defendants to foreign countries for trial, including U.S. citizens as well, but the proportion is much lower because many nations cannot sustain a viable prosecution against many of these powerful traffickers.

The most dramatic example of this type of international law enforcement action was the Manuel Noriega case where he was delivered to the U.S. court system for trial on drug charges after being apprehended by the U.S. military. This case, like no other, set the stage for the interrelationship of drug law enforcement, national security, and diplomacy. Recently, extraditions have also been very successful against Southeast Asian heroin traffickers from Hong Kong. Singapore, for the first time, extradited three very significant heroin traffickers who are Thai nationals.

The future of this type of activity will most likely be more formalized as countries assert their sovereignty and judicial systems are strengthened. In each country, the void of prosecution and meaningful incarceration of traffickers must be filled; however, we are struggling in that direction with mixed results. It is hoped that some day viable prosecution in any country will be a reality, and this remains our goal.

Taking the Profits

In the 1970s, DEA initiated new efforts to address the illicit profits of drug trafficking. Traditionally, we had the authority to seize the automobiles, planes, and boats of violators, but we were not able to reach their assets and profits without the legislation that exists today. Asset removal has been a difficult objective, but today DEA alone is seizing about $1 billion in trafficker assets each year. This success is based on the philosophy that asset removal is a part of every investigation, along with seizing drugs and prosecuting defendants. We have also determined that the best leads to the assets are usually developed out of the traditional drug case itself.

The migration of asset removal and money laundering cases overseas has been difficult, but ultimately successful. To be successful, it was necessary to change significantly the traditional and legal ways of doing business in many financial safe havens throughout the world. Forcing this change was no small task and could not have been accomplished without the drug issue being elevated to the political/diplomatic level. Switzerland first began working with DEA in 1976 to provide drug financial information. Others, such as the Bahamas, Cayman Islands, and Hong Kong have followed. Today, our ability to move freely across financial frontiers is nearly as strong as with other law enforcement techniques.

Once again, we begin to look more like each other than separate nations in the disposition of seized assets. DEA has shared seized assets with cooperating state and local agencies in the United States, and in 1991 over $190 million were shared. We now have begun to do the same thing with our international colleagues, as in 1991 the United States shared $2.5 million with the United Kingdom, $1.8 million with Canada, and $1 million with Switzerland. Sharings are pending with Argentina, Cayman Islands, Colombia, Egypt, Guatemala, Israel, and Paraguay. The Swiss also shared over $10 million with the United States, which was not forfeitable in that country, but was in the United States.

Precursor Chemical Control

DEA established the need for control of precursor and essential chemicals, especially those used to process cocaine and manufacture methamphetamine. Early efforts were voluntary as we probed this avenue under Operation "Chem Con," an acronym which stood for chemical control. A substantial percentage of all chemicals reaching the cartel laboratories in Latin America was being supplied by U.S. corporations. Ultimately, the Chemical Diversion and Trafficking Act of 1988 was passed in the United States and now is the basis for substantial progress. The number of clandestine laboratories seized in the United States dropped by one-half, mostly as a result of our chemical control efforts. The Colombian traffickers now manufacture their own chemicals or recycle them as a result of the restricted availability. As with many of the techniques discussed previously, chemical control was exported as a concept to our counterparts in law enforcement. It too reached the diplomatic agenda and has been institutionalized in the Vienna Convention.

Perhaps the most rewarding aspect of our achievements in chemical control and financial investigations is the fact that we have joined hands with those legitimate worldwide industries which have recognized the greater good. They did not always volunteer, but by-in-large, as a group they are moving in the right direction.

Intelligence

The Narcotics and Dangerous Drugs Information System of the Drug Enforcement Administration was discussed earlier as the informal, but functional worldwide data base for drug traffickers with over three million records today. This fundamental capability has been complemented with enhanced intelligence programs at all levels of sophistication. For example, special emphasis is placed on sharing intelligence for developing detailed "targeting data" for laboratory raids and sharing strategic analysis on chemical and asset movement. A new formal concept for intelligence sharing has also been developed which is called the Joint Information Coordination Center (JICC) program. The formula for JICC is to collocate personnel and commingle data from police and military agencies in a country with special emphasis on the movement of people, drugs, money, and other support commodities. The first JICC was established in 1985 and now this program exists in 16 countries. Most of these units receive U.S. financial support and are interfaced electronically to the El Paso Intelligence Center (EPIC). EPIC has 11 charter U.S. agencies and accesses to multiple federal data bases. It is managed by a DEA special agent in charge and other supervisors from participating agencies. The JICC program represents another unique international capability to share information and work together against the trafficker organizations. In essence, we are gaining equal footing with an enemy who respects no borders.

We have further enhanced our own U.S. intelligence capability with the establishment of Tactical Analysis Teams in several U.S. embassies. These units augment DEA's limited analytical resources with intelligence experts from the military who work under the direction and control of the DEA country attache. These units also allow DEA to interface with some of the other assets of our government and in turn supply excellent intelligence to the foreign counterparts for action. This has been especially successful in interdiction and other drug suppression activities.

Drug Suppression Programs

In the past ten years, there has also been a dramatic escalation of the sophistication of cooperation between nations as it relates to interdiction of drug production capability and transportation. As an example, Operation Bahamas and Turks and Caicos or "OPBAT," as it is known, is a joint effort between the United States, Bahamas, and the British.

This program was established in 1982, after experimentation with less formal efforts in the Bahamas and Mexico. Its uniqueness lies in the fact that multinational resources of police and military agencies can be blended into a successful program if the parties have the will to do so. Dramatic legal change is not required. Much can be done within existing institutions if we are motivated to act and exercise a little flexibility. OPBAT has had active participation over the years by Bahamian police, Bahamian military, DEA, the U.S. Coast Guard, the U.S. Army, the U.S. Air Force, and the U.S. Customs Service. Bahamian officers have been stationed in the United States with the U.S. Customs Service as well. The program is managed by the DEA country attache in Nassau and the U.S. ambassador provides the leadership and diplomatic liaison with the governments involved. The success of this interdiction program against drug-laden boats and airplanes is clearly a major factor in the shift of a good percentage of the flow of cocaine from being almost exclusively via the Caribbean to significant routes via Mexico. The concepts of OPBAT have migrated and evolved to other areas of the hemisphere and feature ever-increasing use of national defense assets, such as radar detection by participating countries. Procedures also have been streamlined to authorize ship boarding of a flag vessel by an interdiction asset of another country. These programs show once again that when nations respond as one we can have success.

Evolving, in part, from the concept of OPBAT, the DEA initiated Operation SNOWCAP in 1987. This effort focused its primary energy in Peru and Bolivia and has as its objective the initiation of drug suppression programs at the source. DEA, once again, is the catalyst for U.S. resources, which are provided by the State Department, various elements of the U.S. Defense Department, and others, such as the Coast Guard and U.S. Border Patrol of the Immigration and Naturalization Service. The State Department provides air support and material, the military provides training, intelligence support, and expertise. The Coast Guard provides riverine experts and the Border Patrol provides road interdiction expertise. DEA once again is the leader of the coalition of U.S. personnel and is the primary interface with host country police, and military to some extent, on operational matters. DEA agents are very active in the field with their law enforcement counterparts and are the principal source of actionable intelligence on drug production laboratories and trafficking organizations.

These programs are not clones of one another as each is developed by each country consistent with the trafficking problem reflected there, the laws and policies of the country, and the critical issue of political will which is often driven by economic issues. Bolivia and Peru each provide us with rich and unique examples of what can be done in response to the problem.

In Bolivia, U.S.-provided helicopters are piloted by Bolivian Air Force pilots to transport Bolivian UMOPAR police forces to carry out law enforcement actions. These actions are often the result of U.S.-provided intelligence. DEA agents participate as a management catalyst and provide additional intelligence support, medical assistance in the field, and coordination with other countries. The State Department provides financial support, the ambassador is the leader of the U.S. country team, and spearheads the diplomatic interface. The U.S. military provides training of the UMOPAR troops and Bolivian Air Force pilots and other support activity as well.

Peru hosts similar activities primarily out of a jointly established base camp at Santa Lucia in the Upper Huallaga Valley—the world's principal coca-growing area. In the case of Peru, air support is flown by U.S. State Department contract personnel and the majority of the operational activity is carried out by the Peruvian police with less Peruvian military involvement. These two programs have been successful in continuing to disrupt traffickers in these coca growing and processing areas and seizing laboratories. The real potential of these programs will be realized as other more sophisticated pieces of the puzzle are put in place, such as radar detection and apprehension of the small aircraft, which is vital to the functioning of these source areas.

The concept of Operation SNOWCAP is being utilized or considered for use in a number of countries in Latin America. In the past year, Mexico has established a program known as the Northern Border Response Force (NBRF) for the purpose of carrying out the apprehension phase of interdiction of the cocaine aircraft flying from Colombia to Mexico. Guatemala has established an interdiction program with similar features known as Operation CADENCE.

Programs, such as OPBAT, SNOWCAP, NBRF, and CADENCE, have been nurtured along and today provide the backbone of the U.S. Andean Strategy for cocaine suppression.

Conclusions

The international drug law enforcement community has developed over the past several decades into a coalition of specialists, who together have established the ability to work toward a common purpose. The day-to-day interaction on a personal basis and in each other's judicial systems is a tribute to international problem-solving. In spite of language barriers, political impediments, corruption, and lack of resources, these police agencies press forward to play their part in drug supply reduction.

Over 35,000 foreign police officers have been trained by DEA in the past twenty-five years and U.S. agencies have been strengthened by these associations as well. No doubt the world will see even more cooperation and harmonization of laws which will improve effectiveness in illegal drug supply reduction efforts to the benefit of all future generations of the family of nations. Certainly, a strong foundation has been laid upon which to build.

6

The Role of the Military

Donald J. Mabry

The U.S. military became an instrument of drug foreign policy because civilians could not stop the importation of illicit drugs. In spite of concerted efforts and vast expenditures of money at home and abroad, the use of illicit drugs seemed to be growing exponentially, and citizens, believing that the rising levels of violence in the United States were caused by illicit drug usage, demanded strong action to stop the drug epidemic. All levels of government and the media focused attention on the role of Latin American drug smugglers. By deciding that the U.S. drug epidemic could only be eliminated by reducing the supply of drugs, policy makers opened the door to military involvement, for the U.S. military can and does operate outside the United States.[1]

The U.S. military role in drug foreign policy has two essential components. The first is the mandate to be the lead agency in detecting drug smuggling, a role which is both domestic and foreign policy. The other is aid to key Latin American governments, aid which includes money, equipment, and advisors. Each will be examined in turn after a background introduction.

Background

The military has networks unavailable to civilians. The U.S. military training missions in most Latin American countries provide U.S. military personnel with personal relationships with Latin American counterparts, many of whose officers have been trained by U.S. personnel either in Panama or in the United States. Probably no other U.S. agency has an international network as extensive as that of the Department of Defense (DoD). In addition, the U.S. military patrols the Circum-Caribbean area from its U.S. and foreign military bases. Finally, because of the long-term fear of surprise aircraft or missile attacks, the military has long maintained radar surveillance of the southern border of the United States.

Further, since the national antidrug campaign has been termed a "war," many people expect soldiers to be used. Even those more sophisticated and temperate in their views envision the use of "tough guys" rather than the traditional anti-smuggling agencies. The war metaphor preconditioned people to think in terms of a military solution and kept that idea in the public mind in spite of military protestations that antidrug campaigns were not a military task.

Three successive Defense secretaries argued against military involvement in the antidrug crusade but the Presidency and Congress dragged a reluctant military into it. Frank Carlucci, Caspar Weinberger, and Richard Cheney each argued that military personnel are not and should not be police and that utilizing military personnel for law enforcement activities would detract from military readiness. DoD officials argued that the mission of the armed forces is to protect the nation from foreign armies, not drug smugglers, and that civilian law enforcement agencies should be given the resources necessary to do the antidrug task. Moreover, military personnel warned Congress of the danger of military involvement; General Stephen Olmstead, then Deputy Assistant Secretary for Drug Policy and Enforcement, argued that the military is capable of doing the job but also argued that civilians would not like the way it would be done, for soldiers would use machine guns and not worry about Miranda rights. Merchants and tourists would not like the consequences of search techniques implemented at the borders or on the high seas.[2]

Unpersuaded, the Federal government mandated and subsequently escalated military participation, providing additional funds at each step. The 1981 amendment of the Posse Comitatus Act allowed DoD to loan equipment and to give some logistical support to civilian police. In subsequent years, as civilian law enforcement personnel became less and less able to cope with the drug epidemic, the demand for military involvement increased, as did funding for military antidrug efforts. In 1982, in Operation BAT in the Bahamas, the U.S. military first started aiding in the suppression of drug activities in the Caribbean and Latin America. Four years later, U.S. military personnel played the major role in planning and conducting Operation Blast Furnace in Bolivia. As part of Operation Snowcap, created in 1987, DoD personnel began teaching military skills to Drug Enforcement Administration (DEA) agents who were to be stationed in the Andes. In late 1988, the military was ordered to play a major role in helping interdict drug trafficking into the United States, to create an integrated intelligence and communications network, and to train foreign military personnel and both U.S. and foreign police forces.[3]

Through the Omnibus Drug Act and the Defense Authorization Act in 1988, Washington decided to convert some military personnel into policemen and spies in the hope that the military could disrupt, if not end, this illicit enterprise. These laws not only required the military to loan even more equipment to civilian law enforcement agencies and provide additional logistical aid, they also brought state National Guard units directly into the antidrug campaign, gave the military the major role in drug interdiction, and expanded military antidrug activities overseas.

In light of world events in 1988–1990, use of military resources for nonmilitary purposes became more attractive. Between the 1989–1990 collapse of the Soviet Empire and the beginning of the Persian Gulf Crisis in August 1990, many Americans believed that the U.S. military had little use for its multi-trillion dollar installed capacity and sought a "peace dividend." Some believed that moving the military further into the antidrug business was one way to collect that dividend. The decline of a military threat frightened the Pentagon and its supporters, for they feared the possible loss of budgets, power, and influence. Although as late as October 1989 the Pentagon continued to argue that its traditional mission of defending the nation against foreign militaries,[4] the toppling of the Iron Curtain and Cheney's November 1989, announcement of plans to cut the DoD budget by $180 billion over five years sent shock waves through the military. By February 1990, DoD offered to fund much of the proposed full surveillance system out of its existing budget. By the summer of 1991, DoD was extending its surveillance activities, providing coverage of the Caribbean Basin, much of the Andes, and searching for more platforms in Latin America from which to launch spy planes. As part of Operation Support Justice, DoD and Latin American governments were trying to prevent cocaine smugglers from using northbound air corridors.[5]

Anti-Smuggling

Because the drug trade is illicit, data on the amounts smuggled into the United States are scarce and unreliable. No one knows how much cocaine, marijuana, and heroin enters the United States. Reported data are guesses based on uncertain methodology. The Drug Enforcement Administration (DEA) estimated that between 348 and 400 metric tons of cocaine hydrochloride are produced annually in Latin America, that most is destined for the United States market, and that over 100 tons were seized in 1988 (55 tons by U.S. authorities). DEA estimated imports as being between 3,545 and 9,000 metric tons, a range which indicates guesswork. Mexico produces 45–55 metric tons of heroin, accounting for 41 percent of total U.S. supply. Even a quick perusal of other sources of narcotics statistics produces different figures. Officials can only agree that too much is imported.[6]

U.S. officials do not know exactly how the drugs are imported into the United States. At one point, they believed that 45 percent of the cocaine seized came via private aircraft and about 20 percent of the cocaine seized came by private vessels. These statistics have limited meaning, for figures based on seizures do not necessarily reflect how the successfully smuggled cocaine arrived; if the bulk of cocaine shipments were entering via cargo containers or via the Mexican land border and if the United States had no effective system of detecting such shipments, large quantities could be entering undetected. This was certainly one possible explanation for the discovery and confiscation of twenty tons of cocaine from a Los Angeles warehouse in September 1990, and tons more in New York a few months later. How did these massive amounts of cocaine arrive? Only the traffickers know for sure.

Trying to stop drug smugglers in the Caribbean Basin is a formidable task. The Gulf of Mexico and the Caribbean Sea together equal about 46 percent of the land area of the United States. The Basin contains, or is bordered by, many sovereign nations, many of which are known smuggling sites. For the United States, sorting out the smugglers and the contraband from licit traffic is very difficult since each year 355 million people, over 100 million vehicles, 220 thousand vessels, and 635 thousand aircraft enter or reenter the country; in addition, 8 million cargo containers enter the United States. Only some of this traffic crosses the southern U.S. border or transits the Caribbean Basin, but so much of it does that closely monitoring it using the traditionally lax practices of the United States is a herculean task.[7]

Whereas the United States has considerable latitude in implementing anti-smuggling efforts on the high seas or airspace of the Caribbean Basin, it does not along the 1900-mile U.S.-Mexican border, the other major smuggling route. Mexico limits U.S. antidrug activities within Mexico and reluctantly cooperates on border issues. The complicated state of U.S.-Mexican relations is not within the scope of this chapter.[8] Suffice it to say that Mexican self-protectiveness vis-à-vis the United States means that the United States must put a premium on patrolling its side of the border and on the use of radar to detect flights coming in from Mexico.

Faced with this formidable task, Washington chose a high technology, military solution even though preventing smuggling is a civilian police function. Civilian agencies control the national borders, including anti-smuggling efforts, except during wartime emergencies. The Coast Guard, for over two hundred years, has been the nation's first line of defense against smugglers. Agents of the Customs Service, stationed in seaports, international airports, and land border crossings, have been trained to detect smugglers and contraband and either tax or seize the latter. Although the Border Patrol serves principally to control immigration, it also works in anti-smuggling activities. Drug smuggling overwhelmed all three, for they could not obtain the personnel, equipment, and budget necessary to meet the challenge. The military has the political clout necessary to get funding; virtually all members of Congress have defense contractors or military bases in their districts and can garner votes by supporting military appropriations. These civilian agencies do not, for few congresspersons gain much by supporting the Coast Guard, Customs Service, and Border Patrol.

From a personnel and resource management perspective, the Defense Department seemed ideal to create a unified, well-coordinated Control, Command, Communications, and Intelligence (C3I) system. Years of wrestling with inter-service rivalries and, at times, of coordinating with foreign military commanders, taught DoD executives how to lead disparate groups to achieve a common goal. Moreover, because the Coast Guard and state National Guard units would form an integral part of this anti-smuggling effort, DoD could easily reach into the civilian sector since both of these groups were also military units[9] and accustomed to working with DoD. Since DoD has an existing C3I structure for these units, its task under the new assignment would be to fold the intelligence-gathering and communications efforts of civilian law enforcement agents into a system directed against drug smuggling.

Another presumed advantage in making DoD the lead agency for detecting drug smugglers was its extraordinary technical capabilities developed from its long experience in monitoring the skies and the waters for incoming Soviet or other hostile military aircraft, warships, and missiles. As events in Operation Desert Storm demonstrated, the U.S. military's ability to use its integrated satellite, radar, and communications technology may be unsurpassed. Acquisition of the ability to react against suspected smugglers in "real time" (fast enough to intercept them before they crossed the U.S. border or escaped) is clearly desirable and comparable to the mission of such agencies as NORAD, whose goal is to detect hostile military acts against the United States quickly enough for the military to react. Thus, proponents of making DoD the lead agency envisioned simply adding the ability to alert law enforcement agencies to the presence of suspected drug smugglers to an existing detection system along the southern U.S. border and in the Caribbean Basin.

Because the new system would utilize much of the existing human and material resources of both DoD and civilian agencies, it appeared relatively inexpensive and more effective. Intelligence data collected by one agency would henceforth be shared automatically with *all* agencies involved in anti-smuggling via a common communications system rather than being gathered and used by one agency because it was unable or unwilling to share. In addition, routine military patrols in the Basin could more easily be diverted to investigate suspicious craft and alert authorities closer to the United States. In sum, by putting DoD in charge, Washington envisioned an anti-smuggling net through which drug criminals would rarely pass.

DoD argued against becoming involved in creating such a net. In an April 1989 report to the House and Senate Armed Services Committees, it estimated that such a net would cost between $480.4 and $760.5 million annually, require the use of one-third of the Navy's fleet, and employ nearly 100 army battalions and, when finally completed in 1992, would only increase detection capability by 25 percent.[10]

Few believed, however, that this enhanced detection ability would do little more than harass drug smugglers and, thus, raise their and their customers' costs. The very high profit margin on cocaine meant that smugglers could sustain very heavy losses and still operate at a profit and that the effect on street-price inside the United States would be negligible. In a December 1991 report, the General Accounting Office raised serious concerns about when, if ever, the DoD interdiction communications systems would be effective and at what cost. Because interdiction has not stopped the flow of cocaine into the United States, the Inter-American Commission on Drug Policy recommended reducing funding for interdiction.[11]

Inside Latin American Nations

Washington drug foreign policy rested more on destroying crops and laboratories in Latin America in the belief that the cheapest and most efficient solution to the desire of Americans for illicit drugs was to eliminate their supply at the source. Washington officials understood such a policy, for they had been using it with varying degrees of success and failure for many years in various parts of the world.[12] My comments on the role of the U.S. military inside Latin American nations are limited to the Andean region; its role in other nations has been so minor that they are not within the scope of this chapter. Although Mexico plays a very active role in international drug control strategy, it has been able to limit the number of U.S. officials and the scope of their activities because of its internal strength and fierce nationalism. Mexican police and military personnel jealously preserve the right to police Mexico even while accepting financial aid from the United States. Panama is a special case, for it is a nation whose government exists at the sufferance of the United States and its military. Although the United States went to war against Panama in December 1989, ostensibly to capture General Noriega, the motives for that military action were more complex.[13]

Throughout Latin America the supply-reduction foreign policy has been difficult to achieve because Washington cannot control events abroad. Because no nation wants foreigners eradicating crops, destroying laboratories, and arresting traffickers on its own territory, Washington pressured producing and transit nations to use their own personnel to accomplish these tasks. Further, DEA and other U.S. officials (including military personnel) were sent as advisors and proctors. In the Andes, the United States, in conjunction with host governments, created special drug police, hired coca eradication workers, and provided a wide range of other technical assistance. The Bureau of International Narcotics Matters of the State Department developed its own air wing for use in the antidrug campaigns in Bolivia and Peru. U.S. military personnel began advising local police and military on techniques to protect field workers against the inevitable violent reactions of those whose source of income was being destroyed. Often, host country security forces could not or would not protect antidrug agents. Control of events rests in the hands of Andean governments and their security forces, those growing the coca or processing it, and the drug merchants. In Colombia and Peru, guerrilla movements sometimes control events.

Washington could not stop the ability of drug traffickers to corrupt police and military officers. One reason that Colombia has been unable to capture its principal traffickers has been their ability to buy intelligence information and protection from bureaucrats, cops, and soldiers. The same problem exists in Peru. Narcotics corruption in Bolivian official ranks is "pervasive" according to the U.S. Department of State. Washington is so cognizant of the ties between the former military dictatorship of General Luis García Meza (1980–1982) and international cocaine trafficking that it obtained the resignation of García Meza's former army intelligence chief Faustino Rico Toro almost immediately after Rico Toro was appointed in early 1991 to head the National Council Against Drug Abuse and Trafficking. Corruption permeates the Anti-Narcotics Special Forces (FELCN) according to its commander. In other words, Washington lacks a reliable security force in each of these nations, one uninfluenced by drug money and unintimidated by the threat of violent retribution.[14]

To increase the personal safety of anti-drug workers, the United States created Operation Snowcap in 1987. As part of Snowcap, some DEA agents were trained in military tactics by U.S. special operations personnel and Special Forces teams were sent to Peru (and Bolivia) to give on-site advice and, when necessary, to protect antidrug workers. Because the number of Special Forces personnel has intentionally been kept low, their presence has not exacerbated nationalistic tensions. At Santa Lucia in the Upper Huallaga Valley (UHV) of Peru, the United States built a fortified base to protect Peruvian and American antidrug workers. U.S. personnel maintain the helicopters (loaned to the State Department by DoD) utilized in antidrug campaigns. But Operation Snowcap does not work, according to the House Committee on Government Operations.[15]

In 1988, Washington increased the amount of antidrug military aid to Latin America to stiffen the will of local security forces in Latin American "drug countries." One million dollars was authorized to arm foreign aircraft for defensive purposes in narcotics interdiction and eradication campaigns, two million dollars for education and training in the operation and maintenance of antinarcotics equipment and to pay for DoD mobile training teams to teach tactical operational skills for narcotics interdiction, and another three and one-half million was authorized for military assistance to more general antinarcotics efforts in Latin America. The bulk of the money was destined for Colombia because of its unique role in the cocaine business. When Colombian president Virgilio Barco's August 1989 crackdown was countered by a large, sustained wave of violence by these Colombian criminals, President Bush responded by sending $65 million in military equipment and other forms of aid. If the Colombian traffickers could be beaten, then "victory" was possible in the drug war.[16]

The Andean Initiative

The Colombian confrontation was fortuitous, for it lent urgency to Bush's Andean Initiative, planned months before but announced in the September 1989 National Drug Control Strategy report and by Bush on national television. The Initiative made it clear that the U.S. planned "to the greatest extent possible, ... [to] disrupt the transportation and trafficking of drugs *within* [emphasis added] their source countries, since the interdiction of drugs and traffickers en route to the United States is an immeasurably more complicated, expensive, and less effective means of reducing the drug supply to this country."[17] Specifically, the cocaine trade from the Andean countries of Colombia, Bolivia, and Peru was the target. The Initiative called for increased repression, much of it to be accomplished by military personnel. About $141 million of the aid destined for Colombia, Peru, and Bolivia was military equipment—such as helicopters, patrol boats, and ammunition—and $13.5 million in "intelligence aid"—radar, electronic sensors, secure communications equipment, and computers. More U.S. military advisors were sent to train Andean armies in the use and maintenance of the American equipment. To avoid anti-American sentiment and getting drawn into local political conflicts, Special Forces advisors were forbidden to accompany host nation forces when the latter go on antidrug missions.

The United States increased antidrug aid to Colombia, Bolivia, and Peru. President Bush proposed $68.3 million for FY90 and $132.2 million in FY93 to Colombia, $66.6 million and $184.2 million, respectively, to Peru, and $96.7 million and $183.5 million, respectively, to Bolivia. The majority of each of these aid packages was to be for non-military purposes, but the increases in military aid were to be dramatic. Between FY88 and FY93, military aid to Colombia was to go from $4 million to $60.2 million, to Peru from $0.4 million to $34.7 million, and to Bolivia from $0.4 million to $40.9 million. The actual expenditures changed, in part, because Peru refused military aid in 1990.[18]

Why Bush opted for a more military-oriented policy is not clear. Perhaps he responded to growing American frustration with the inability to repress the drug trade in the United States and Latin America. Neither interdiction nor eradication were working and Americans knew it. Appointing William Bennett as the first director of the National Drug Control Policy Office certainly signaled a harder line, for Bennett rarely spoke softly or advocated timid methods. Perhaps Bush was trying to counter campaign charges that he was indecisive and weak. Bush understood that the United States had been substituting military muscle for diplomacy in Latin America for generations. His predecessor had done so in Grenada, El Salvador, and Nicaragua and had sent troops to Bolivia in 1986 to aid DEA agents and Bolivian police in destroying a number of drug labs.[19] Thus Bush experienced firsthand the idea of a military solution to drug interdiction, crop eradication, and Latin American domestic political problems exacerbated by drug trafficking.

Bush got lucky. The Colombian political crisis beginning in August 1989 gave the Bush administration the serendipitous opportunity to dramatically announce its antidrug policy within the context of Colombian criminals directly and violently challenging the authority of the Colombian state. The traffickers instigated their killing spree against selected fellow countrymen in an effort to force the Barco government to reverse its decision to implement the U.S.-backed extradition treaty. Rather than yield, Barco struck back and used international television to appeal for immediate aid. Television networks flooded screens with images of the havoc being wreaked in Colombia by the traffickers, shocking Americans and creating instant public support for Bush's decision to send $65 million in military aid to Colombia. A few weeks later, when Bush announced his antidrug policy on national television, he could do so as a decisive national leader who was rescuing a neighboring ally and preventing a similar occurrence in the United States.

Video images of the death and destruction wreaked by the terrorism campaign of Colombian traffickers lent credence to the argument that Colombia was threatened by narcoterrorism, an idea that Washington had promoted for years. The Reagan administration, unable to obtain sufficient cooperation from Latin American governments, had begun arguing that there were direct links between drug traffickers and leftist guerrillas and, thus, that these countries were threatened by "narcoterrorism." Few paid much attention to the narcoterrorism argument until Colombian events seemed to prove the Reagan administration prophetic.

These same Colombian events opened the door to a greater U.S. military role in Latin America, for the narcoterrorism argument provided the rationale for using military resources to stifle the drug business. Antiguerrilla campaigns are a military specialty. Although guerrillas were not the protagonists in the drug terrorism campaigns of 1989–1990 and counter-terrorism is a police specialty, few made these distinctions as bombs exploded and people were shot in Colombia. Confusing matters further was the fact that the Colombian National Police is a branch of the Colombian military and, thus, army generals wrote the final shopping list when Bush promised the $65 million in emergency aid. By the time the Colombian crisis began, U.S. civilian agencies had begun to realize that they were stalemated, at best, and that only a more active DoD role might give them the resources necessary to break the impasse. Allying with DoD would guarantee consistently larger funding for the drug war.

Colombia

Colombian reality, however, did not support the U.S. narcoterrorism thesis. Conservative businessmen, not leftist guerrillas, were conducting the highly publicized attack against the state institutions of Colombia. In spite of some isolated instances of cooperation between one or more guerrilla movements, on the one hand, and drug gangsters, on the other, the two are not integrally related nor has the Colombian government treated them as such. Of the two, the Colombian government has viewed the guerrilla movements as the more serious threat. Guerrilla movements were active for many years before narcotrafficking and its violence became an issue. The Colombian military has fought the Revolutionary Armed Forces of Colombia (FARC), the 19th of April Movement (M-19), the National Liberation Army (ELN), and the People's Liberation Army (ELP) for years. Colombian police fight criminals, be they narcotraficantes or more ordinary crooks, and account for eighty percent of drug busts. In fact, one of the most serious problems faced by the police was the military-narcotraficante cooperation to kill their common enemy, leftist guerrillas. Military officers sometimes compromised police raids in exchange for trafficker information on the location of guerrilla bands.

Colombia accepted both police and military aid, for it faced danger from gangsters and guerrillas, but refused to increase U.S. military activity. Bogotá has consistently argued that it does not need nor want foreign troops on its soil and that its principal need in the antidrug fight was more equipment for its police and judicial systems. Colombian Defense Minister General Oscar Botero, on September 1, 1989, made it clear that Colombia did not need "foreign troops to solve our domestic problems," including the American military advisors sent by President Bush.[20] Later in 1989, when the United States proposed stationing an aircraft carrier in international waters off the Colombian Caribbean coast to improve antidrug electronic surveillance, the Colombian nationalistic response was so strong that Washington had to abandon the plan. Although U.S. military personnel no doubt played a role in Colombia's crackdown on its drug traffickers by providing intelligence information and logistical support, both governments downplayed it. Colombian politicians understand that self-respect demands that Colombians find a solution to Colombian problems.[21]

The Colombian military has little to fear from drug businessmen. The narcotraficantes do not intend revolution nor replacing the existing military establishment with a revolutionary one. Instead, the narcotraficantes aid the military against their common enemy, leftist guerrillas. Moreover, some Colombian military officers have taken bribes from the traffickers. This may explain why the Colombian military received 84 percent of the $65 million in emergency aid in 1989 when it only accounted for 20 percent or less of antidrug efforts. Bush administration officials insisted that the Colombian government demanded the equipment which many consider inappropriate for antidrug efforts. If true, it may reflect military pressure on the Barco government to insure military and not police supremacy inside Colombia. That the military subsequently used this equipment primarily for anti-guerrilla campaigns would seem to support this proposition.

Although the crackdown which began in August 1989 achieved some success, the price was so high that in 1990 the Colombian government began seeking a non-violent solution to its domestic problems. The government started serious negotiations with the traffickers and, more importantly, adopted a new constitution in 1991 in hope of incorporating guerrillas into the electoral system. In the convention elections, the former M-19 guerrilla movement became the nation's third largest political party. The Peoples' Liberation Army agreed on January 29, 1991, to lay down its arms and take two seats in the constituent assembly. Negotiations with the ELN and FARC have been unsuccessful, however, and the Colombian army attacked the FARC ferociously in the fall of 1990, partly as an attempt to force FARC leaders to negotiate. Apparently, it used U.S. equipment which had been supplied by the United States for antidrug purposes. President Gaviria, while still threatening drug gangsters with extradition to the United States, has promised that those who surrender would be tried in Colombian courts and imprisoned only in Colombia. By March 1991 the three Ochoa brothers had accepted the offer and surrendered to Colombia police; Pablo Escobar surrendered in June 1991, after the Colombian Constitutional convention adopted an anti-extradition provision for the new constitution.[22] His 1992 prison escape and 1993 threat to renew drug cartel violence if the government continued to try to capture cartel members made it uncertain that the Gaviria administration's strategy would work. However, Escobar's death in December 1993, prior to capture by government authorities, provided new incentives for traffickers to surrender peacefully and abstain from violent conduct.

Peru

Peru provided a much better argument for the use of the military, for it is both the principal source of coca and a place where guerrillas are involved in the drug enterprise. When Peru did not eradicate crops quickly enough, the United States sent its own personnel to make sure that the job was done. The crop and lab destroyers in Peru soon faced two serious problems. Farmers planted fields and traffickers built labs in new and more isolated locations. More serious, however, was the inability or unwillingness of Peruvian security forces to protect antidrug workers against the violent resistance which inevitably occurred, especially that of Sendero Luminoso. If the crop eradication and lab destruction program was to succeed, the Upper Huallaga Valley (UHV) had to be made secure.[23]

Many UHV residents welcomed the arrival of Sendero in the Valley. When coca growing and trafficking boomed in the lawless UHV and tensions were subsequently raised by the antidrug campaign, Sendero Luminoso moved into the Valley and imposed order, something the Peruvian government had not done. Colombian traffickers, who had been abusing the growers, were disciplined and taxed; Sendero thus gained support from the growers and income with which to pursue its political ends. In a very real sense, Sendero became the government of the UHV. The Peruvian military could not dislodge them.

The Peruvian military failed largely because it was ordered to follow a contradictory policy. It could fight Sendero or engage in antidrug efforts but not both. Antidrug efforts drove people into the protective arms of Sendero while attacks on Sendero gave the drug producers a free hand to pursue their business. Peruvian military leaders, by and large, preferred to concentrate on Sendero, believing that Sendero was the serious threat to national security and one that the military was trained to fight. The United States, however, more interested in destroying drugs and protecting antidrug workers, pressured Peru to focus on drugs.

Because of Sendero's tactical involvement with the drug business in the UHV, it is easy to ignore why it exists. It is a radical response to the course of Peruvian history. Peru has been badly governed for centuries by an assortment of Spanish viceroys, civilian and military dictators, and an occasional democratically elected president. Peruvian elites, largely European in origin, have excluded the bulk of the population from political and economic power and practiced their own brand of apartheid against the majority of the population. Such a policy produced severe income inequality and, consequently, economic stagnation, prompting the military, in 1968, to overthrow the civilian government and start a social revolution. Although this effort ultimately failed for a variety of reasons and the military returned power to civilians in 1980, the experience raised the expectations of the masses. That same year, long before the UHV became important to coca production, Sendero began its guerrilla campaign. For Peru, and thus for U.S. foreign policy there, it is important to recognize that eliminating Peruvian drug production will not eliminate Sendero, eliminating Sendero will not eliminate drug production, and eliminating both may not be possible.[24]

By 1990, faced with the continued threat of Sendero to Peruvian antidrug efforts and the commensurate inability to eradicate crops, Washington unsuccessfully tried to up the ante through a proposed $35 million military aid package. DEA had reported in late 1989 that Peru was unlikely to militarize its antidrug campaign, but the new proposal called for the construction of a military training base near Santa Lucia to train six Peruvian strike battalions and a second base on the Tombo and Ene rivers. The United States would also supply more river patrol boats, refurbish ground-attack jets, and install more radar in the Valley.[25] In other words, Washington thought more force would solve the problem. Some Americans began arguing that the Peruvian situation was low-intensity conflict (LIC), the current military euphemism for counter-insurgency warfare.

The newly elected government of Alberto Fujimori rejected the proposed aid in September 1990, arguing that Peru's problems could only be solved by political and economic, not military, means. Peruvian officials believed that combining the antidrug campaign and the anti-Sendero war was the road to disaster. Sendero has power in communities whose residents believe that they have been abused by the government, so the key to defeating Sendero lay in the Peruvian government regaining the confidence of its people. Military campaigns, especially if directed by U.S. soldiers, would have the opposite effect. When Fujimori balked, Washington threatened to cancel all aid to Peru.[26] In May 1991, Fujimori capitulated; Peru's severe economic crisis left him little choice.

Relations between the Fujimori and Bush administrations soured even more, however. Not only did the Peruvian economy worsen in 1992, but Sendero also increased its urban terrorist attacks, especially in Lima. Because of the increased desperation of the local situation, Fujimori used the February 1992 San Antonio drug summit to sharply criticize the U.S. focus on coca eradication and to demand more economic aid. On April 4, Fujimori, with the aid of the Peruvian military, suspended the constitution and declared martial law. Washington responded with a suspension of all military and non-humanitarian aid and withdrew about two dozen Special Forces trainers. Later that month, Peruvian jets fired upon a U.S. anti-drug plane, killing one person. Incensed, Congress began to question the extent to which Peru was an ally. In June, the United States ended all Foreign Military Financing aid to Peru.

Conflict between Lima and Washington was unlikely to lead to the withdrawal of all U.S. aid. Neither Washington nor Lima wants a Sendero victory. Peru wants to expand its licit trade with the United States whereas the United States will continue to want to end the cocaine trade. The two nations are likely to skirmish diplomatically until a mutually acceptable agreement can be reached.

Bolivia

The U.S.-Bolivian decision to seek a military solution perhaps best illustrates the militarization of U.S. drug foreign policy in Latin America. One cannot make the narcoterrorism argument, in either of its forms, for, unlike Colombia and Peru, Bolivia does not have a guerrilla threat or substantial narcotraficante violence. Bolivia is very important to the suppression of the cocaine trade, however, because it is the second-largest coca producer. In the 1990 agreement between Washington and La Paz, Bolivia agreed to accept $32.2 million in military aid in exchange for militarizing its antidrug efforts, supplanting UMOPAR, the antidrug police. As one of the poorest nations in the hemisphere, Bolivia could not risk losing foreign aid. Moreover, to a nation historically controlled by its military, the offer of additional money and equipment for that military must have been irresistible. Although the Bolivian government has been democratically elected since 1981, civilian power is extraordinarily weak. That Colombia and Peru have not been as compliant as Bolivia does not belie the fact that Washington has greater faith in Andean militaries than it has in Andean policemen.

In Bolivia, opposition to the implementation of U.S. drug policy, particularly the use of military units, comes from democratic forces—political parties, farmers' syndicates, and labor unions. In the Chapare region, where most of Bolivia's illicit coca is grown, the coca farmers' syndicate represents at least 40,000 families. Coca growers belong as well to the CSUTCB, the nation's largest farmer organization, and have ties to the COB, one of the nation's largest labor organizations. The CSUTCB voted in May 1991, to stage a national blockade of roads and trains in June to protest use of the military in antidrug activity. Opposition political parties court the coca farmer syndicates, giving the latter still another entree into national democratic politics.[27]

The Low-Intensity Conflict Argument

Some analysts advocate an even larger military role in the antidrug campaign, arguing that it apply its low-intensity doctrine in the Andes. One argument is that the traffickers are equivalent to guerrillas. In this view, the illicit drug trade destabilizes these governments through bribery, intimidation, and the flaunting of authority to the extent that the traffickers have become a "state within a state." Further, the traffickers conduct economic warfare against these countries when they use their illicit profits to purchase farms, factories, and business firms, for the state is robbed of revenue and legitimate business cannot compete on even terms. Moreover, the influx of narcodollars induces inflation and "dollarizes" local economies. Finally, the traffickers not only possess better weaponry than public security forces but also have demonstrated their willingness to use it, as they have done in Colombia. LIC proponents assert that police techniques cannot overcome the traffickers because the police, unlike the military, lack sufficient discipline, adequate technology, and a unified command and control system. These proponents point to the operational success of Operation Blast Furnace as proof of the applicability of LIC doctrine. Other pro-LIC writers agree but argue that the presence of leftist guerrillas requires the use of LIC techniques because police forces cannot successfully prosecute a counterinsurgency campaign. They argue that the traffickers and guerrillas must be attacked simultaneously because the two are interrelated, something only the military can do.[28]

LIC doctrine has been used to attack the drug trafficking problem in Latin America. Special Operations units are sent to Andean countries to teach LIC techniques to local antidrug police, DEA personnel, and some military units. Although forbidden to accompany their pupils on raids, it is likely that some U.S. military personnel have done so. In Colombia, the U.S. military has probably given important intelligence data and logistical aid not only in such efforts as the killing of Gonzalo Rodríguez Gacha but also for counterinsurgency campaigns. Panama was invaded in December 1989. DEA, the State Department, and the Office of National Drug Policy began advocating a more substantive military role in the Andes instead of just the logistical help they had previously wanted from DoD and testified to Congress in favor of the administration's 1990 proposal to increase military aid to Andean nations. By the summer of 1990, General Maxwell Thurman, commander of the Southern Command (SOUTHCOM) and planner of the Panamanian invasion, had begun planning a low-intensity conflict in Colombia, Bolivia, and Peru, one in which local military forces, aided by the U.S. military, would launch simultaneous strikes against drug traffickers.[29] By 1991, a version of that plan, Operation Support Justice, was under way in the Andes.[30] Certainly, the proposed increases in military aid in 1990, which included the training of strike battalions, was part of this new interest in using LIC doctrine although it is possible that the Thurman plan was just one more instance of contingency planning by the military.

The advantage and problem in using low-intensity conflict doctrine is the fuzziness of the concept. In 1981, the United States Army defined two types of low-intensity conflict, both of which said it was aid to prevent efforts "aimed at internal seizure of power." Michael T. Klare points out, however, that the definition adopted by the Joint Chiefs of Staff is so broad that it is virtually meaningless. David Silverstein, writing for the Heritage Foundation, asserts that the maintenance of an intimidating, large military force is LIC because it threatens potential opponents, a definition which means that the United States has been engaged in low-intensity conflict with virtually every nation in the world, since each nation is a potential opponent of the United States. This is nonsensical. Bernard McMahon uses a more workable definition: "political-military confrontation between contending states or groups at a level below conventional warfare but above routine peaceful competition among states."

The very vagueness of LIC doctrine, however, provided the means of justifying the use of the military in law enforcement. As Richard J. Barnet so aptly understood, LIC doctrine has been redefined to give police functions to militaries.[31] Representative of this argument is that made by U.S. Army Colonel Michael Abbott, who argued that the drug infrastructure in a major producing country must be seen as an insurgency and LIC doctrine must be applied.[32]

These proponents point to the operational success of Operation Blast Furnace as proof of the applicability of LIC doctrine. In Blast Furnace, U.S. Army soldiers flew helicopters carrying Bolivian and U.S. policemen in successful strikes against coca processing labs. Blast Furnace disrupted Bolivian processing sufficiently to force down coca leaf prices and, most importantly, demonstrated that the U.S. military could coordinate a binational, multi-agency effort against the drug business. No traffickers were captured, one of the goals, because corrupted policemen warned them of impending strikes and they fled. Some analysts believe, however, that a completely military operation, relying upon intelligence gathered by the military, can avoid this occurring in any future operation. That the traffickers fled suggests that they will not fight military units.[33]

Guerrilla armies do fight, so LIC proponents argue that military units must be involved when guerrillas are present in a drug region because guerrillas and the drug business are interrelated and must be attacked simultaneously. To them, police forces are not capable of conducting counter-insurgency warfare, something only the military can do, much less chase crooks while also defending themselves against guerrillas. Instead, an LIC campaign, in which police and military forces conduct coordinated attacks, is the most effective approach. They would point to Colombia as an example. Although the vast majority of the campaign against the traffickers and their labs has been conducted by the Colombian National Police, the Colombian military has also played an important role, destroying labs and trying to capture traffickers. Simultaneously, the military has been fighting FARC and ELN, thus preventing them from assisting the traffickers. Through this joint police-military effort, easier in Colombia than in some other nations because the National Police are part of the Defense Ministry, traffickers have been captured or been encouraged to surrender and the international cocaine business has suffered.[34]

The two wars fought by the Bush administration increased interest in a military solution, for both were short and successful. The success of the Panamanian invasion (Operation Just Cause) heightened interest in a military solution. The DEA, the State Department, and the Office of National Drug Policy began advocating a more substantive military role in the Andes to condition Congress and the public to accept a military solution and then later testified in favor of the administration's 1990 proposal to increase military aid to Andean nations. Operation Desert Storm, conducted by the Central Command, generated tremendous popular support in the United States for its military but it also undercut the Southern Command, which specializes in low intensity conflict. Although LIC teams were used in Desert Storm, their work went largely unnoticed and LIC commanders had to make a special effort to obtain any publicity. If SOUTHCOM and LIC are to have a future, a successful LIC operation is needed. SOUTHCOM cannot point to its involvement in the Salvadoran civil war or the Contra effort as great successes. SOUTHCOM personnel are anxious to get involved in the Andes in order to prove their capability.

Even popular fiction may have encouraged the use of LIC doctrine. In Tom Clancy's best-selling novel, *Clear and Present Danger*, U.S. Spanish-speaking light infantry soldiers were infiltrated into Colombia to destroy cocaine laboratories and kill enough drug traffickers in an effort to start a civil war within the ranks of the traffickers. The Bush administration may have considered using Bolivian, Colombian, and Peruvian soldiers instead of Hispanic-Americans. Under U.S. supervision, these battalions would launch a simultaneous strike against drug traffickers. By being centrally coordinated by the United States, the planners believed that the traffickers could be captured, killed, or forced to flee the Andes. These simultaneous attacks would so disrupt the trafficking organizations that coca leaf prices would drop so low that farmers would voluntarily quit growing coca.

This is the thread which explains why the United States insisted that these nations allow the United States to create and deploy special light infantry battalions even though doing so created great risks for those nations. Washington policy makers believed those LIC theorists who argued that special operations units and counter-insurgency techniques could be successfully applied against criminal organizations. The targets were not the gunmen or guerrillas in Colombia nor guerrillas and farmers in Peru nor farmers in Bolivia. Even by proxy, the United States did not want to go to war against the Andean civilian population. The target was the higher echelons of the cocaine business and their labs.[35] In Bolivia, for example, these units were deployed not in the Chapare, the heart of illicit coca growing, but in the Beni and other lab locales in order to avoid conflict with farmers.

Although it is not possible to know exactly how these battalions were to be used, for such information is classified, many important, obvious questions can be raised. How long would such forces exist? Would their existence create unwanted tensions within their own military establishments? Would these battalions attack fellow military personnel or police or politicians or businessmen who are involved in the drug trade? If they were successful in capturing or killing drug kingpins, would the lieutenants of the latter simply replace their bosses, as happened in the Clancy novel? As these battalions were deployed, would the business headquarters and laboratories in these three nations move to safer haven in Ecuador, Chile, Paraguay, Argentina, Venezuela, and Brazil? Would the United States then try to pursue the same policies there? If the price of coca leaf drops sufficiently to drive farmers out of business, would they meekly acquiesce or would they fight back? If guerrilla movements were as dependent upon drug money as some suggest, would they fight to preserve their sources of income and weaponry? If, for example, Peruvian farmers and Sendero join forces to fight, how many soldiers would be necessary to defeat them? Would Bolivian coca farmers conduct armed resistance?

Regardless of the answers to these questions, the Bush strategy represented a militarization of antidrug efforts in the Andes and a threat to democratic government there. Although proponents asserted that the military would only be supporting civilian agencies, such is unlikely to be the case. To succeed, such campaigns must have a centralized command and control system, a role that each national military would insist upon playing, for no military would voluntarily subject itself to police control. Military officers would then be the chief law enforcement agents in the nation. The United States, by insisting that the civilian police forces in these nations are incompetent to destroy what the United States itself terms criminal organizations, telegraphed the message that militaries are more important than civilian institutions. Militaries do not practice democracy within their own ranks and, in the Andes, they have consistently been the most powerful anti-democratic force. Enhancing their power, which this initiative did, diminished democratic governments there. To the extent that U.S. soldiers coordinate the actions of these battalions, democracy is also diminished for they are not elected by these nations to be in control. If there is to be a trinational, simultaneous strike against traffickers, U.S. advisors, in direct and constant contact with SOUTHCOM, would have to coordinate the forces. If that occurs, then the important decision making power would have passed from Bogotá, La Paz, and Lima to the United States.

LIC does not work against drug crime for a number of reasons. Too many people have a vested interest in the continuance of the trade. Besides the obvious examples of the criminals and the drug consumers, there are also the numerous persons who sell all kinds of goods or provide services to drug farmers, processors, transporters, bankers, and so forth. One tenet of LIC is "winning the hearts and minds" of the people in order to deny support to the opponent. Opposition to drug traffickers in Latin America emanates primarily from their use of violence, not from the fact that they are engaged in drug trafficking. If, for example, there are 300,000 persons benefitting financially, directly or indirectly, from the drug trade in Bolivia, then at least 30 percent of the economically active population has a vested interest in the continuance of the trade. In Peru, at least 15 percent of the economically active population benefits from the trade. The fact that coca-chewing is part of Andean culture makes gaining popular support even more unlikely. LIC units need other militaries to fight. The goons used by traffickers are not armies, even guerrilla armies. Although the United States has the physical capability of destroying coca fields in short order, the tactic could only be used if the United States also wanted mass uprisings against it. Destroying coca-processing labs is more difficult for they are dispersed and relatively easy to replace. If, for example, all the Colombian and Peruvian labs were destroyed, would the United States then penetrate Brazil, Ecuador, and Chile, where some labs currently exist and more would be sure to follow? Colombia, Bolivia, and Peru are not small nations; combined, their land area equals one-third of that of the United States, the area east of the Mississippi River. The number of troops required would be large. If the United States tried to use local troops, it would inevitably find operations compromised by the influence of nationalism, familial ties, and money. Finally, although drug trafficking is a serious political problem for Bolivia, Colombia, and Peru, the application of LIC doctrine by the United States would be even greater.

Conclusions

Interdiction

The Caribbean Basin is too vast, the U.S.-Mexican border too long, and the number of persons, vehicles, aircraft, and seacraft approaching or crossing the U.S. border too large for effective detection and interception unless the military were allowed to operate under wartime conditions. Were it allowed to use whatever force it deemed necessary, such as killing anyone who did not obey orders to stay within certain travel lanes or to stop, the military could substantially reduce drug smuggling. Shooting down innocent civilian aircraft or sinking innocent cabin cruisers would produce an anti-military and, perhaps, an anti-government backlash that no one wants to risk. DoD and Congress do not want that.[36]

Will interdiction work; will it significantly reduce the supply of illicit drugs in the United States? The Pentagon and the General Accounting Office do not think so. Peter Reuter, the principal economist studying the issue, argues that even if non-land smuggling routes became too risky, the retail price of cocaine would only increase 3 percent and even more smuggling traffic would shift to the Mexican land border. Given the economics of the cocaine business, one could reasonably expect smugglers, if necessary, to shift their routes out of the Caribbean Basin altogether. Cocaine could be flown through other Latin American nations and then around the radar screen to land further north on the Atlantic and Pacific coasts of the United States. Since cocaine smuggling routes to Europe currently exist, one might well expect transshipment to the United States from London or Madrid or some other European site. Surveillance and interdiction harass smugglers but do not stop them. The 1989 National Drug Control Strategy report recognized the limits of interdiction: "indeed, our recent experiences with drug interdiction have persuasively demonstrated that interdiction alone cannot prevent the entry of drugs, or fully deter traffickers and their organizations."[37]

Intelligence data are both the linchpin and the weakness of the strategy. Military satellites, radar, and tracking planes can monitor aircraft and seacraft leaving South America, but cannot determine if such craft are transporting illicit cargo. That information has to come from espionage activities within source and transit countries. Someone has to inform the proper authorities about the nature of the cargo being shipped. Informants risk death, making it difficult to recruit them. Drug corruption within the ranks of police and military forces within these countries has long compromised them as sources of information.³⁸

In spite of claims to the contrary, the increased military interdiction role had no demonstrable impact. Stephen Duncan, Coordinator for Drug Enforcement Policy and Support, DoD, in response to questions in the spring of 1990 about how effective the military has been in reducing drug smuggling into the United States, dodged the question, finally argued that military efforts had forced the traffickers to shift their smuggling routes to Mexico. However, the smugglers had begun that shift at least as early as 1985 because of the effectiveness of the South Florida Task Force, an essentially civilian effort. That success led to the creation of Operation Alliance, a multi-agency task force based in El Paso, Texas, in an effort to replicate this success. Even the military only claimed a 25 percent increase in the interdiction rate once its system was fully installed in 1992.³⁹

The Persian Gulf War demonstrated the inherent problem in making the military the lead agency in antinarcotics smuggling. The military's Defense-in-Depth surveillance and interdiction strategy requires the use of large numbers of aircraft and ships. Using these resources is easy, albeit expensive, when the military is in a waiting status but in wartime many of these resources must be quickly reassigned to war zones, thus creating holes in the surveillance net. During the Persian Gulf War, AWACS planes and navy ships were redeployed to the war theater, reducing coverage of the Caribbean Basin.⁴⁰

One solution is for Washington to strengthen the appropriate civilian agencies so that they can better accomplish their missions. If the drug problem is ever solved, the general smuggling problem will still exist. Building a civilian anti-smuggling system for the long-term makes more sense than institutionalizing border control as a military task.

Military Aid to Latin America

The strategy of using Andean militaries to suppress the drug business in Latin America is problematical at best. It assumes a mutuality of interest between the United States, on the one hand, and Andean militaries, on the other, which does not exist. Further, it incorrectly links drug traffickers and guerrillas and, by doing so, inadvertently aids both. Finally, it threatens democracy in Latin America, a long-term foreign policy goal of the United States.

Some Latin American military officers do not want to get involved in the antidrug crusade. Meeting at American University in June 1988, fifty Latin American military officers agreed that the military should not get involved in antidrug campaigns because military involvement would strengthen the military vis-à-vis civilian government and make the military more autonomous.⁴¹ Although these particular officers are a small portion of all officers, their views are consistent with the behavior of Latin American armies. Only the Mexican army has consistently engaged in drug suppression. Bolivian, Colombian, and Peruvian militaries have not, nor are they likely to do so, even with increased U.S. aid. Like their U.S. counterparts, they do not want to be policemen. The Colombian and Peruvian militaries prefer counter-insurgency operations.

Counter-insurgency warfare in Colombia and Peru, even with U.S. aid, will not end the drug trade, for leftist guerrillas and rightist businessmen are natural opponents who have only occasionally cooperated for mutual convenience. Traffickers want the guerrillas beaten; the guerrillas raise the cost of doing business and attract too much attention from the government, thus complicating normal business operations. The traffickers can reach accommodations with the military.

To varying degrees, the militaries of these nations are riddled with narcocorruption, as the 1991 *International Narcotics Control Strategy Report* points out. The Colombian armed forces have long been abusing the population. One report asserts that the military, in league with right-wing death squads, terrorizes and kills innocent people in Uraba state. The level of corruption can reach quite high; the Bolivian military government of 1981 was implicated in the cocaine trade. Military commanders in the Upper Huallaga Valley have been accused of being allies of the traffickers. Communication systems are insecure and fast helicopters and high-powered weapons are of marginal utility when someone picks up the telephone to warn traffickers that a raid is about to take place.⁴²

Using militaries to arrest criminals and destroy crops and factories further institutionalizes militaries as the authority within those states, encouraging them to marginalize or replace civilian government. This is a serious concern. Bolivia was governed by a series of military dictatorships between 1964–1982. Civilian government is of recent vintage in Peru; the military ruled from 1968–1980. Colombia has not had a military dictatorship since that of General Gustavo Pinilla's of 1954–1958. Colombia's military has only 60,000 members for an almost thirty-two-million-person population, and Colombian civilians seek to keep it under their control. Nevertheless, the military often ignores its civilian commanders. Military dictatorship is a long-standing scourge in Latin America that the United States should not encourage through its antidrug policy.⁴³

The solution of the insurgency problems in Peru and Colombia must come from those countries, not the United States. Both the Peruvian military and Sendero Luminoso are Peruvian, and the Peruvian government should be able to find Peruvian military leaders smart enough to outwit fellow countrymen. There is no evidence that Sendero has received outside aid; in fact, Sendero obtains its weaponry by buying or stealing it from the Peruvian military. Although Peruvian counter-insurgency measures attack the symptoms of Peru's problems, the civilian government has to deal with the causes of the insurgency, something the Fujimori administration wants to do. Colombia has begun using political accommodation as well as repression to solve its insurgency problem; it is too early to estimate its potential success, but the entry of M-19 into electoral politics suggests that other guerrilla movements might also be persuaded to make a similar move.

Militaries are killing machines not police forces; they are trained to kill people in sufficient numbers to convince the survivors not to fight. Military personnel are not trained nor suited to nation-building. Is there any evidence from any country that suggests that military units are good economic entrepreneurs? Are these bureaucratic entities, dependent as they are upon convincing governmental leaders and the public that the latter should transfer some of their wealth into the military, people who know how to farm and market the resultant products, to start and foster business enterprises, etc.? In real wars, the military is unleashed like a pit bull and then rechained once the conflict is over, but the "drug war" is not a war and will not end quickly. The Bush antidrug strategy called for a greatly enhanced military establishment performing a civilian function indefinitely. The anti-smuggling screens and the maritime-aerial patrols would have to be sustained else drug smuggling would resume if demand for foreign drugs continued or could be regenerated. If true military emergencies occur, either even more resources would have to be devoted to the Pentagon or the military's antidrug mission would have to be compromised. Moreover, the smuggling problem is not just a drug smuggling problem. The nation has little control over its borders. American enterprise is being undercut by smuggled goods. Terrorists and weapons can easily enter the country.[44] Should the military be given so much potential authority over civilian commerce?

The very fact that militaries are being used for civilian law enforcement is an admission of the failure of civilian government. This is particularly true for the United States with its historic tradition of keeping the military out of civilian affairs. Civilian government officials failed to resist the seductiveness of the popular image of the military and the personal political gains which come from supporting the military establishment. Dazzled by the glitter, glory, and gold of a possible military solution, these leaders fail to see that illicit drug use is a domestic, civilian problem, both in the United States and Latin America, one wherein free enterprise capitalists are servicing consumers. Using the military for the police function of illicit drug suppression emanates from anger, not reason.

Future Military Role

Americans are unlikely to sustain their fear and anger about illicit drug usage. They will become bored with drug news and divert their attention to other issues, especially as they slowly adjust to the reality that a certain percentage of the population, even though higher than they might wish, will always use illicit drugs. The drug problem pales in comparison to other national problems even though it received an inordinate amount of attention in the 1980s. The drug issue was part of a much larger issue in U.S. society, that of social control. The Reagan and Bush administrations represented, among other things, an effort to restore social control. Many Americans believed that life had gotten out of hand. Americans wanted their national government to fight those things which they believed threatened the "American way of life," whether those things were the intrusive role of the national government in the conduct of business and industry (hence the demand for deregulation), threats from the "Evil Empire" (hence the massive military buildup directed against the Soviet Union and intervention against leftists in Central America), international terrorism (hence the bombing of Libya), or sexual activity outside marriage and drug usage (hence the anti-abortion, anti-alcohol, and anti-illicit drugs crusades). In the 1990s, the nation must decide what, if anything, it will do about its educational system, the persistence of poverty, deterioration of its economic infrastructure, reduced clout in the international economy, urban decay, environmental pollution, budget deficits, and what role it will play in international affairs.

Congress became more critical of Bush's drug foreign policy, reflecting declining congressional interest in the issue. Congress followed public opinion and the public was less interested in drug foreign policy and what happened in Latin America. Americans care little about Latin America and ignore it until a "crisis" occurs. The crises occurring with the emergence of free nations in Eastern Europe, the consequences of the dismemberment of the USSR, the Persian Gulf War and the restructuring of Middle Eastern politics, and the economic shock waves pulsating through the U.S. economy as a result of the 1992 consolidation of Common Market economies and growing Japanese economic might shove Latin America, including its role as a drug source, into the background. Only a leftist victory in a Latin American nation is likely to again focus as much U.S. attention on Latin America as occurred in the 1980s.

The Bush administration appeared to be interested in a larger role for militaries. Laura Brooks reported that "Southcom says 'discussions are under way' to support unidentified antidrug forces in Central America with special forces military training."[45] Latin American militaries, through the Interamerican Defense Board and the Armies of the Americas program, both sponsored by the United States, discussed this possibility at the March 1991 meeting of twenty-five Latin American military officers in Montevideo, Uruguay. The decline of military dictatorships have left these military establishments (except in a few cases) with little to do.[46]

The Clinton administration indicates that it will shift more resources to tackling the *causes* of illicit drug use in the United States. It is likely to continue conducting surveillance and paying for the training and deployment of Latin American military units against the drug business, for they give the appearance of action. The amount spent is small by U.S. terms, making it easy to appropriate, but is very large in Latin American terms, giving the United States significant leverage in those nations. So many Washington agencies get a piece of the antidrug money pie that reducing the size of the pie will occur slowly. Neither the DEA nor the State Department's Bureau of International Narcotics Matters, to take two examples, has a bureaucratic interest in reducing the international antidrug budget. Neither does the DoD. In a time when its budget is being reduced, it has incentive to preserve as much of its budget as possible. Further, while there is no solid evidence that military involvement has made a significant difference, there is also no evidence that it has not. Supporters of the military's role can argue that the situation would be worse if the military were withdrawn. Put another way, DoD occupies an ideal bureaucratic position, for it can ask for more and more funds without having to prove that its programs are effective. Clinton, however, will listen to his Democratic party constituency, especially city mayors, who have long argued that money should be spent in their jurisdictions. He and Congress are likely to focus more on education, rehabilitation, and fiscal aid to law enforcement.

Notes

1. Another reason for trying to solve the U.S. drug epidemic abroad is the historical belief that foreigners and U.S. ethnic minorities cause the epidemics; see Douglas Clark Kinder, "Nativism, Cultural Conflict, Drug Control: United States and Latin American Antinarcotics Diplomacy Through 1965" in *The Latin American Narcotics Trade and U.S. National Security*, ed. by Donald J. Mabry (Westport, CT: Greenwood Press, 1989).

2. General Stephen Olmstead, USMC, makes this point in Congressional Research Service, *Narcotics Interdiction and the Use of the Military: Issues for Congress* (Washington: GPO, 1988), 15, 24. For a scholarly warning, see Morris J. Blachman

and Kenneth Sharpe, "The War on Drugs: American Democracy Under Assault," *World Policy Journal* (Winter 1989–90), 135–163.

3. Donald J. Mabry, "Andean Drug Trafficking and the Military Option," *The Military Review* (March 1990), and "The Possible Roles of the U.S. Military in the Andes," *The Andean Drug Strategy and the Role of the U.S. Military. Proceedings of a seminar held by the Congressional Research Service (November 9, 1989)*. Report of the Defense Policy Panel and Investigations Subcommittee of the Committee on Armed Services, House of Representatives, 101st Congress, First Session. Washington: Government Printing Office (January 1990), pp. 39–41. See also "The U.S. Military and the War on Drugs in Latin America," *Journal of Interamerican Studies and World Affairs* 30:2 (Summer–Fall 1988).

4. Stephen Duncan, Testimony to hearing of Subcommittees on Legislation and National Security and Government Information, Justice and Agriculture, U.S. House of Representatives, October 17, 1989, 101st Congress, 1st Session. Mimeo.

5. Charles Lane, et al., "The Newest War," *Newsweek*, January 6, 1992, 21.

6. John Martsh, as quoted in United States Senate. Select Committee on Narcotics Abuse and Control, *Drugs and Latin America: Economic and Political Impact and U.S. Policy Options*, report of the Select Committee on Narcotics Abuse and Control, 101st Congress, 1st Session (Washington D.C.: U.S. Government Printing Office, 1989), 22; W. R. Surrett, *The International Narcotics Trade: An Overview of Its Dimensions, Production Sources, and Organizations*. Congressional Research Service Report No. 88-643-F. (Washington D.C.: Library of Congress, 1988), 5, 8.

7. Office of National Drug Control Policy, *National Drug Control Strategy* (Washington, D.C.: ONDCP, 1989), 73. Hereafter cited as ONDCP, *1989 National Drug Control*.

8. On U.S.-Mexican drug foreign policy, see the following articles by Richard B. Craig: "Human Rights and Mexico's Antidrug Campaign," *Social Science Quarterly*, 60 (1980), 691–701; "Illegal Drug Traffic," in *Borderlands Sourcebook: A Guide to the Literature of Northern Mexico and the American Southwest*, ed. by E. R. Stoddard, R. L. Nostrand, and J. P. West (Norman, OK: University of Oklahoma Press, 1983), 209–13; "*La Campaña Permanente:* Mexico's Antidrug Campaign," *Journal of Interamerican Studies and World Affairs*, 20 (1978), 107–31; "Operación Intercepción: una política de presión internacional," *Foro Internacional*, 22 (1981), 203–30; "Operation Condor: Mexico's Antidrug Campaign Enters a New Era," *Journal of Interamerican Studies and World Affairs*, 22 (1980), 345–63; and "Mexican Narcotics Traffic: Binational Security Implications," in *The Latin American Narcotics Trade and U.S. National Security*, ed. by Donald J. Mabry (Westport, CT: Greenwood Press, 1989), 27–41. On the history of U.S.-Mexican relations, see Robert J. Shafer and Donald J. Mabry, *Neighbors—Mexico and the United States* (Chicago: Nelson-Hall, 1981).

9. In peacetime, the Coast Guard is civilian and under the jurisdiction of the Transportation Department but it uses a military organization to facilitate its conversion to a military unit in wartime. State militia (National Guard) are military but are not impeded by the Posse Comitatus Act (1878) which forbids the national military from engaging in civilian law enforcement.

10. Department of Defense (DoD), Report to House and Senate Armed Services Committee, accompanying April 20, 1989, letter from J. D. White, Office of Na-

tional Drug Control Policy, to Les Aspin, Chairman, Committee on Armed Services, House of Representatives.

11. U.S. General Accounting Office, *Drug Control: Communications Network Funding and Requirements Uncertain* GA)/NSIAD-92-29 (Washington: GAO, December, 1991); Inter-American Commission on Drug Policy, *Seizing Opportunities.* San Diego, Institute of the Americas, 1991, 9.

12. William O. Walker III, *Drug Control in the Americas,* rev. ed. (Albuquerque: University of New Mexico Press, 1989).

13. On the Panamanian invasion, see Bruce Watson and Peter Tsouras, *Operation Just Cause* (Boulder: Westview Press, 1991).

14. *International Drug Control Strategy Report* (Washington: U.S. Department of State, 1991), 26, 80, 97, 99, 114-15, 118-19); Comisión Andina de Juristas, "Bolivia: The Army Readies Itself," *Drug Trafficking Update,* May 6, 1991, 3.

15. United States. Congress. House. Committee on Government Operations. *Stopping the Flood of Cocaine With Operation Snowcap: Is It Working?* 13th Report (Washington: GPO, 1990), 101st Cong., 2d Sess., HR 101-673.

16. See United States, Antidrug Abuse Act of 1988; HR 5120, *Congressional Record-House*; House of Representatives, *Conference Report to Accompany H.R. 4481*; and United States, National Defense Authorization Act for FY 1989.

17. ONDCP, *1989 National Drug Control.*

18. United States. House. Committee on Government Operations. *United States Anti-Narcotics Activities in the Andean Region.* 38th Report. (Washington: GPO, 1990), 17. Hereafter cited as Government Operations, *Anti-Narcotics Activities;* and Raphael Perl, "United States International Drug Policy: Recent Developments and Issues," *Journal of Interamerican Studies and World Affairs,* 32:4 (1990), 123-135.

19. On Operation Blast Furnace, see Lt. Col. Sewell H. Menzel, "Operation Blast Furnace," *Army,* 39:11 (November, 1989), p. 25; and Major Mark P. Hertling, "Narcoterrorism: The New Unconventional War," *Military Review,* LXX:3 (March, 1990), pp. 16-28.

20. Associated Press Dispatch, *Clarion-Ledger,* September 2, 1989. Colombia also wanted $19 million to buy equipment to protect its juridical system; see John M. Gushko, "Colombia Asks Help in Protecting Judges," *The Washington Post,* August 30, 1989.

21. Colombia cracked down on the traffickers in the mid-1980s but the public eventually tired of the effort. During the course of the crackdown, the drug kingpins went into hiding, mounted a massive nationalistic propaganda campaign within Colombia to portray that government as a tool of the United States, and tried to bargain for amnesty. The Colombian government made no deal but did ease up on its attacks on the traffickers. See Guy Gugliotta and Jeff Leen, *Kings of Cocaine* (New York: Simon and Schuster, 1989), 170-77, and Bruce M. Bagley, "Colombia and the War on Drugs," *Foreign Affairs,* 67:1 (Fall 1988), 70-92. Fabio Ochoa made a similar offer after the August 1989 crackdown began; see Eugene Robinson, "Kin of 'Extraditables' Calls for Negotiations; Bombings in Medellin," *The Washington Post,* August 30,1989.

22. Bruce Bagley, "Colombia and the War on Drugs," 87.

23. For a more detailed examination of the coca enterprise and U.S. drug policy in Peru see: Rensselaer W. Lee III, *The White Labyrinth: Cocaine and Political Power*

(New Brunswick: Transaction Publishers, 1989); and Edmundo Morales, *Cocaine: White Gold Rush in Peru* (Tucson: University of Arizona Press, 1989).

24. The literature on Sendero Luminoso is growing at a rapid pace. The best single book on the subject is Gustavo Gorriti E., *Sendero: historia de la guerra milenaria en el Perú, I* (Lima: Editorial Apoyo, 1990). A summary analysis can be found in Gustavo Gorriti, "The War of the Philosopher-King," *The New Republic* (June 16, 1990), 15–22. Tina Rosenberg, "Guerrilla Tourism," *The New Republic* (June 16, 1990), 23–25, is based on her interviews with Senderistas.

25. *New York Times*, April 22, 1990. On the DEA assessment of Peru's priorities, see *DEA Review*, December 1989), 60–61, as quoted in Government Operations. *Anti-Narcotics Activities*, 38.

26. Alex Emery, "Fujimori: Won't Sign U.S. Military Aid Agreement to Combat Drugs," Associated Press Dispatch, published by peru@ATHENA.MIT.EDU, September 13, 1990. Emery quotes U.S. Ambassador Anthony Quainton as having said in an interview with the news magazine *Caretas* that if Peru "does not sign the agreement, the aid would go to other countries." See also Michael Isikoff, "Talks Between U.S., Peru On Military Aid Collapse," *Washington Post*, September 26, 1990. César Atala, Peruvian ambassador to the United States in 1989, argued that a better solution to the coca-growing problem in his country was for the United States to buy the entire crop; see his testimony in United States. Congress. Senate. Committee on Governmental Affairs. Permanent Subcommittee on Investigations. *U.S. Government Anti-Narcotics Activities in the Andean Region of South America. Hearing before the Permanent Subcommittee on Investigations of the Committee on Governmental Affairs, United States Senate, 101st Cong. 1st sess. September 26, 27, 29, 1989.* S. Hrg. 101–311 (Washington: GPO, 1989), 74. Gustavo Gorriti testified in the same hearings, arguing that mixing drug eradication and counterinsurgency was akin to pouring fuel on a fire; see his testimony on pages 128–132.

27. Eduardo Gamarra, "U.S. Military Assistance, the Militarization of the War on Drugs, and the Prospects of the Consolidation of Democracy in Bolivia," *Congressional Record-Senate* (May 9), 102nd Cong, 1st sess., S 5687; Kevin Healy, "Political Ascent of Bolivia's Peasant Coca Leaf Producers," *Journal of Interamerican Studies and World Affairs*, 33:1 (Spring 1991), 104–108, 111–113; and James Painter, "Peasants Protest US Role in Bolivia's Drug War," *Christian Science Monitor* (May 17, 1991), 7.

28. Bernard McMahon, "Low-Intensity Conflict: The Pentagon's Foible," *ORBIS* (Winter, 1990), pp. 3–4; Abbott, "The Army and the Drug War," 4; Menzel, "Operation Blast Furnace," 25; Hertling, "Narcoterrorism," 16–28. Moreover, there has been some support in the Senate for the military to assume this role; see Benjamin F. Schemmer, "Senate Leaders Ask Scrowcroft for New White House Focus on Low-Intensity Conflict," *Armed Forces Journal International*, 126:8 (March 1, 1989), pp. 66–67.

29. "Risky Business," *Newsweek* (July 16, 1990), 16–19.

30. Lane, "The Newest War," 18–23. The best book on U.S. military efforts in the Andes is Washington Office on Latin America, *Clear and Present Dangers: The U.S. Military and the War on Drugs in Latin America* (Washington, October, 1991).

31. Department of the Army, Field Manual 100–20, *Low Intensity Conflict* (Baltimore: U.S. Army Adjutant Publications Center, 1981); U.S. Army Training and

Doctrine Command, U.S. Army Operational Concept for Low Intensity Conflict. TRADOC Pamphlet No. 525-44 (Fort Monroe, VA, 1986), 2; Richard J. Barnet, "The Costs and Perils of Intervention," in *Low-Intensity Warfare*, ed. by Michael T. Klare and Peter Kornbluh (New York: Pantheon Books, 1987), 53; Bernard McMahon, "Low-Intensity Conflict: The Pentagon's Foible," *ORBIS* (Winter, 1990), pp. 3-4; and David Silverstein, "Preparing America to Win Low-Intensity Conflicts," *Backgrounder*, No. 786, August 31, 1990.

32. Donald J. Mabry, "Andean Drug Trafficking and the Military Option," *Military Review*, LXX:3 (March 1990), 29-40; Donald J. Mabry, "The Role of the Military in the War on Drugs," in *The Latin American Narcotics Trade and U.S. National Security* (Westport: Greenwood Press, 1990), edited by Donald J. Mabry, pp. 75-88; IDCSR, 1991; Michael H. Abbott, "The Army and the Drug War: Politics or National Security," *Parameters*, XVIII:4 (December, 1988), 108-11.

33. Abbott; Sewell H. Menzel, "Operation Blast Furnace," *Army*, 39:11 (November 1989, 25.

34. Abbott, 108; Menzel, 25; Mark P. Hertling, "Narcoterrorism: The New Unconventional War," *Military Review*, LXX:3 (March 1990), 16-28; Schemmer, 1989; Benjamin F. Schemmer, "Senate Leaders Ask Scrowcroft for New White House Focus on Low-Intensity Conflict," *Armed Forces Journal International*, 126:8 (March 1, 1989), p. 66.

35. Departments of Defense and State, "Andean Drug Efforts: A Report to Congress," *Congressional Record* (March 7, 1991), 102nd Cong., 1st sess.

36. Senator Mitch McConnell did propose a bill in the summer of 1989 to empower the military to shoot down suspected drug-smuggling aircraft but Congress refused to let it out of committee; see J. Baker, "The 'You Fly, You Die' Debate," *Newsweek* (October 2, 1989), 26. The executive branch later made it clear that: "consistent with international law and in the interests of aviation safety, no action may now be taken to stop or interrupt the progress of a target aircraft in flight"; see ONDCP, *1989 National Drug Control*, 76.

37. Department of Defense (DoD), Report to House and Senate Armed Services Committee, accompanying April 20, 1989 letter from J. D. White, Office of National Drug Control Policy, to Les Aspin, Chairman, Committee on Armed Services, House of Representatives; General Accounting Office, *Drug Smuggling: Capabilities for Interdicting Private Aircraft are Limited and Costly.* (GAO/GGD-89-93). (Washington, D.C.: GAO, 1989). The analysis of Reuter and his RAND colleagues appears in a number of places: Peter Reuter, Testimony to Committee on Government Operations, U.S. House of Representatives. October 17, 1989, Mimeo, 12-13; Peter Reuter, and Mark Kleian, "Risks and Prices: An Economic Analysis of Drug Enforcement," *Crime and Justice* (July 1986), 293; Peter Reuter, Gordon Crawford, and Jonathan Crane, *Sealing the Borders: The Effects of Military Participation in Drug Interdiction* (Santa Monica: Rand Corporation, 1988); Peter Reuter, *Eternal Hope: America's International Narcotics Effort* (Santa Monica: The Rand Corporation, 1987); Peter Reuter, "Quantity Illusions and Paradoxes of Drug Interdiction: Federal Intervention into Vice Policy," *Law & Contemporary Problems* (Winter 1988), pp. 233-52. The quote is from ONDCP, *National Drug Control Strategy Report* (Washington: ONDCP, 1989).

38. J. Dillin, "Task Force Steps Up Drug War," *The Christian Science Monitor* (October 24, 1989), 7.

39. Stephen Duncan, Coordinator for Drug Enforcement Policy and Support, Department of Defense, testimony in United States. Congress. House. Committee on Armed Services, *Military Role in Drug Interdiction (Part 4)* (Washington: GPO, 1990), hearing held April 19, 1990. 101st Cong., 1st sess. H.A.S.C 101–671. pp. 47, 54, 62. Duncan argued that determining effectiveness was very difficult. By 1986, long before the U.S. military was given the leadership role in drug interdiction, drug smuggling was shifting to the U.S.-Mexican border; see United States. Congress. Senate. Committee on Appropriations, *Drugs and Domestic Terrorism Threat to Arizona and the Southwest Border: Hearings before a Subcommittee of the Committee on Appropriations,* 99th Cong. 2d sess., January 7, 9, 1986 (Washington: GPO, 1986) 1–6, 55, 58; United States. General Accounting Office, *Report to the Chairman, Subcommittee on Information, Justice, Agriculture, Committee on Government Operations. House of Representatives. Drug Smuggling: Large Amounts of Illegal Drugs Not Seized by Federal Authorities,* GAO/GGD-87-91 (Washington: GPO, 1987), 15; and United States. House. Select Committee on Narcotics Abuse and Control, *The Federal War on Drugs: Past, Present, and Future: Hearing before the Select Committee on Narcotics Abuse and Control.* 99th Cong., 2d sess., October 3, 1986 (Washington: GPO, 1987), 79–82. The only scholarly analysis of the creation of Operation Alliance is Horace D. Nash, "Congress and the Southwest Border War on Drugs: Operation Alliance, 1986–1988," unpublished paper, Department of History, Mississippi State University, December, 1990.

40. The Pentagon both admits that coverage was reduced and denies that its reduced coverage had any effect!

41. L. Goodman, and J. Mendelson, "Whose Drug War Is It, Anyway?" *The Christian Science Monitor* (July 22, 1988), 12.

42. The problem of drug-related corruption in public security forces in the United States or Latin America is well documented. For some examples, see Government Operations, *Anti-Narcotics Activities,* 40–43, and the quotation from the *DEA Review* (December 1989), on page 60 of the same report; Kevin Healy, "Coca, The State, and the Peasantry in Bolivia, 1982–1988," *Journal of Interamerican Studies and World Affairs,* 30: 2 & 3 (Summer 1988), 111; and Coletta Youngers, "Colombia Military's Link with Drug Dealers," *The Christian Science Monitor,* September 11, 1989.

43. Augusto Varas, ed., *Hemispheric Security and U.S. Policy in Latin America* (Boulder: Westview Press, 1989); Karen L. Remmer, *Military Rule in Latin America* (Boston: Unwin Hyman, 1989); and Brian Loveman and Thomas M. Davies, Jr., eds., *The Politics of Antipolitics: the Military in Latin America,* 2nd ed., rev. and expanded (Lincoln: University of Nebraska Press, 1989).

44. J. Dillin, "U.S. Paying Stiff Price for Porous Borders." *The Christian Science Monitor* (October 10, 1989), 1–2.

45. Laura Brooks, "U.S. Military Extends Drug War into C. America," *Christian Science Monitor,* June 25, 1991, 1.

46. Samuel Blixen, "Southern Cone Militaries Find Common Ground: MERCOSUR Allows For Growing Military Autonomy," *Latinamerica Press,* 23: 21 (June 6, 1991), 1.

7

The Role of Economic Development: Policy Options for Increased Peasant Participation in Peru and Bolivia

Kevin Healy

Economic development has been at the top of Third World government agendas for many decades. This chapter presents some central policy issues and considerations about the role of economic development in relation to international cocaine trafficking and drug policy with particular attention to Peru and Bolivia.

The concept of national economic development for Third World governments is synonymous with the notion of progress bringing an increase in output of goods and services and improved levels of living for citizens. Indicators such as national investment, savings, per capita incomes and energy consumption have served to measure these developmental changes during modern history. Social equity, participation and environmental dimensions have been added to the concept of economic development in more recent times.

The economic development concept also has become part of the framework of anti-drug policies. The expansion of the drug industry itself over the past decade has been a form of economic development for various Third World countries. The runaway growth in the illegal industry generates economic benefits which are in scarce supply in the developing world. Despite the many ills and economic distortions which the drug industry spreads, nation-states with massive levels of unemployment and underemployment, with prolonged economic recessions, and sizeable peasant populations may be understandably ambivalent about the vigor with which they deal with this issue.

The author would like to thank David Bray for his helpful comments on this chapter. The author's views do not necessarily reflect those of the Inter-American Foundation.

Supressing drug production is to deny gains in increased employment and incomes, foreign exchange, lower consumer prices from dollar laundering and increased circulation of income. In nations with large numbers employed in the illegal industry's laborforce or where its economic weight in the national economy is substantial, the disincentives are especially strong for liquidating illicit economic structures.

Peasant producers represent the social group which best illustrates this argument. The peasant farmer has become an important economic actor and a major concern of anti-drug policy-makers. Peasant cultivators, responding to First World demand, produce the coca leaf which initiates the multi-tiered chain of cocaine production and trafficking activities. The elimination of coca leaf holdings for hundreds of thousands of peasant cultivators is a guarantee of political fall-out to states pursuing national development goals. To protect themselves from such economic losses, states have signed bi-lateral and multi-lateral agreements of programs for alternative development in coca growing regions supported by increased foreign economic aid. In theory, alternative development represents legal economic development programs (livestock, agriculture and other activities) which are economically viable enough to replace illicit crop production.

Yet there are some inherent difficulties and dilemmas to this rural development approach to the drug problem. Under normal conditions, the record over the past four decades of foreign aid agencies and Third World states to improve the agrarian economies and incomes of the peasant sector has been poor. The presence of an illicit money making crop makes rural development even more complicated and its goals less attainable. Luring peasant producers away from a profitable crop which has no competitive rival adds to the difficulties in bringing about effective rural development with legal crops.

States endorse alternative development strategies also to avoid exclusive reliance on the use of police and military force for curbing drug trafficking. Using a single policy of repression for combatting drugs would undermine the national credibility of Third World leaders, portraying them as pawns of the powerful Northern states. This problem of subordination to a more powerful nation's interests also makes economic development programs an imperative for anti-drug strategies in the Third World.

The chapter focuses on economic development and drug trafficking issues in the nations of Peru and Bolivia.[1] These two countries combined produce 90 percent of the coca leaf and processed coca paste used by the international cocaine industry. Their strategic economic roles in the illegal industry have made them a principal focus for anti-drug policies in the Western Hemisphere.

This chapter will offer some considerations on economic development issues which are often ignored in the debates over U.S. drug policy. This author argues that both architects and critics of drug policy fail to address some critical economic issues in relation to combatting drugs, issues which go to the heart of peasant motivations and the socio-economic conditions which shape them.[2] Assuming that the Andean states and their First World sponsors will forge ahead with alternative development programs to curb drug production, this chapter offers some lessons for policy analysis from the field of Andean rural development during recent decades.

The first part of the chapter focus is on the patterns of rural modernization and economic change in the Andean countries in recent decades. It gives attention to the regional and social biases of national public policies which have shaped the developmental changes and beneficiary populations. This background material presents the public policy and socio-economic context for understanding both the expansion of the coca-cocaine economy and the implementation of alternative development programs, both past and present.

After the critique of prevailing rural development policies, the chapter discusses some alternative policies and institutional arrangements to address the developmental needs and socio-economic interests of the peasantries in Peru and Bolivia. The macro and micro level of analysis will include the necessary political requirements, the experience of integrated rural development projects and alternative development projects and the critical role of non-governmental development and grassroots organizations for engendering peasant-based rural development strategies.

A final section of the chapter presents a case study of effective grassroots development with cocoa bean production in a non-traditional coca growing area of Bolivia. Thus the chapter's progression moves from the macro level of analysis down to the micro-level of grassroots development.

Recent Economic Trends for Peru and Bolivia

An assessment of a drug related economic development strategy must begin by placing the two countries in the context of their decade-long crises. Peru and Bolivia have been in the throes of economic turmoil and near collapse during the 1980's. A recent World Development Report measures the deterioration in a variety of ways. Their figures show a drop in the rate of growth in the Gross National Product between the periods 1965–1980 and 1980–1989 of 3.9 percent to .4 percent in Peru and 4.4 percent to –0.9 percent in Bolivia.

In the agricultural sector, whose performance has important implications for coca production, both countries showed significant food deficits and zero growth in per capita food production leading to major increases in food imports and donated international food aid. In energy production and consumption, manufacturing, gross domestic investment, Bolivia and Peru demonstrated serious declines, in most cases, falling to negative rates (World Bank 1991:218). Between 1980 and 1989, both per capita consumption and per capita incomes for the two countries fell to the level of 1970.

The International Monetary Fund's stabilization and economic recovery plans were adopted as solutions to these profound crises. The IMF plan went into effect in Bolivia in 1985 and in Peru several years ago in 1990. Through major increases in export earnings, the elimination of hyperinflation and positive economic growth rates, Bolivia has achieved a modest record of success. However, extremely high social costs such as the increase in unemployment rate from 17 percent to 25 percent, enormous growth in the urban informal sector, and a plunge in the minimum wage have raised serious questions about the social equity and political viability of the policies (Iriarte 1989; Horton 1989:190). The adjustment "shock treatment" in Peru has been equally harsh and dramatic since the shock began in 1990. Although inflation has fallen from 60 percent to 5 percent per month, Peru has had two consecutive years with negative economic growth rates. The standard of living of the population fell by 24 percent, which compounded a decline by 53 percent that had already occurred between 1985–1990. In mid-1992, only 10 percent of Lima's population was adequately employed.

During the 1980's decade, the illegal coca-cocaine industry expanded rapidly to occupy a central place in both economies. Coca leaf cultivation increased from 30,000 ha. to 150,000 ha. in Peru and from 12,000 ha. to 70,000 ha. in Bolivia. In 1990, some 700,000 or 5 percent of the Peruvian workforce participated in the coca-cocaine industry and in Bolivia 250,000 people or 7 percent of the workforce participated. In Bolivia, coca growers have increased 2 percent to 10 percent of the total peasant population. In both countries, masses of peasant farmers in drug producing regions have moved upstream into the value-added processing of coca paste to further integrate themselves into the international cocaine economy. Moreover, recent State Department findings point to additional vertical integration of the cocaine industry in Bolivia through the processing of 25 percent of coca leaf production into refined cocaine. The value of earnings from the industry invested in the two national economies reach hundreds of millions of dollars in each country and are an especially high percentage of total exports in Bolivia (Andreas, Betram, Blackman, and Sharpe 1991 and 1992).

Economic Development Strategies in Peru and Bolivia

To have significant impact on drug production in Peru and Bolivia, economic development process must include a peasant-based rural development strategy. A supply side strategy which fails to take the basic needs and economic opportunity structure of the peasantry into account will be doomed to the same frustrating results of the past decade. The fact that neither country has had an extended history of a broad-based agricultural development strategy benefitting its peasant producers partly explains the massive migrations to coca producing areas and suggests the entrenched interests and political influence of upper income social groups. Perhaps by reviewing briefly some characteristics of Mexico's economic growth, the need for substituting a mainstream agricultural strategy for a peasant-based development strategy will be apparent.

The Mexican case illustrates the impact of conventional economic growth strategies on the tendency by peasant producers to engage in illicit crop production. Mexico has twice the per capita income level of Peru and three times that of Bolivia. If by achieving high economic growth levels, the two Andean countries equalled Mexico's per capita income, would the raw material production for the drug industry by the peasantry disappear or be significantly reduced? Given the widespread persistence of rural poverty in Mexico and an estimated 35,000 ha. of opium poppy production, the answer to that question would have to be no.

Between 1965 and 1989, Mexico maintained an impressive 3.5 percent annual rate of growth in GNP. Unfortunately, this pattern of urban and industrial development left out or adversely affected the mass of peasant producers who often migrated to Mexico's urban centers and the United States. Mexico's impressive economic growth ran counter to a peasant-based development strategy. Solon Barraclough, a longtime analyst of Mexican rural development concluded that in spite of this rapid industrial growth and agricultural modernization nearly three-fourths of the rural population in 1980 did not have sufficient income to meet their basic needs and over half did not have access to adequate food supplies (Barraclough 1991:22).

Peasant migration patterns from highland Andean communities to the main coca growing areas, the Upper Huallaga of Peru and the Chapare zone of Bolivia, raise similar questions about whether or not the peasant impact of conventional agricultural development and modernization strategies are consistent with achieving the ambitious drug related goals. Despite a substantial flow of foreign aid in both countries during various decades (Bolivia being one of the highest per capita aid recipients in the Third World), available financial and economic resources and related agricultural production opportunities tended to benefit disproportionately the large and medium size commercial operators (Hopkins 1981, Alvarez

1983). For example, the strong preference to channel economic and financial investments to the export sectors similarly express the anti-peasant bias of state policy.

The Peruvian state policy provided support to the modernization and expansion of coastal commercial farms in lieu of peasant agriculture. The small plot producer of the highlands was a victim rather than a beneficiary of the state's agricultural development plans. Caballero demonstrates how this agricultural policy bias caused coastal capitalist agriculture to displace some important Andean food crops in urban markets. For example, highland potatoes dropped from 46 percent to 11 percent of the total share in urban markets between 1971 and 1978 (Caballero 1984:15). Another study shows that during the 1970s and 1980s Peruvian regimes whether using both heterodox and orthodox economic policies heavily favored public investments in coastal agriculture which discriminated against the peasants in highland areas (Wilson and Wise 1986).

When Peruvian regimes ostensibly championed peasant interests for ideological reasons, the results were also the same. For example, Velasco Alvarado's populist government channeled 50 percent of the total national agricultural investments one year for four large coastal irrigation projects (Wilson and Wise 1986). In the mid-eighties, the APRA government declared its objective of using guaranteed farm prices as a way to redistribute national expenditures to the highland producers. However, the two-year program collapsed in the face of the political power of coastal interest groups in determining the allocation of state resources. While 70 percent of the total price subsidies supported rice production, predominantly on medium and large coastal farms with mechanized and irrigated operations, only 4 percent bolstered highland crops (Maranon 1989:90).

Historians argue that the state bias in agricultural investment policy has deep roots in the Peruvian social structure. During Peru's history as an independent nation the government showed little incentive to invest in sectors like small manufacturing and agriculture in the sierra, which neither belonged to elites nor were viewed as offering the economic potential of mining and coastal agriculture (Berry 1992:52). More recently a Peruvian sociologist, Guillermo Monge, argued that it took the guerrilla threat of the Shining Path (Sendero Luminoso) to put the highland peasantry for the first time in history on the national agenda.

In similar ways, the Bolivian state has demonstrated anti-peasant and corresponding regional biases by its selective financing of the expansion of commercial agriculture in the lowland Santa Cruz region. Since the 1950's, credit, exchange rate, investment, pricing, fiscal, agricultural research and export policies have supported the rapid expansion and capitalization of medium and large commercial farms in Santa Cruz while starving peasant producers of the needed technology and capital to improve their small farm production and marketing capacity (Dandler, Blanes, Prudencio, and Munoz 1987). Such policies also had negative environmental effects on the tropical Santa Cruz region which seriously jeopardized the future of peasant farming. Regardless of whether national policies consist of industrial import substitution or structural adjustment, the bottom line result has been to enrich the Santa Cruz agricultural elites and exclude a peasant producer class which presently supplies 70 percent of Bolivia's national agricultural production. This distribution of agricultural resources follows the concentration of power and wealth among influential groups within the Bolivian social structure. When the Bolivian state showed a committment toward social change in the highland areas during the land reform era of the 1950's, Santa Cruz elites retained their national influence to capture the lion's share of agricultural investments (Gill 1989).

Public policies of peasant colonization and resettlement over four decades also have stimulated the migration of highland peasant populations to the tropical lowlands of the Amazonian basin, the areas which subsequently became national centers of coca expansion for the drug industry. The colonization policies also manifest the anti-highland peasant bias in national development and belief in the lowland jungle areas as a key to future progress in the two countries. Through his Amazon basin development project, the Carretera Marginal, former President Beleunde of Peru made his own personal crusade into a national cause and vision of his country's future developmment. Peru and Bolivia's ranking among the top three countries in Latin America in terms of new cropland brought into production between 1961 and 1979 underscore the importance of colonization programs (Grindle 1986:90). The erroneous assumption underlying the strategy of the Bolivian government and its primary supporter, the United States Agency for International Development (USAID) for the regional population shift was the belief in the superior economic potential of the lowlands for increasing national production and rural employment (USAID 1974). Ironically, this assumption turned out to be true mostly for coca leaf whose expansion backfired because of the spreading cocaine industry and environmental degradation of the rain forest areas of the Amazonian basin, thereby turning a noble dream into a national as well as international nightmare.

Another policy mechanism which undermined peasant agriculture in the highlands and other regions of Peru and Bolivia was the policy of cheap food established to benefit the urban consumer and foster a subsidized industrialization strategy. Such policies have been common throughout Latin America for many decades (de Janvry 1981; Grindle 1986). In Peru, food price controls manifest this state policy bias (de Janvry 1981). In Bolivia, the terms of trade favoring urban consumers have been a common thread of agrarian history of the past four decades of the modernization era. The fact that not a single Latin American country has been able to reverse the unfavorable terms of trade for the peasantry suggests the structural basis of the problem.

This structural imbalance and consistent policy discrimination has led throughout the Third World to a net transfer of income from the peasant producer regions to the expanding modern sectors. Viewed from the level of the individual peasant household, peasants pursue strategies such as migration and off farm employment to shore up the falling rural incomes from these policies (Figueroa 1986). The peasant impulse to leave their home highland communities to alleviate low income and employment opportunities represent the factors pushing the massive migration behind the rapidly expanding coca frontier in the Upper Huallaga and Chapare regions.

Peru's importation of meat, rice and wheat flour is another manifestation of the cheap food policy (Painter 1983: 202). Indeed, between 1970 and 1984, 67.3 percent of food subsidies in Peru went for imported products (Maranon 1989). As a result, producers were unable to compete with subsidized food imports and domestically produced foodstuffs sold at controlled prices (Painter 1983: 203). At the national level, this anti-food production policy generated an increase in cereal imports and donated international food aid (World Bank 1991).[3]

Mayer and Glave's research on the diffusion of high-yielding potato varieties developed by the International Potato Center (IPC) of Peru illustrates the difficulties for peasant farmers in overcoming the unfavorable terms of trade when new and improved agricultural technologies are available to them (Mayer and Glave 1992). Despite advances in potato productivity in recent decades in Peru, this data shows that because of cheap food policies and rising agricultural input prices only a minority of upper income peasants in the highlands were able to use profitably the new technology. For the vast majority, the economic risks represent an irrational investment, compelling them to use other economic strategies.

Viewed in structural terms, the Andean peasant predicament has been referred to as internal colonialism. Economic discrimination fits within a web of social and cultural discrimination. In return for cheap labor and food provided to the cities and the modern sector, peasants receive negligible state investment in their communities and, adding insult to injury, as discrete ethnic groups, endure soci-cultural discrimination in schools, courts, hospitals, banks, markets and public offices, etc. Moreover, public agencies ostensibly operating to promote agriculture in the highlands have provided inefficient and scant services and resources for the peasant sector.

Adjustment Programs and Peasant Agriculture

The International Monetary Fund's stabilization and structural adjustment policies (the New Economic Policy or NEP) have been adopted in the two Andean countries to reverse the declining economic trends of the eighties. For the purpose of our analysis on coca growing, the impact of the NEP on the peasant agricultural performance is important to examine. From the foregoing policy analysis, there are perhaps reasons that structural adjustment programs would improve the conditions of peasant producers. For example, the elimination of subsidies for the urban consumer and agricultural elite producer take policy benefits away from these traditional constituents of state policy.

Bolivia presents an easier case to evaluate since results are available for a five year implementation period. Available findings show that peasant agriculture has been adversely affected by the new NEP measures. A recent World Bank report indicated that both the volume and value-added of the goods produced by the poor fell during the adjustment period worsening peasant welfare (World Bank 1990a:32). This deterioration of the standard of living of peasants is also due to climatic catastrophes in Bolivia.

At the same time, exorbitant interest rates made agricultural loans prohibitive and the peasantry faced decreasing access to the public and private banking system for productive activities (Healy 1993). The small minority of agrarian elites from the Santa Cruz region once again captured the lion's share of state resources for agricultural development investments such as large-scale land-clearing (deforestation) and soybean production schemes. While the peasantry experienced reduced access to sources of formal credit, non-peasant soybean producers obtained the lion's share of tariff rebates for their exports and economic benefits from loan programs of the Inter-American Development Bank and World Bank.

In Peruvian agriculture, after two years of implementation of structural adjustment programs, preliminary findings also show a fall in peasant production and income although at a slower rate than large commercial farm groups (Escobal and Castillo 1992). Large highland areas of Peru suffered from climatic changes from the El Niño currents which had negative affects on peasant agriculture during this same period.

The cumulative effects of public policies unfavorable to peasant agriculture have led to such problems as agricultural stagnation, increasing food deficits, rural unemployment and underemployment, social polarization, and regional social and economic disparities. Highland migration in search of employment and income becomes a rational response within a context of severe economic crises on top of decades of discrimination by state policies.

In short, whereas the migration to the Upper Huallaga and Chapare for coca leaf cultivation has been stimulated by the relative high prices for coca, the push factor of extreme poverty in highland communities is also part of the equation.[4] Andean public policies have led to decades of exploitation and marginality creating the necessary pre-conditions for expanded coca growing. In view of this background, it appears that only a fundamental reordering of national and regional agricultural priorities will enable economic development to play an effective role in drug reduction.

Peasant-Based Development Strategies

In facing the tremendous challenges on many fronts to their future development prospects, Peruvian and Bolivian analysts have called for a neo-Marshall Plan (Gorriti 1989; García Sayan 1989; GOB 1990). They have argued that to arrest the continued growth of the coca-cocaine industry requires an enormous transfer of external financial and economic resources to lift Peru and Bolivia out of their economic crises. Only within a context of effective economic recovery and a major economic development upswing, they argue, will a drug policy have a chance to work.

However, missing from their macro-level economic picture is any allusion to the need for fundamental changes in agrarian policies and recognition of the critical role of popular participation for effective broad-based agricultural development. It is unlikely that huge resource transfers will have an important impact on peasant economic behavior without structural reforms, and related agricultural policy changes.

New public policies based upon the real conditions of local economies would provide affordable credit to peasant producers even if it meant re-introducing financial subsidies removed by the IMF adjustment programs. Highland infrastructural investment in roads, communications and storage facilities would have the highest priority in national agricultural policy. Investments would go to industries with linkages to small-scale peasant production and for production and consumption needs of peasants. (Barraclough 1991). Preferential trade agreements with Western industrial countries would be attained for products (coffee, cocoa, quinoa, etc.) produced on peasant farms, and whenever possible peasant producers should participate in direct marketing through grassroots organizations.

How does one set into motion a participatory approach to agricultural development without having it railroaded by the economic and political elites benefitting from status quo policies? An essential step would be the organization of a political coalition around peasant economic interests and socio-political participation. A government that adopts a peasant-based strategy is likely to look to the peasantry for a large part of its political support and must be able to mobilize that support both in achieving power and maintaining it (Pearse 1980). Thus the most effective way to compete with the economic interest groups controlling agricultural policy and key rural development institutions is to have a national alternative development program with the weight of peasant social and political mobilization behind it.

Such a coalition-building effort would be an easier task in Bolivia than Peru given the active national peasant *sindicato* network and the crucial role peasant producers play in national food production.[5] However, in Peru there are perhaps increasing possibilities to forge urban political alliances with institutions interested in arresting the spread of coca paste consumption in urban neighborhoods not to mention police and political corruption and revenues for Sendero Luminoso. Given their high priority of drug related concerns, U.S. and Western European governments have to put their donor weight behind this political praxis of democratization for crop reduction during the 1990's.

The requirements at the local or micro-regional level for an effective agricultural development strategy also are in need of change.[6] The programs for "alternative rural development" in the Chapare and Upper Huallaga resemble what was known in Latin America during the seventies as integrated rural development projects (IRDs). The IRDs were put into vogue in Latin America by multilateral agencies such as the World Bank and Inter-American Development Bank (de Janvry 1981). The project design, established for a given province or micro-region, provided access to credit, extension services, water, roads, markets, health facilities, education for their children and non-farm sources of rural employment (Grindle 1986:161). Part of their inspiration and conception came from the former World Bank's president Robert MacNamara, in his 1973 address for aid to the rural poor of the Third World. MacNamara's thesis was that large programs and projects would reduce rural poverty without the need for structural change bringing a redistribution of power and wealth in the social system. However, the academic rural development literature on this experience concludes that the results of IRDs were a failure in terms of achieving the social and economic development goals established for the projects.

The IRD projects encountered insoluble problems of bureaucratic competition, personal ambitions, political interference, weak inter-agency coordination and clientelistic practices (Grindle 1986). At their best, they benefitted only a minority of the better-off peasants (de Janvry 1981). The IRDs were also faulted for their lack of experience in encouraging participation as well as the long experience of top-down planning and implementation (de Janvry 1981). Moreover they did not intend for the scope of participation to go beyond the local level and demonstrate to the State and society more generally that peasants should be taken into account as actors in national development (de Janvry 1981). It is interesting to note that similar problems are undermining the alternative rural development programs sponsored by the Andean states in the Chapare and Upper Huallaga areas.

Examples from the highland region of Bolivia illustrate what can happen as a result of unmet expectations in such ambitious project undertakings. In the altiplano region, three World Bank financed IRDs were unable to sustain community consensus behind their work ultimately leading to a fundamental rupture in relations with the local populations. During the early eighties, local *sindicatos* of the Aymara ethnic group staged occupations in each of these projects to protest their lack of participation in decision-making and control over resources (Healy 1989).

Similarly, in the alternative development programs of the Chapare region, peasant participation in planning and execution has been a controversial political issue. During the past four years, there has been an ongoing struggle between the peasant *sindicato* federations and the state over the terms of participation in the rural development programs established to replace coca production (Healy 1988b, 1991).

The coca leaf producers have mobilized various protest events to pressure the state to create councils within the Ministry of Agriculture and Peasant Affairs (MACA) which place their leaders in decision-making positions to share power with high-level government officials in relation to the alternative development programs. They have also attempted to institute local councils of government-peasant representation in the Chapare. At one point, frustrated by the slow pace of the institutional reforms, the ineffective state-sponsored alternative development programs and the threat of military intervention in the Chapare, the peasant organizations signed agreements of cooperation with non-governmental actors such as a regional coalition of NGOs, the Comite Cívico, which is the most prominent regional citizens' committee, and the regional public development corporation, CORDECO, to make some progress in participatory development without relying upon official channels.

Conflicts between the peasant *sindicatos* and the Bolivian state have been a major obstacle to attaining more widespread cooperation and participation in the crop-reduction programs and establishing a broad-based rural development strategy. However, there is little evidence that the failures and shortcomings experienced by the IRDs have had any influence over the state's project designs in the Upper Huallaga and the Chapare.

There is also little evidence of recognition by the state or the United States government for another important role which the peasant *sindicatos* play in preventing violent strategies similar to Sendero Luminoso terrorism in the coca growing Chapare. According to Peruvian analysts such as Carlos Iván de Gregori, Sendero Luminoso has been weakest in those areas with strong grassroots organizations. The rural *sindicato* has been Bolivia's bulwark against incursions from national or Peruvian terrorist groups.

An evaluation of the alternative development programs in the Chapare conducted by a commission comprising peasant leaders and representatives of the Catholic Church in 1992 concluded that the programs were a failure (Informe R 1992). They visited some 38 small-scale projects and concluded that only 2.5 percent of the population were benefitting from the development programs, that government technicians were apathetic and irresponsible and their offices overly bureaucratic, and that excessive political instead of developmental criteria influenced the allocation of resources. Another conclusion was that for the majority of projects peasant participation in decision-making for planning and project execution was non-existent and as a result various small-scale projects turned out to be overscaled white elephants (Informe R 1992).

A concrete example of this top-down planning problem was the followup agricultural credit provided to 1,050 peasants who participated in the voluntary coca leaf reduction campaign in 1991. The peasants were unable to repay their loans because the repayment schedule did not take into account the time requirements for the maturation of the substitute crops and many seedlings failed to survive their transplanting for lack of technical assistance (Los Tiempos 1991). Facing these results, the Proyecto de Desarrollo Alternativo Regional (PDAR) and USAID's PL-480 program stopped disbursing the credit to the borrowers and shortly thereafter disbanded the program altogether. Such oversights could have been avoided through planning the credit program via peasant consultation and joint decision-making. One peasant leader remarked that borrower delinquency had given the peasants a new incentive to increase coca leaf production for earnings to repay the loans.

In Peru, analyst Edmundo Morales cited low financing, dishonesty, lack of discipline, bureaucratic corruption as reasons for the Peruvian government's failed alternative development program (Proyecto Especial del Alto Huallaga, PEAH) which invested $25 million between 1981 and 1986 (Morales 1989:154). On a similar pessimistic note, an agricultural scientist reported that the ten years of field research in the Upper Huallaga has failed to identify an economically viable crop which could compete with the coca leaf (Hoy 1992).

Strategies with Local Development Organizations

Non-governmental development organizations (NGOs), an important, underutilized resource in Peru and Bolivia, should have a major role in micro-development strategies for alternative development. Many of these organizations have been managing participatory development projects for over a decade throughout the Andean highlands and lowlands.[7] They have designed sophisticated local development programs and strategies and maintained detailed documentation about micro-regions and ecologies.

Their rural development experiences have yielded impressive systematized knowledge on important topics such as the local peasant economies. In recent decades, NGOs have developed innovative methodologies for grass-roots organizing, appropriate social communications for poorly educated groups, participatory agricultural extension with paraprofessionals, and have accumulated specialized knowledge about local cropping systems.

The NGOs have made giant strides in accomplishing what the states of Latin America and the Andean region find most difficult—fostering peasant empowerment at the micro-regional and local levels. Within a peasant-based national development strategy such an NGO role will help to insure greater social equity and improved local development planning and project results. Above all, the NGOs have helped the Andean peasantry to organize, defend their economic and socio-political interests and develop project planning and implementation skills.

Thus the creation in the Andean world of new peasant organizations strengthening the veteran ones owes much credit to the work of NGOs. The attention by social scientists given to the role of local peasant organizations in development has increased during the eighties (Esman and Uphoff 1984; Korten and Klauss 1984; Annis and Hakim 1988). This interest in peasant participation issues has added legitimacy for major international lending agencies such as USAID, the World Bank and the United Nations although the practice of these agencies typically lags far behind their rhetoric.

The arguments for the important role in rural development of local organizations focus on federated community-based organizations rather than the primary group of producers (Esman and Uphoff 1984). Such organizations comprising grassroots groups and often organized by NGOs have achieved an important status among rural development practitioners and analysts in the Third World.[8]

Unfortunately, these lessons have not influenced the alternative development strategies in the Chapare and Upper Huallaga regions during the decade of the eighties. Closing the organization gap in local agricultural development terms becomes as important as the price gap or technology gap (Esman and Uphoff 1984). Within this view, local organizations assume a dynamic role, carrying out tasks such as resource management, control of bureaucracy, resource mobilization, planning and goal-setting which have been the prerogative of the state in conventional rural development programs (Esman and Uphoff 1984).

The participatory approach of NGOs in Peru and Bolivia has also employed other rural development elements which have the potential to be utilized on a broader scale. The two Andean republics rest on the foundations of highly sophisticated pre-columbian agrarian civilizations, an agricultural knowledge base which has only recently been tapped by some of the national political elites.

In recent decades, the rediscovery and recovery of some important agricultural technologies such as raised-field agriculture and terraced farming have had promising results. The raised-field agriculture trials in Peru and Bolivia have demonstrated multiple advantages over modern agricultural production techniques for achieving productivity increases, increased rural employment, lowering costs of purchased inputs, improved environmental management and food production security. These discoveries represent a pattern of utilization of native resources which had been overlooked during the rush by Andean states to adopt imported models of rural modernization. In addition to technologies, the elements of the Andean model which have resurfaced in recent years include resources (crops, trees, shrubs) and socio-cultural values (such as indigenous languages for rural schooling, traditional organizations, etc.).

These efforts in the Andean countries are being reinforced by a discovery in the First World of formerly obscure Andean crops which have high nutritional value and environmental importance to the Andean ecosystem and the world food supply (National Research Council 1989). The growing international interest has led to the opening of new foreign markets for Andean peasant producers. These important initiatives and programs should be provided greater resource support to increase their scale of application and favorable impact on the peasant population.

A Case of Peasant-Based Development at the Micro-Level

To find an example of participatory rural development as alternative to the IRD approach and its less than successful counterpart in the Chapare and Upper Huallaga, one would have to journey to to the Alto Beni, a tropical micro-region in northern Bolivia. Although not a traditional coca growing area, the Alto Beni does have tiny plots of clandestine coca leaf production. However, this illicit production expansion has been held in check during the decade of the eighties by an effective grassroots development experience which has benefitted thousands of peasant producers in the micro-region. The Central de Cooperativas Agrícolas-Industriales, El Ceibo, is a local organization which has been successful at marshalling various development resources and an effective participatory development program based on the local production and processing of cocoa beans (Healy 1987, 1988b). Moreover, as a tropical tree crop on individual peasant farms, cocoa is environmentally benign.

El Ceibo consists of 37 multi-ethnic, peasant co-operatives, each of which is an autonomous organization in its own right with its own service program. The El Ceibo federation provides marketing, training, agricultural extension, transport and export services to its member co-operatives. Federation trucks transport fermented and classified cocoa beans over rugged terrain in a ten hour drive to their warehouse and industrial complex in the city of La Paz. Here under peasant cooperative management, the beans are manufactured into cocoa powder, chocolate candy, baking chocolate, cakes, and cocoa butter.

They also sell their beans to Bolivian chocolate industries and to international buyers in South America, Western Europe and recently the United States. In 1990, they exported $600,000 worth of organic and non-organic products. By controlling the various farm to export market functions themselves, the federation insures that the peasant communities capture the lion's share of economic benefits from their production. As a foreign-aid financed project, El Ceibo has received support from the Swiss government and the Inter-American Foundation, a public corporation of the U.S. government, and continuous technical assistance from German volunteer agronomists and economists.

El Ceibo also has attained advanced educational training for members of its staff in agronomy, business administration and accounting. The federation employs a variety of participatory mechanisms to insure that peasant members themselves manage the various service sections and prevent entrenched, corrupt leadership practices, the bane of Third World cooperatives, from taking hold. As a self-managed business and service organization, El Ceibo's training programs supply the local cooperatives with bookkeepers and accountants and the localities with agricultural extensionists to improve productivity of cocoa and other crops.

The participatory structures and organizational autonomy are not the only explanations for success in participatory rural development. A necessary but not sufficient condition are the above-world market prices for its products. They have entered the subsidized Alternate Marketing Organizations (AMOs) store networks set up by Western European foreign aid and other programs and subsequently the emerging segmented markets serving natural health food store chains. El Ceibo would be unable to sustain its business and service operations without these premium prices for its products. This example from Bolivia underscores the importance of legal export incentives for Andean peasant producers which can be offered by cocaine consuming nations of the North.

There are various lessons from the El Ceibo experience applicable to discussions about a long term view of alternative development in the Upper Huallaga and the Chapare. By training and making accountable its own technicians, El Ceibo is not dependent on the whims of government officials and the political instabilities inherent in government rural development programs. By managing and owning the industry themselves, they capture the value-added profits which lift earnings beyond the normal level achieved by peasant producers.

A final lesson in the El Ceibo case is that the institutional development of small producers organizations into a federated network should be a crucial ingredient to coca-inspired alternative development programs. Since it is highly unlikely that a wonder crop exists whose high prices would be competitive with an illicit crop such as the coca leaf, other aspects of rural development such as institutional growth through local organizations and intensive capacity-building programs should achieve prominence. An organizational framework and set of practices such as those exhibited by El Ceibo, are the guarantee that economic benefits will have broad distribution, unlike the IRDs or the alternative development programs whose benefits have not reached beyond a small minority of better-off peasants. However, the caveat to this approach is that local organizations such as El Ceibo do not emerge overnight but represent years of painstaking trial and error organization-building.

The alternative development programs in the coca growing areas during the eighties typically have overlooked this institutional dimension in their project designs. Only until very recent times in the Chapare have producer associations been encouraged to perform this all-important participatory role. However, this effort is incipient and superficial, currently reaching only 280 families out of a possible 40,000. In addition, sometimes the interests of these new groups clash with the local peasant *sindicatos* and their federations, the most representative peasant organization of the area.

Conclusions

Economic development has come to occupy a central role in counter-drug strategies in Third World countries. The national interest in fighting drugs becomes a highly ambiguous concept when a state faces massive unemployment, underemployment, and increasing rural poverty among its citizens. Political conflicts invariably loom large for states attempting to reduce drug related employment and income opportunities in socioeconomic contexts of widespread poverty. Alternative development has been used as a policy device to save Third World states from having to absorb self-inflicted wounds while curbing drug production and trafficking within their national borders.

Since cocaine and various other illicit drugs are agricultural-based products, policy-makers must analyze the impact of national agricultural policies on the peasant producer sector. Policy-makers must take into account what is happening to peasant economies locally in response to broader regional and national socio-economic changes. Peasant migration to areas producing the raw material for the illegal drug industry occurs not only because of relatively attractive income-earning opportunities but also due to the deterioration of living conditions in home communities from national policies.

The case studies of Peru and Bolivia shed light on these important economic issues while providing interesting lessons about the prospects for alternative development as a strategy for weaning peasant farmers away from producing the coca leaf. Both countries were caught in the throes of deep economic crises during the 1980's. Moreover, the structural adjustment programs, established to redirect the national economies on more solid footing, have increased poverty levels, especially in rural areas. These economic trends have contributed to the continued heavy migration to the coca growing regions of the Upper Huallaga of Peru and the Chapare in Bolivia to expand the international cocaine industry. Structural adjustment and anti-drug policies seem to be working at crosspurposes yet there appears to be little recognition of this inherent conflict by policy-makers.

Another example of how past lessons for rural development in the Andean countries have been missed by policy-makers is in the design and implementation of the state-led alternative development programs in coca growing regions. This local development approach resembles the integrated rural development (IRD) programs which came into vogue in Latin America through the World Bank and other international financing during the 1970's. Just as the IRDs floundered to yield disappointing results, the alternative development programs, especially in Bolivia which has been free from guerrilla driven violence, have been spinning their wheels for over a decade (Tropical Research and Development 1986).

Bolivian and Peruvian policy-makers must opt for a peasant-based rural development strategy which requires policy and program changes at both macro and micro levels. Changes in national agricultural policy necessarily involve the formation of political coalitions which would tip the national balance of power toward peasant interests. Social and political mobilization of the peasantry behind new agricultural policies would lead to a reassessment of the structural adjustment program, especially its components of trade liberalization and removal of possible price subsidies for peasant crops. First World states suffering from the effects of drug trafficking in their communities should use their foreign aid leverage over national governments to support a peasant-based development strategy as a break with the decades old policies of agricultural modernization which have increased rural poverty, social inequity, and consequently peasant migration to coca growing areas.

At a level of the micro-region, there are other important elements of a peasant-based strategy. During the decade of the 1980's, there has been a proliferation of non-governmental development agencies (NGOs) in the countryside of both countries. These organizations are a relatively new and widespread phenomenon and possess advantages over the state in the design and implementation of rural development programs for finetuning operations to local conditions and for involving substantial peasant participation in project decision-making.

In the two Andean countries, the NGOs have helped to spread a greater appreciation for and utilization of Native-American resources, technologies, socio-cultural values, and knowledge which have been critical in the past to the evolution of sophisticated agrarian systems in this part of the hemisphere. Such NGO rural development activities on behalf of peasant producers should be supported on a much larger scale in both the highland and the lowland areas of Peru and Bolivia.

The NGOs have also helped to improve rural development through support for membership grassroots organizations. Methodologies for group formation and training in self-management and social communications skills have advanced greatly over the past decade and have led to various co-managed and self-managed rural development programs and projects with interesting results. The alternative development programs in the Chapare and Upper Huallaga have either ignored or at best de-emphasized the role of grassroots organizations. In the Chapare, directors of alternative development programs for over a decade have been locked in conflict with the local peasant *sindicatos* (the most representative small farmers organization) over the lack of participation in decision-making and poor developmental results. Because of their well established legitimacy within the socio-political context, the sindicatos' marginalization from state programs, despite official agreements to the contrary, have worked to undermine the alternative development programs.

The best example from the two Andean countries of the important role of grassroots organizations in rural development is El Ceibo, a peasant cooperative federation in the Alto Beni micro region of Bolivia. The El Ceibo experience of the past sixteen years demonstrates what can be accomplished through a peasant-based development strategy in a clandestine coca growing area. The El Ceibo members are peasant cocoa bean producers who autonomously manage programs in agricultural extension and training, transport, agro-industry, and an export business. They process their beans into cocoa powder, chocolate candy, baking chocolate, and other products and export to the European Alternative Marketing Organizations (AMOs) and natural health food trading companies which offer them a premium price for their products. Because of El Ceibo's participatory organizational style, economic benefits are widely distributed among their membership and network of communities.

By incorporating such rural development lessons from the macro and micro levels and underutilized resources in Peru and Bolivia, the two governments and their international supporters in the United States and Western Europe would stand a chance for greater peasant cooperation in schemes for coca leaf reduction and making significant progress in their anti-narcotics strategies. By continuing to ignore these lessons, official efforts on the economic front of the drug war will remain self-defeating.

Notes

1. The author is aware of the constraints on rural development in the Upper Huallaga from the terrorist activity of Sendero Luminoso. However, this chapter will not be analyzing that important political factor in presenting the material on economic development. The author's position is that even without Sendero Luminoso, the economic development problems and issues indicated in this chapter would persist.

2. A good example of giving short shrift to complex rural development issues associated with the drug crisis analysis is the report produced by the Institute of the Americas called *Seizing Opportunities, A Report of the Inter-American Commission on Drug Policy*, La Jolla, California. A rare example of serious treatment of economic development issues was the GAO publication of "Drug Policy and Agriculture, U.S. Trade Impacts of Alternative Crops to Andean Coca" (U.S. GAO 1991).

3. A World Bank report which analyzed the Peruvian agricultural sector for the 1970's concluded the following: "Throughout the 1970's the performance was weak. Overall production expanded at an average rate of .07 percent per year. All these trends translate into sharply declining per-capita production and increasing dependence on food imports" (World Bank 1981:48).

4. Painter's work shows the deterioration in Bolivia's southern upland valleys which has resulted in part from macro-policy biases against the highland populations over various decades.

5. The Bolivian peasantry in most rural areas has been organized into sindicatos since the 1952 social revolution. Sindicatos incorporate all the families in rural communities and have representation of their political and economic interests at the local, sub-regional, regional and national levels.

6. A recent example of the rural development strategy for a micro-region which ignores completely the issues of participation and the vital role of local organizations is a project proposal prepared by consultants (several ex-ministers of the state) to the Peruvian government called Propuesta de Desarrollo Rural Integrado Alternativo a la Economiá de la Coca (Watson 1991).

7. One note of caution is the increasing practice among Andean governments to create overnight pseudo non-governmental organizations (NGOs) to support their cronies and extend control of the rural development activities. There is also a tendency for government officials to prefer to work with strong local power brokers ("cacique") in lieu of dynamic representative grassroots organizations.

8. The author endorses the USAID position in Bolivia that alternative development must involve the highland agricultural areas, especially the areas with strong migration linkages to the Chapare such as in Cochabamba. The environmental carrying-capacity of the Chapare has been assessed to have reached its limits by a geographer observing the zone since the 1960's (Henkel 1993). This observation has important implications for the rural development strategies of alternative development.

References

Alvarez, Elena. 1983. *Política, Economía y Agricultura en Perú, 1969–1979*, IEP, Lima.
Andreas, Peter R., Eva C. Betram, Morris F. Blackman, and Kenneth E. Sharpe. 1991 and 1992. "Dead-End Drug Wars," *Foreign Policy*, Number 85 inter 1991–1992, pp. 106–128.
Annis, Sheldon, and Peter Hakim, eds. 1988. *Direct to the Poor, Grassroots Development in Latin America*, Lynne Rienner Publishers, Boulder.
Barraclough, Solon. 1991. *An End to Hunger, The Social Origins of Food Strategies*, Zed Books, New Jersey.
Caballero, Jose Maria. 1984 "Agriculture and the Peasantry under Industrialization Pressures: Lessons from the Peruvian Experience," *Latin American Research Review*, Volume XIX, Number 2, pp. 3–43.
Dandler, Jorge, Jose Blanes, Julio Prudencio, and Jorge Munoz. 1987. *El Sistema Agroalimentario en Bolivia*, CERES.
de Janvry, Alain. 1981. *The Agrarian Question and Reformism in Latin America*, Johns Hopkins University Press, Baltimore.
Escobal, Javier, and Marco Castillo. 1992. "Política de Precios en al Agro, Distribucion del Ingreso e Inserción al Mercado: Una Nota Metodológica," (mimeo) Grupo del Analysis Para El Desarrollo, Lima.
Esman, Milton J., and Norman T. Uphoff. 1984. *Local Organizations, Intermediaries in Rural Development*, Cornell University Press.
Figueroa, Adolfo. 1984. *Capitalist Development and Peasant Economy in Peru*, Cambridge University.
García-Sayan, Diego, ed. 1989. *Coca, Cocaina y Narcotrafico, Laberinto en los Andes*, Narco Trafico y Region Andina: Una Vision General Comision Andina de Juristas, Lima, Peru, pp. 17–48.
Gill, Lesley. 1989. *Peasants, Entrepreneurs and Social Change: Frontier Settlement in Lowland Bolivia*, Westview Press, Boulder.
GOB (Government of Bolivia). 1990. *Estrategia Nacional del Desarrollo Alternativo 1990*, Presidencia de la República, La Paz.
Gorriti, Gustavo. 1989. "How To Fight the Drug War," *Atlantic*, volume 263, Issue no. l, July, pp. 70–76.

Grindle, Merilee S. 1986. *State and Countryside, Development Policy and Agrarian Politics in Latin America*, Johns Hopkins University Press.
Healy, Kevin. 1987. "From Field to Factory, Vertical Integration in Bolivia," *Journal of Grassroots Development*, Volume 11, No. 2, pp. 2–11.
_____. 1988a. "A Recipe for Sweet Success, Consensus and Self-Reliance in the Alto Beni," *Journal of Grassroots Development*, Volume 12, No. 1, pp. 32–40.
_____. 1988b. "Coca, the State, and the Peasantry in Bolivia, 1982–88," *Journal of Interamerican Studies and World Affairs*, Volume 30, Numbers 2 and 3, Summer/Fall 1988, pp. 105–177.
_____. 1989. *Sindicatos Campesinos y Desarrollo Rural, 1978–85*, HISBOL, La Paz.
_____. 1991. "Political Ascent of Bolivia's Peasant Coca Leaf Producers," *Journal of Interamerican Studies and World Affairs*, Volume 33, Number 1, spring 1991, pp. 87–133.
_____. 1993. "Public Policies in Conflict: Structural Adjustment and Alternative Development in Bolivia," in *Privatization Amidst Poverty: Contemporary Challenges in Latin American Political Economy*, North-South Center, University of Miami (forthcoming).
Henkel, Ray. 1982. "The Move to the Oriente: Colonization and Environmental Impact," in J.D. Ladman, ed., *Modern-Day Bolivia: Legacy of the Revolution and Prospects for Future*, Arizona State, Tempe.
_____. 1993. "Environment and Cocaine in the Chapare," paper presented at Symposium at the New York Botanical Garden, June 23–26.
Hopkins, Raul. 1981. *Desarrollo Desigual y Crisis en la Agricultura Peruana 1944–1969*, Instituto de Estudios Peruanos, Lima.
Horton, Susan. 1989. Labor Markets in an Era of Adjustment: Bolivia (manuscript), Toronto.
Hoy. 1992. "EEUU Aun No Encuentra Forma de Sustituir Cocales en Peru," March.
Informe R. 1992. "Participacion Campesina en el Desarrollo Alternativo," Ano XII 240 CEDOIN, La Paz.
Institute of the Americas. 1991. *Seizing Opportunities: Report of the Inter-American Commission on Drug Policy*, La Jolla, California.
Iriarte, Gregorio. 1989. *Analysis Critico de la Realidad, Esquemas de Interpretacion*, Secretariado Nacional de Pastoral Social CENPAS-CEB, La Paz.
Korten, David, and Rudi Klauss. 1984. *People Centered Development, Contributions Toward Theory and Planning Frameworks*, Kumarian Press.
Los Tiempos. 1991. "Creditos del PL-480 Imposibilitan Que Cocaleros Cambien Cultivos," November.
Maranon, Boris. 1989. "Los Subsidios en el Agro-1986–87," *Debate Agrario*, 85–103, Lima.
Mayer, Enrique, and Manueal Glave. 1992. "Rentabilidad Económica en La Producción Campesina de Papas," pp. 29–213, in Enrique Mayer, ed., *La Chacra de Papa, Economia y Ecologia*, Centro Peruano de Estudios Sociales, Lima.
Morales, Edmundo. 1989. *Cocaine, White Gold Rush in Peru*, University of Arizona Press.
Morales, Juan Antonio. 1990. "Bolivia: Ajustes Estructurales en la 1990 Agricultura," Centro Peruano de Estudios Sociales, pp. 121–162, Lima.

National Research Council. 1989. *Lost Crop of the Incas, Little Known Plants of the Andes with Promise for Worldwide Cultivation,* National Academy Press, Washington, D.C.

Painter, James. 1993. *Bolivia and Cocaine: A Study in Dependency,* Lynne Rienner Publishers, Boulder (forthcoming).

Painter, Michael. 1983. "Agricultural Policy, Food Production, and Multinational Corporations in Peru," *Latin American Research Review,* Volume XVIII, Number 2, pp. 201–219.

———. 1991. "Upland-Lowland Production Linkages and Land Degradation in Bolivia, Institute of Development Anthropology," working paper, No. 81, November.

Pearse, Andrew. 1980. *Seeds of Plenty, Seeds of Want, Social and Economic Implications of the Green Revolution,* United Nations Research Institute for Social Development (UNRISD), Geneva.

Perez-Crespo, Carlos. 1991. "Why Do People Migrate? Internal Migration and the Pattern of Capital Accumulation in Bolivia," Institute of Development Anthropology, Binghamton.

Rasnake, Roger, and Michael Painter. 1989. "Rural Development and Crop Substitution in Bolivia: USAID and the Chapare Regional Development Project," Institute for Development Anthropology, Binghamton.

Tropical Research and Development. 1986. "Evaluation of Chapare Regional Development Project," unpublished report prepared for USAID Bolivia, Gainesville.

USAID. 1974. *Agricultural Development in Bolivia, A Sector Assessment.* USAID Mission to Bolivia, La Paz.

U.S. General Accounting Office (GAO). 1991. *Drug Policy and Agriculture, U.S. Trade Impacts of Alternative Crops to Andean Coca,* October, Washington, D.C.

Watson, Eduardo, Eduardo Toledo Carlos Amat, and Jose Toledo. 1991. "Propuesta de Desarrollo Rural Integrado Alternativo a la Economía de la Coca (unpublished manuscript), Lima.

Wilson, Patricia, and Carol Wise. 1986. "The Regional Implications of Public Investment in Peru, 1968–1983," *Latin American Research Review,* Volume XXI, Number 2, pp. 93–117, University of New Mexico, Albuquerque.

World Bank. 1981. *Peru, Major Policy Development Issues and Recommendations,* A World Bank Country Study. World Bank, Washington, D.C.

———. 1984. *Bolivia, Agricultural Pricing and Investment Policies,* a World Bank Country Study. World Bank, Washington, D.C.

———. 1990a. Bolivia Poverty Report, Report No. 8646, internal document.

———. 1990b. Bolivia Updating Economic Memorandum, internal document.

———. 1991. *World Development Report 1991, The Challenge of Development,* World Bank, Washington, D.C.

8

World-Wide and Regional Anti-Drug Programs

Irving Tragen

For nearly a century, the community of nations has been seeking to develop an effective framework for inter-country cooperation to deal with the illicit drug trade. As has been apparent since the Opium Wars of the nineteenth century, the drug trade is a transnational phenomenon which requires cooperation between and among governments to bring it under effective control.

Illicit drug trafficking is a complex chain of operations from producer to consumer which seldom is confined to the boundaries of any sovereign state. Production in one country is often processed in a second country, manufactured into a narcotic drug or psychotropic substance in a third, transported through others to reach distribution and marketing centers for sale to the users with the profits laundered and invested in just about every hospitable site around the world.[1]

Without close intergovernmental cooperation to combat the sophisticated criminal organizations which practically monopolize illicit trafficking world-wide, there is little hope that any government acting by itself can effectively curtail the flow of drugs. The Secretary General of the United Nations when he inaugurated the seventeenth special session of the UN General Assembly in February 1990 estimated that the volume of this illicit traffic world-wide exceeds $500 billion annually—second only to armaments as a category in world trade.[2] Drugs now rank with peace, development, debt and environment at the top of the agendas of multilateral bodies.

The importance flows from the multiple threat which illicit trafficking poses to the operations of key domestic institutions in many countries, in some the stability of the government itself, as well as to relations between governments and the well-being of people. When the drug problem first emerged as an international issue in the late nineteenth century, primary concern focused on the human consequences of drug abuse, especially of opium, as a matter of public health. This initial focus broadened progressively as the scope and impact of illicit drug trafficking took on more ominous dimensions. The multi-billion dollar underground business burgeoned, under the control of powerful criminal syndicates. The enormous profits have systematically bought political influence and economic power as well as corrupted government officials and institutions, financed subversion where appropriate and distorted economies—with little or no tax revenues paid to affected governments. By the last decade of the twentieth century, the world-wide, regional, subregional and country agendas to deal with drugs have become multi-faceted and extend to the political, economic and social as well as the human consequences of illicit trafficking and drug abuse.

Since World War I, multilateral efforts have been concentrated in the paramount world-wide international political body—the United Nations and its predecessor, the League of Nations. The strategy has been to develop universal norms to govern the production, manufacture, transport, import, export, distribution, use and consumption of narcotic drugs and, in later years, psychotropic substances. Effective enforcement has only begun to receive appropriate attention in the last two decades. It is only in the last decade that systematic multilateral attention has begun to focus on action programs to support national governments and to assist them in resolving priority problems on their domestic agendas.

To facilitate analysis of the scope and relevance of current multilateral efforts, this chapter is divided into two parts: The Juridical Framework and Multilateral Programs to Support National Efforts.

The Juridical Framework

The United Nations now administers three universal conventions which provide the world-wide juridical framework for dealing with narcotic drugs and psychotropic substances.[3] These three instruments are:

1. The Single Convention on Narcotic Drugs of 1961 as amended by the Protocol of 1972;
2. The Convention on Psychotropic Substances of 1971; and,
3. The 1988 Convention Against Illicit Traffic in Narcotic Drugs and Psychotropic Substances.

These Conventions are the culmination of nearly a century of worldwide efforts to control drugs. The first major conference on drugs was held in Shanghai in 1909, the Shanghai Conference on Opium. In 1912, the first convention aimed at suppressing the abuse of other substances by controlling their production and distribution was signed at The Hague. The Hague Convention was essentially a voluntary undertaking by governments to prevent the opium trade. It neither specified the production levels nor created any enforcement machinery. It recognized the important role of customs authorities to control imports and exports, but nothing more specific.

From this halting first step, the international community gradually laid the bases for the three instruments now in force. First, under the League of Nations, from 1920 to 1946, three additional conventions were adopted under article 23 (c) of the Convention which established the League. The article provided:

> Subject to and in accordance with the provisions of international conventions existing or hereafter to be agreed upon, the Members of the League ... "will intrust the League with the general supervision over the execution of agreements with regard to ... the traffic in opium and other dangerous drugs."

The three Conventions were:

- The International Opium Convention of 1925;
- The Convention for Limiting the Manufacture and Regulating the Distribution of Narcotic Drugs of 1931; and,
- The Convention for the Suppression of Illicit Traffic in Dangerous Drugs of 1936.

The three Conventions, together with other agreements of more limited scope, gradually broaden the authority of the League and its agencies to take steps to suppress the international illicit narcotics trade. These instruments also set up the first multilateral administrative machinery to deal with this problem. By far, the most important was the 1936 Convention which represents the first international attempt to distinguish between licit and illicit trade in drugs and to focus on measures needed to suppress illicit trafficking. It was the first multilateral Convention to provide criminal penalties for those who engage in the illicit manufacture, conversion, extraction, preparation, possession, distribution, purchase, sale, transport and trafficking of those narcotic drugs covered by the instrument. The Convention entered into force in October 1939 after the outbreak of World War II and the de facto demise of the League.

Secondly, in the United Nations, in February 1946, the Economic and Social Council of the United Nations (ECOSOC) set up the Commission on Narcotic Drugs. In December of the same year, the Protocol of Lake Success was signed under which the governments party to various League of Nations Agreements, Conventions and Protocols transferred to the United Nations the functions that had been exercised by the defunct League. The Division of Narcotic Drugs was established to exercise these functions and to serve as Secretariat to the Commission of Narcotic Drugs.[4]

Between 1946 and 1960, only one additional Protocol was prepared by the Commission, namely, the 1953 Protocol for Limiting and Regulating the Cultivation of the Poppy Plant, the Production of, International and Wholesale Trade in, and Use of Opium. By the late 1950's, attention was focused on the need for eliminating contradictions, overlapping and ambiguities among the various Agreements, Conventions and Protocols then in force. This led in 1960–1961 to the preparation of a new, unified instrument to govern international cooperation and measures on narcotic drugs, the Single Convention on Narcotic Drugs of 1961, subsequently amended by the Protocol of 1972, which in its Article 44, terminated and replaced the earlier international instruments which had been in force since 1912.

Hence, the provisions for world-wide control of addictive narcotic drugs is a product of the Twentieth Century. They evolved progressively into an international juridical system under the aegis of multilateral authorities. The adoption of the Single Convention in 1961 and its Protocol in 1972 set in place machinery to deal with narcotic drugs. The 1971 Convention on Psychotropic Drugs provides the framework for controlling Psychotropic Substances. And the landmark 1988 Convention Against Illicit Traffic in Narcotic Drugs and Psychotropic Substances invests the world community with tools needed for inter-governmental cooperation, with multilateral support, to curtail the current drug explosion.

Widespread support for and adherence to this juridical system is evidenced by the 135 states that are Party to the Single Convention (108 of which also ratified the Protocol of 1972) and by the 107 states which have ratified the Convention on Psychotropic Substances. Seventy-seven states signed the 1988 Convention which entered in force in November 1990 after 20 countries had ratified it. As of July 1992, 62 states and the European Community have ratified, acceded to or approved the 1988 Convention; and, a substantial number are in varying stages of their respective domestic ratification accession or approval process.

The Single Convention of 1961 as Amended by the Protocol of 1972

The Single Convention essentially sets up a universal system to control the cultivation, production, manufacture, export, import, distribution of, trade in, use and possession of essentially three families of narcotic substances: the opium poppy, coca leaf and cannabis. It obligates parties not only to apply the Convention in their national territories but also to cooperate with other States in its application. Controlled drugs under the Single Convention can be legally used only for medical and scientific purposes; and the Convention set up an international authority to determine and allocate annually quotas of controlled drugs among countries for their legal cultivation, production, manufacture, etc.

The Convention requires Parties to license the production and manufacture of controlled substances. It further establishes stringent regulations over their export and import, including specific government authorization for export and corresponding certificates for import by receiving countries. Legal shipments require the matching export authorizations with import certificates. For domestic markets, trade and distribution require a license by the appropriate governmental authorities, and individual users require medical prescriptions.

The Single Convention stipulates that "the Parties shall not permit the possession of drugs except under legal authority."[5] Indeed, it establishes norms for governmental supervision and inspection of all persons who obtain licenses, authorizations and certificates as well as for record-keeping by governmental authorities, manufacturers, traders, scientists, scientific institutions and hospitals.

Clearly, the underlying thrust of the Single Convention is to prevent illicit trafficking in the narcotic drugs scheduled under it. Building on the experience since 1912, Parties are to coordinate prevention and enforcement at the national level and are recommended to designate "an appropriate agency responsible for such coordination."[6] It calls for bilateral and multilateral cooperation in suppressing the illicit trade, the prosecution of drug dealers and "maintaining a co-ordinated campaign against the illicit traffic."[7]

At the center of the international system, the Single Convention created a multilateral authority within the United Nations, the International Narcotics Control Board (INCB), to oversee its implementation. INCB is a technical body of thirteen specialists from parties to the Convention, who are elected for five-year terms by the UN Economic and Social Council (ECOSOC) and supported by the expert advice of the World Health Organization (WHO). It has the authority annually to assess world-wide scientific and medical requirements for controlled substances and to allocate quotas among the States Party for their legal cultivation, production, manufacture, export, import, distribution, trade in, use of and possession. It can and does establish norms and procedures and require reports from Parties.[8]

INCB is further empowered to modify the lists of controlled substances. It may also examine the compliance record of Parties and call the attention of the ECOSOC, the Commission of Narcotic Drugs and the Parties themselves to the problems encountered, including non-compliance with its decisions. It may require reports from Parties on illicit drug activities in their countries, including information on illicit cultivation, production, manufacture and use of and on illicit trafficking in drugs. It can appeal to world opinion. But it does not have its own police power to enforce. It does not enjoy supranational enforcement or penal powers.

Indeed, the power to enforce and to punish remains under the domestic jurisdiction of each Party. The constitutional limitations of each state determine specific offenses and punishment as well as the applicability of extradition and other means for bringing violators to justice. The differences in norms and procedures at the national level and the limited effectiveness of intergovernmental and international cooperation in enforcing the Convention have contributed substantially to the weakness of worldwide efforts to deal with the current drug crisis.

The Single Convention calls upon the Parties to declare as punishable offenses the "cultivation, production, manufacture, extraction, preparation, possession, offering, offering for sale, distribution, purchase, sale, delivery on any terms whatsoever, brokerage, dispatch, dispatch in transit, transport, importation and exportation of drugs contrary to the provisions of this Convention, and any other action which in the opinion of such Party may be contrary to the provisions of this Convention." It further includes as eligible for punishable offenses: "intentional participation in, conspiracy to commit and attempts to commit, any of such offenses, and preparatory acts and financial operations in connexion with the offenses referred to in this article."[9]

Thus, the multilateral juridical framework is now in place for establishing the parameters of legal production, shipment and use of narcotic drugs at each step of the transnational drug chain. INCB is an efficient and competent international authority. It can initiate consultation with a member state, provide expert services needed to study specific problems and recommend remedial measures. It can promote cooperative actions by the Parties to deal with specific problems. However, the national state remains the arbiter of what action is to be taken. Multinational authority is essentially limited to persuasion, and international cooperation remains voluntary.

The Convention on Psychotropic Substances of 1971

This is the companion instrument to the Single Convention. It establishes international machinery to control psychotropic substances, entrusting to INCB the responsibility for insuring the implementation of its provisions, with the technical support of the WHO.

World-Wide and Regional Anti-Drug Programs

This Convention establishes controls over the manufacture, trade in and distribution of natural or synthetic substances which cause dependency and produce central nervous system stimulation or depression which result in hallucinations or disturbance in motor function, thinking, behavior and perception or mood.

The Convention establishes four schedules of controlled substances, with those on Schedules I and II subject to the strictest controls. The lists may be increased, reduced or amended by the Commission on the Narcotic Drugs on the recommendation of the WHO. Those substances included on any of the four schedules must be licenced by governments for manufacture, trade and distribution, with governments reporting annually to INCB. The Convention further requires that Parties notify each other, through the Secretary General of the United Nations, of any prohibitions or restrictions that may be established on the import or export of any controlled substance. In addition, Parties are to require medical prescriptions for the supply or dispensing of any substance on Schedules I, II and III.

The Convention seeks to limit the use of the controlled substances to medical and scientific purposes. For those on Schedule I, the Parties shall "prohibit all use except for scientific and very limited medical purposes by duly authorized persons, in medical or scientific establishments which are directly under the control of their Governments or specifically approved by them."[10] For those on Schedules II, III and IV, each Party is "to limit by such measures as it considers appropriate the manufacture, export, import, distribution and stock of trade in, and use and possession in schedules II, III and IV to medical and scientific purposes."[11]

The Convention once again establishes norms and procedures for applying controls, including licensing, domestic use, export, import, inspection, record-keeping and reports. INCB is empowered to oversee the application of the provisions of the Convention. However, the authority to apply the Convention remains essentially with each sovereign state. The control, inspection and enforcement are functions which are the responsibility of each State Party. It is the domestic legislation that defines punishable offenses and deals with violators. INCB receives reports and can provide advice, guidance and assistance. The Convention repeatedly calls for cooperation among the Parties, but it leaves to the option of each government to select the most appropriate mechanisms in accordance with its constitutional requirements and its assessment of the local situation.

The 1988 United Nations Convention Against Illicit Traffic in Narcotic Drugs and Psychotropic Substances

The third Convention in force was adopted on December 20, 1988, and focuses specifically on the problem of illicit drug trafficking. The first two

Conventions established the world-wide machinery for fixing annual limits to licit cultivation, production, manufacture, etc. of the controlled substances and impose obligations on States Party to take those measures indicated by INCB to comply with its determinations. However, the 1988 Convention is designed to set up multilateral machinery to facilitate the suppression of activities prohibited under the two earlier instruments.

The issue of effectiveness, in light of explosion of illicit trafficking in the 1970's and 1980's, led the member states of the United Nations and the Organization of American States to consider additional multilateral worldwide and regional instruments and mechanisms to deal with this increasingly dangerous problem. Almost simultaneously in 1984, Colombia and Venezuela undertook initiatives in the UN Economic and Social Council and the OAS General Assembly for the preparation of new international instruments to deal specifically with illicit trafficking. In early 1985, both organizations initiated work on such an instrument. The OAS, in view of the world-wide scope of the problem and the expeditious response of the UN, elected to develop a comprehensive regional action program to spearhead regional cooperation, rather than a Convention or other international instrument.

The preparation and negotiation of the 1988 United Nations Convention Against Illicit Traffic in Narcotic Drugs and Psychotropic Substances was completed in almost record time. It represents a major step forward in international penal law and in defining the framework for inter-governmental cooperation to deal with criminal activities whose operations transcend the jurisdiction of any single sovereign state.

The speed with which the world community reached consensus on this complex thirty-four-article document reflects the deep concern of governments and people with the increasing tide of illicit trafficking and drug abuse and their nefarious impact on political stability, economic development and the well-being of people, especially children. The Convention recognizes that "illicit traffic is an international criminal activity, the suppression of which demands urgent attention and the highest priority."[12] Its Preamble spells out the rationale and need for multilateral action and inter-governmental cooperation to deprive criminals of the proceeds of their crimes and to eliminate the root causes for the problem.

Many of the thirty-four articles of the Convention are based on concepts, principles and obligations which were initially broached in the 1936 Convention and rather generally covered in the Single Convention and that on Psychotropic Substances. It is in this Convention that the concepts of the 1936 Convention are developed into full scale commitments, with procedures to facilitate their compliance.

It is an agreement by sovereign states "to promote cooperation among the Parties so that they may address more effectively the various aspects of illicit traffic in narcotic drugs and psychotropic substances having an international dimension," in a context that ensures full respect for each state's sovereignty, domestic legislative systems and territorial integrity.[13] Commitments to work together are clearly expressions of national political will and require domestic legislation to implement.

The main thrust of this Convention is the obligation on the Parties to establish as criminal offenses all activities which contravene the other two UN Conventions in force. Article 3 sets the tone of the Convention by requiring that each ratifying state should adopt necessary measures to establish as criminal offenses under its domestic law, all intentional acts in the entire chain of illicit trafficking from cultivation, production, manufacture, extraction, preparation, offering, offering for sale, distribution, sale, delivery on any terms whatsoever, brokerage, dispatch in transit, transport, exportation or importation of narcotic drugs or psychotropic substances, as well as their use and possession. This requirement extends to the manufacture, transport or distribution of equipment, materials and specific substances used in illicit cultivation, production or manufacture. It further comprehends the management and financing of illicit activities, including conversion or transfer of property, money laundering and participating or conspiring knowingly therein.

The Convention provides guidelines for national authorities to follow in shaping domestic legislation on asset seizure, money laundering and forfeiture of proceeds derived from illicit trafficking. It spells out rules and procedures for controlling the diversion of precursor chemicals and other chemical substances from licit to illicit uses. It recommends measures to eradicate illicit cultivation and to eliminate demand. It further allows Parties to adopt more strict or severe measures than those provided by the Convention.

Moreover, it builds a sound basis for inter-governmental cooperation by:

1. Spelling out the jurisdiction of Parties over criminal actions in complex situations;
2. Setting ground rules for extradition;
3. Defining areas of mutual legal assistance and other forms of judicial, police (including controlled deliveries) and technical cooperation;
4. Establishing ground rules for handling drug cases in specialized situations such as in free zones and free ports, on the high seas, and the postal system as well as on merchant ships and other commercial carriers; and
5. Prescribing rules for the handling of drug shipments by merchant ships and commercial carriers and the labelling of exports.

The UN Commission of Narcotic Drugs and the INCB are invested with the responsibility to oversee compliance with and implementation of this Convention. The Board has the specific responsibility of constantly reviewing country performance and may invite a Party or Parties to furnish relevant information and to consult with it. The Board is further empowered to render annual, as well as special, reports to the Commission on compliance, "with such comments as it sees fit."[14]

With the adoption and entrance into force of the 1988 Convention, three unique UN instruments provide the world community with a juridical framework for intergovernmental cooperation in combatting illicit trafficking and drug abuse. However, the effectiveness of this legal framework depends on compliance with its provisions, and compliance depends on enforcement measures by the States Party to the Convention.

In this context, the multilateral juridical framework which has evolved since the early years of this century can orient, influence and even convince governments of the policies, norms and procedures which they should follow in combatting illicit trafficking and drug abuse. However, it is each sovereign state that ultimately decides by its own legislative, executive and judicial actions what laws and decrees are to be adopted, enforced and applied in its national territory. Hence, the effectiveness of multilateral conventions continues to depend on the actions taken by each sovereign state, on the basis of its national will and interests.

Multilateral Support for National Programs

In spite of the three UN Conventions and international machinery which they have set in place illicit drug trafficking and drug abuse have raged unabated—increasing in absolute and qualitative terms over the past thirty years. Based on this experience, the world community has now begun to take additional measures to promote inter-governmental and grass-roots cooperation to understand, apply and comply with the conventions.

Those additional measures are applying to the international arena the experience learned in the promulgation and application of domestic legislation. The efficacy of a law is not only its substance, but the degree of compliance—voluntary or enforced. So, with conventions, unless a sustained effort is made to promote compliance, the instruments remain little more than an enunciation of principles and precepts.

Up to the 1960's international efforts to promote compliance were limited, including occasional seminars, training programs and technical assistance by various multilateral world-wide bodies especially within the UN system. There were few sustained, systematic multilateral activities to assist governments and people either to develop coherent strategies and programs for domestic compliance or to facilitate cooperation across national boundaries.

The first UN body established was the Division of Narcotic Drugs (DND), whose primary functions were to serve as the Secretariat for the Commission of Narcotic Drugs.[15] In the 1960's, with the adoption of the Single Convention, the International Narcotics Control Board (INCB) was established to oversee treaty compliance; the INCB's powers have been expanded under each new Convention.[16] In 1971, the Fund for Drug Abuse Control (UNFDAC) was created to finance action programs.[17]

UNFDAC funds came from voluntary contributions from UN member states and other public and private entities. In its first decade, contributions to it were small; and, it operated projects limited in scope and impact. Since the early 1980's, UNFDAC's programs multiplied, contributions rose—and its annual budget has grown to over US$70,000,000 a year. Although its budget represents a relatively small amount of money compared to the size of the drug trade and the profits of the drug barons, UNFDAC staked out a critically important role in helping governments and people take the measures needed against illicit trafficking and drug abuse.

Under resolution 45/179 of December 21, 1990, the UN General Assembly merged the three units into a single operational entity, the United Nations International Narcotics Control Program (UNDCP), under the direction of an Executive Director, with the rank of Under-Secretary General.[18] Ambassador Giorgio Giacomelli was appointed to that post in early 1991. The UNDCP integrates the DND, UNFDAC and many INCB secretariat functions into a single operational unit and is responsible for providing effective leadership for all UN drug control activities, ensuring the development of coherent action programs and coordinating anti-drug activities across the United Nations system. Under the adroit direction of Ambassador Giacomelli, UNDCP became operational in 1991.

The importance of the UNDCP is underlined by the recommendations of the International Conference on Drug Abuse and Illicit Trafficking (ICDAIT), which was held in Vienna, June 17–26, 1987. Representatives of 138 countries, a score of intergovernmental and regional bodies and over 200 non-governmental organizations prepared and adopted the Comprehensive Multidisciplinary Outline of Future Activities in Drug Abuse Control (CMO).[19] This provides the first world-wide programmatic framework for cooperative multilateral, regional, national and local efforts to prevent drug abuse and reduce demand, control supply, suppress illicit trafficking and treat and rehabilitate drug addicts.

Complementing UN efforts, specialized multilateral world-wide bodies have also evolved since World War II, such as the International Police Cooperation Organization (ICPO/INTERPOL)[20] and the Customs Cooperation Council (CCC).[21] Their focus has been almost exclusively to work with national governments in their efforts to deal with specific aspects of the drug problem.

In addition over the past two decades a significant network of regional multilateral bodies has been developed and is rapidly acquiring experience and linkages with governments and private groups which offer promise for better progress in the future than that achieved to date—especially if effective working relations can be developed with the world-wide bodies and adequate financial and technical resources can be mobilized to provide the sustained support which governments need.

Thus, multilateral cooperation with governments and people to apply the Conventions and improve national anti-drug programs is a relatively new dimension in world-wide and regional anti-drug efforts. As governments become increasingly aware of the need for inter-country cooperation in controlling this transnational criminal activity, the importance of multilateral mechanisms to assist them in the process will correspondingly increase. Let us look at some of the programs that are already taking shape.

United Nations Programs

One of the major considerations for Under Secretary General Giacomelli is how the provisions of the CMO will be carried out. With its focus on concrete, substantive actions needed to deal with drug abuse and relevant trafficking, the CMO expressly recognizes that the Conventions and the international administrative mechanisms which have been created to administer them are not a sufficient multilateral response to the burgeoning drug problem now faced by the world community. The CMO is divided into four component chapters: the first, dealing with prevention and reduction of illicit demand; the second, control of supply; the third, suppression of illicit trafficking; and, the fourth, treatment and rehabilitation.

In each chapter, the nature of the problem and challenge to the international community is spelled out. Specific targets which demand immediate action are identified, with recommended courses of action at the national, regional and international levels. Indeed, the sum of the 35 targets, established in the four chapters is a comprehensive world-wide action program which could minimize the impact of the drug problem on the world community and on people throughout the world.

The application of the CMO would be the logical complement to the three Conventions. However, limited programming compounded by inadequate financial resources—at the world-wide, regional and national level—have inhibited its comprehensive implementation.

The UN has been seeking appropriate approaches for applying comprehensively the CMO. The seventeenth special session of the General Assembly held in New York on February 19–23, 1990 adopted a global program of action to reinforce the CMO and to set the priorities for immediate action.[22] And the decision in late 1990 to reorganize and integrate the UN administrative structures is part of this process.

The bringing together and rationalizing of the UN efforts in support of the CMO and the global program of action is a major undertaking. It must encompass more than the activities of DND, INCB and UNFDAC and include the United Nations Specialized Agencies, most of which at present have only limited anti-drug programs.[23]

Food and Agriculture Organization (FAO), The International Labor Organization (ILO), the United Nations Development Program (UNDP), the United Nations Educational, Scientific and Cultural Organization (UNESCO), among others, have carried out anti-drug projects. However, only the World Health Organization (WHO) has developed a specific program. It is the technical adviser to the Commission on Narcotic Drugs and INCB "in respect to changes in the control of substances and their scheduling for control purposes. WHO has to assess the dependence liability and therapeutic usefulness of each substance and, after evaluating any public health and social problem related to its abuse, to make a recommendation to the Commission on Narcotic Drugs for its control." In addition, "it is the only specialized agency with a specific programme (prevention and control of alcohol and drug abuse) and full time staff allocated to addiction problems. ... The programme seeks to develop methods of combatting drug dependence and collaborates directly with individual countries in their efforts against it."[24]

Within the UN system, there are other specialized programs which deal with specific aspects of the drug problem, such as the UN Crime Prevention and Criminal Justice Branch. These programs can play pivotal roles in expanding traditional law enforcement activities and directly involving judges, legislators and prosecutors in inter-country cooperative activities. The United Nations Institute for Latin America for the Prevention of Crime and the Treatment of Delinquents (ILANUD),[25] for example, has developed a broadly based Inter-American program which brings together judges and prosecutors from the region to analyze the complex legal, judicial and penal questions which are so important to effective intergovernmental cooperative action against transnational illicit trafficking. Nonetheless, the principal multilateral actor world-wide and the primary source of assistance to governments is the UNDCP.

The UNDCP actively promotes the development of comprehensive anti-drug programs at the world-wide, regional and national levels. It has formulated a programming system, called the Masterplan, to assist countries in the analysis of their problems and the identification of their priority needs. It supports multilateral agencies and governments in the implementation of specific programs, through both technical and financial support. In fact, the UNDCP is the primary multilateral banker for combatting illicit trafficking and drug abuse. It is the coordinating force for multilateral assistance efforts and funds much of the effort by UN and other multilateral bodies.

The funds of UNDCP are currently concentrated in projects aimed at (1) eradicating illicit production and alternative development in producer countries; (2) improving the effectiveness of law enforcement; and (3) supporting multi-country and national programs of education for the prevention of drug abuse and public awareness of the problem. This distribution of resources reflects the priorities applied by UNFDAC, and, as new priorities are identified this may well change.

The UNDCP program includes training seminars and workshops at the regional level for drug enforcement officers and officials involved in drug demand reduction and arranges for fellowships as well as specialized study for scientists and law enforcement personnel on technical and forensic aspects.[26] It prepares and distributes relevant training materials to complement drug control programs. It undertakes specialized studies and prepares the draft reports for the INCB on compliance with the requirements established under the three Conventions. In addition, it serves as a world-wide clearinghouse for the collection and dissemination of information on developments of international drug control.

The UNDCP also co-ordinates international efforts to control drugs. It consults and collaborates with the secretariats of UN specialized agencies on matters of mutual concern. It promotes and supports regional cooperation among governments in the various regions of the world and serves as the Secretariat for the annual meetings of subsidiary regional bodies created by the Commission on Narcotic Drugs.

It is the INCB which advises governments on technical questions related to the implementation of the Conventions and conducts training programs for national officials on reporting and other requirements established under the Conventions and by INCB to administer them.[27]

Other World-Wide Multilateral Organizations

In addition, there are other world-wide multilateral bodies which provide technical services to and cooperate with governments on drug matters. Two of special importance are the International Police Cooperation Organization (ICPO/INTERPOL) and the Customs Cooperation Council (CCC).

- *ICPO/INTERPOL*, created in 1923 and reorganized after World War II has a special section which deals with illicit drugs and drug traf-

ficking, and seeks to promote mutual assistance among law enforcement agencies engaged in the prevention and suppression of this transnational problem. It provides training and technical assistance to law enforcement agencies, facilitates cooperation and coordination in the arrest and extradition of traffickers and maintains an international communications system for the rapid interchange of information among police agencies.
- CCC, created in 1950 is the world-wide multilateral organization which encourages cooperation among customs services of its 108 members. It focuses on the necessary controls over the flow of goods into and out of countries and the detection of contraband. It has sponsored expert groups which have elaborated important recommendations on cooperation, coordination of enforcement measures and exchange of intelligence among customs officials, which have been widely adopted and applied by governments. It oversees the development of standardized nomenclature for international commerce. CCC also conducts seminars and training programs, operates an information exchange program, and prepares manuals and catalogues for dealing with customs issues, including those related to the smuggling of narcotic drugs and psychotropic substances.

Several world-wide private institutions also assist and support national efforts to combat drugs. Many, such as the International Council on Alcohol and Addictions (ICAA), provide a network of resources which play an important role in sharing program experiences across national frontiers. Unfortunately, most of them have limited funding.

The CMO has provided the world community, including the private sector, with a blueprint for sustained and coordinated action to deal with the priority dimensions of the drug problem; but, without resources, it is doubtful that the measures called for world-wide, much less at the regional and national levels, can be effectively implemented.

Regional and Sub-Regional Programs

Over the past two decades as the seriousness of the drug problem deepened and governments became more concerned about its effects on political structures, social conditions, economic developments and the welfare of people, groups of governments have signed regional and subregional accords to coordinate national programs and to cooperate with each other in combatting drug trafficking and the impact of drug abuse. Most of the regional bodies are focused on the specific needs within their areas; but, some have broadened the scope of regional programs to deal with almost every facets of the drug chain from illicit production, manufacture, transit, distribution, marketing and use to money laundering. These regional bodies are the complementary mechanism to the UN, ICPO/INTERPOL and CCC normative functions world-wide and provide appropriate multilateral machinery for working directly with the member states in applying norms and in strengthening the fabric of inter-governmental cooperation in each of the geographic areas.

With the UN Resolution 45/179 of December 21, 1990, which integrates the three UN agencies under the IDCP, it may now be opportune for a similar restructuring of UN relations with regional organizations.

Since 1973, the UN Commission on Narcotic Drugs has set in place a series of regional consultative mechanisms. The first was the Sub-Commission on Illicit Drug Traffic and Related Matters in the Near and Middle East. It was created in 1973 to study the implementation of recommendations of the ad hoc Committee on Illicit Traffic in the Near and Middle East and to submit additional recommendations to the Commission for dealing with the drug problem in the area.[28]

In addition, the Commission has set up HONLEAs (Heads of National Law Enforcement Agencies), to advise it on the promotion and strengthening of regional and interregional cooperation and coordination in suppressing illicit trafficking and other law enforcement matters. Their paramount function is to recommend courses of action to the Commission and member governments. They also provide an excellent forum for dialogue among law enforcement chiefs and inter-country contacts so essential to improved inter-governmental cooperation.

The first HONLEA was created for the Asia and Pacific Region in 1974.[29] HONLEAs have since been established for Africa, Latin America and the Caribbean and the European Region since the mid-1980's.[30] The Sub-Commission for the Near and Middle East, *inter alia*, covers the functions of the HONLEA in the other regions.

HONLEA participants are usually the top government law enforcement officials, but do not necessarily include all of the component agencies in each country engaged in combatting illicit trafficking and drug abuse. HONLEAs meet annually at the regional level, and, every third year, an interregional HONLEA brings them together to discuss issues which transcend law enforcement in individual regions. It should be pointed out that other world-wide specialized organizations such as ICPO/INTERPOL and CCC as well as most of the regional bodies discussed in the following paragraphs also convene their own annual regional meetings—sometimes with similar agendas, the same participants and the same frequency as the HONLEAs.

The reorganization of the UN administrative machinery offers the Commission an appropriate opportunity to review the structure and scope of its and HONLEAs' relations with regional bodies and their programs.

One of the first regional bodies to establish a broadly based anti-drug program was the Colombo Plan. This 26-member intergovernmental organization founded in 1950 by six developed countries and 20 developing countries, created in 1973 a Drug Advisory Program (DAP) and a Drug Advisor to consult with member governments and help develop cooperative drug prevention and control programs.[31] The DAP encompasses law enforcement, prevention, supply reduction, treatment and rehabilitation. It provides technical support to member states, including advisory services on up-dating and harmonizing legislation, establishing special drug units and coordinating systems and procedures. It sponsors training programs for technicians in all relevant fields, through fellowships for graduate study, seminars, workshops, study exchange programs and research projects. DAP has spearheaded public awareness campaigns and involvement of the media, the community, non-governmental organizations and voluntary groups in anti-drug programs. These various activities are closely coordinated with the UN drug agencies and Specialized Organizations, ICPO/INTERPOL and other inter-governmental world-wide and regional bodies concerned with the drug problem in the countries which are members of the Colombo Plan.

Another of the regional mechanisms created in the 1970's was set up by Association of South-East Asian Nations (ASEAN). ASEAN, which was established by five governments in 1967, in its 1975 meeting in Manila adopted the ASEAN Declaration of Principles to Combat the Abuse of Narcotic Drugs, and set up the Asian Drug Experts Group Meeting to translate the Declaration into practical action programs. In 1985, the Expert Group was renamed the ASEAN Senior Officials on Drug Matters.[32] In addition, ASEAN has established:

1. a Narcotic Desk in Jakarta to serve as a clearinghouse for information on research, expertise and other activities related to combatting the drug problem;
2. a law enforcement training center in Bangkok;
3. a training center on prevention, education and public information in Manila; and
4. a training center for professionals on treatment and rehabilitation at Kuala Lumpur.

Similar regional structures have evolved in the Arab Countries. In addition to the Sub-Commission on Illicit Drug Traffic and Related Matters for the Near and Middle East set up by the UN Commission of Narcotic Drugs in 1973, the Secretariat of the Council of Arab Ministers of the Interior was created in the mid-1980's to coordinate the activities of participating governments. The Secretariat has developed:

1. the Model Arab Law to deal with the drug problem which was adopted by the Ministers of the Interior and referred to member states for adoption;
2. the Arab strategy for combatting illicit traffic of narcotics drugs and psychotropic substances; and
3. a five year work plan in 1987 to apply the strategy and strengthen inter-country cooperation.[33] In addition, a dynamic center has been set up in Cairo to provide training on priority aspects of controlling the drug problem.

The Pompidou Group was set up in 1971 to provide a forum for coordinating Western European approaches for dealing with its escalating drug problem. In the 1980's it became part of the Council of Europe, with membership voluntary. It has grown from 6 to 16 participating countries. Its program[34] is directed by Ministers from the participating governments who meet periodically and is carried out by working groups, seminars, symposia, expert studies and related mechanisms. The Group has dealt with a wide range of law enforcement and drug abuse issues. It helped analyze and coordinate the position of member states on the various components of the 1988 United Nations Convention. It works with the Secretariat of the Commission of European Communities on a wide range of drug issues. Many of its technical papers are breaking new ground, conceptually and operationally, in defining and dealing with the drugs. Some of the issues which the Group has considered are: European cooperation in the control of drug traffic; administrative monitoring systems for the assessment of public health and social problems related to drug misuse; the role of the criminal justice system in responding to the needs of drug misusers; methods of reaching young people at particular risk; care of hard-core addicts; problems connected with drug addicts in prison; problems related to the staffing of treatment and rehabilitation services; and prevalence of AIDS among drug users. In 1989, the HONLEA for Europe was set up and includes all of the countries of the Western and Eastern regions of that continent.

In the Western Hemisphere, the first regional initiative was the South American Agreement on Narcotic Drugs and Psychotropic Substances (ASEP) set up by ten countries of South America in 1976.[35] It has promoted inter-country cooperation in the continent and has co-ordinated studies on and programs to meet the special needs of the member states. ASEP sponsors seven South American training centers:

1. treatment and rehabilitation in Buenos Aires, Argentina;
2. preventive education in Caracas, Venezuela;
3. suppression of illicit drug trafficking in Lima, Peru;
4. documentation in Buenos Aires;
5. customs in Brasília, Brazil;
6. training of dogs for anti-drug law enforcement, Buenos Aires, Argentina; and
7. regulation of the use of licit drugs, Santiago, Chile.

In the Caribbean, the Heads of Government of the Caribbean Community (CARICOM) entrusted its CARICOM Secretariat with the responsibility for developing multi-country programs to deal with law enforcement, epidemiology, education for prevention, and treatment and rehabilitation.[36] CARICOM has initiated an extensive program in each of these fields since the mid-1980's.

In the Central American area, the Chiefs of State of Costa Rica, El Salvador, Guatemala, Honduras and Nicaragua, established in December 1990, the Permanent Central American Commission for the Eradication of the Production, Traffic, Consumption and Use of Narcotic Drugs and Psychotropic Substances, and Related Offenses (CCP), to coordinate national policies and programs as well as to establish necessary intergovernmental cooperative efforts to deal with common drug problems.[37] The CCP has met twice over the past year and is now developing its organization and formulating a program of action.

In the inter-American region, encompassing South America, the Caribbean, Central America, and North America, a major regional program was initiated in 1986.[38] The member states of the Organization of American States (OAS) adopted the Inter-American Program of Action of Rio de Janeiro against the Illicit Use and Production of Narcotic Drugs and Psychotropic Substances, and Trafficking Therein (Program of Rio) and established the Inter-American Drug Abuse Control Commission (CICAD) to implement it.[39]

The Program of Rio spells out a range of measures needed at the national and inter-American levels to reduce the demand and supply of drugs. It further recommends to member governments that they set up national commissions to coordinate domestic efforts. In addition it specifies regional measures needed to support national efforts. CICAD was given the responsibility to develop, coordinate, evaluate and monitor these measures. In 1990, at the Meeting of Ministers Alliance of the Americas Against Drug Trafficking held in Ixtapa, Mexico, progress under the Program of Rio was assessed; and, specific priorities set for CICAD to implement over the next two or three years.[40]

In both the programs of the Rio and Ixtapa, CICAD is repeatedly enjoined to coordinate its efforts with those of other multilateral worldwide, regional and sub-regional organizations working on the drug problem in the inter-American region. The governments have assigned special importance to the principle of inter-agency cooperation and coordination because of the similarity of problems and solutions identified at the world-wide and inter-American levels. The CMO and the Global Plan of Action adopted by the UN in 1987 and 1990 respectively closely resemble the Programs of Rio and Ixtapa. This comparability in goals and focus underscores the need for complementarity in programming and coordination in operations.

To illustrate the importance of this principle, the following description of a regional program is presented. Examples could well have been drawn from several regional programs. However, for coherence and because of the ready availability of operational details, the CICAD Program has been selected. It indeed emphasizes the advantages in combatting illicit trafficking and drug abuse of coordinating, perhaps even in integrating world-wide, regional and sub-regional efforts.

The Inter-American Program of Rio and Ixtapa

In 1984, after years of confrontation among producer, transit and consumer countries in the OAS, the member states agreed that they need to work together to eradicate transnational illicit drug trafficking. In Resolution 699 of the OAS General Assembly in Brasilia that year, illicit drug trafficking was declared to be a crime that affects all of humanity, with all of the legal implications that it entails. In the same Resolution, a Specialized Inter-American Conference on Drug Trafficking was convened for the first quarter of 1986. That conference was held in April 1986 in Rio de Janeiro, and at it the Program of Action of Rio was drafted and adopted.[41] The Program of Rio drew on the relevant world-wide and regional experience to shape a policy and programatic framework for building long term inter-American cooperation to combat drug trafficking and drug abuse at its most critical points.

The Program of Rio defines national and inter-American regional measures needed for a sustained attack on the illicit demand for and supply of drugs, placing the highest priority on measures to reduce demand, including education for prevention, treatment and rehabilitation. It calls for unified national drug control agencies to plan, implement and coordinate comprehensive national policies and programs, and the creation of CICAD at the inter-American regional level. The Program of Rio also emphasizes the need to harmonize the legislation among member states, authorize the forfeiture of assets derived from illicit drug trafficking, control precursors and other chemicals essential for the manufacture of narcotic drugs and psychotropic substances, support crop substitution and eradication of illicit production, and build effective cooperation among anti-drug agencies in and among member states.

The goals and content of the Program of Rio were reaffirmed by the meeting of Ministers at Ixtapa, México in 1990, which also set the priorities for the Inter-American Program in the 1990's. High among those priorities is the early ratification by OAS member states of the 1988 United Nations Convention Against Illicit Traffic. In addition, CICAD is instructed to support member states in harmonizing their laws and procedures for effective application of the Convention, especially to control precursors and other chemical products and to effect forfeiture of assets derived from drug trafficking and money laundering. In addition, specific measures were approved on inter-American cooperation on demand reduction, interdiction and elimination of illicit production, as well as cooperation among the judiciary and enforcement agencies.

CICAD has adopted five priority lines of action to implement the Programs of Rio and Ixtapa: legal development, education for prevention, community mobilization, a uniform inter-American statistical system and an inter-American drug information system. A summary of their focus and development is presented in the following paragraphs.[42] Their component activities are consistent with UN Conventions as well as the CMO.

Legal Development. The framework for this priority line of action was proposed by specialists from the member states in San Jose, Costa Rica, in May 1988,[43] and is directed at building intergovernmental cooperation to:

1. harmonize national legislation, regulations and procedures dealing with illicit drug trafficking and drug abuse and facilitate the application throughout the region of the 1988 United Nations Convention against Illicit Traffic in Narcotic Drugs and Psychotropic Substances;
2. improve the collection, safeguarding and presentation in judicial proceedings of evidence against traffickers;
3. expedite court proceedings against drug traffickers;
4. develop relatively uniform and adequate sanctions and penalties against traffickers; and
5. generate public support for necessary legal action against drug traffickers.

The 1988 UN Convention provides the juridical framework for implementation of this line of action, whose activities are designed to assist member states to work together to apply the Convention. Under this line of action, a group of specialists from 12 member states, working within the framework of Articles 12 and 13 of the 1988 UN Convention, prepared

Model Regulations to Control Chemical Precursors and Chemical Substances, Machines and Materials, which were approved by CICAD in March 1990 and by the Meeting of Ministers in Ixtapa, April 17–20, 1990, and whose early adoption and implementation was recommended to the member states by the OAS General Assembly. CICAD has conducted workshops and training programs to assist member states in the consideration and application of the Model Regulations. Twelve countries have adopted and are applying the Model Regulations and seven more have legislation pending in their national congresses.

Model Regulations have also been prepared to facilitate the application of Article 5 of the 1988 Convention on money laundering and the seizure of assets derived from illicit drug trafficking. An expert group in which thirteen inter-American countries participated presented to CICAD in March 1992 a comprehensive proposal on Laundering Offenses Connected to Illicit Drug Trafficking and Related Offenses. The proposal was approved by CICAD and the General Assembly of the OAS which recommended that the Model Regulations be adopted and implemented by the member states. CICAD is now planning a systematic follow-up program to work with member states in their analysis, adoption and implementation.

CICAD is also seeking to assist Member States in promoting cooperation among their judiciaries as well as in improving their enforcement capability, especially in the collection, safekeeping and presentation in judicial proceedings of evidence against those engaged in illicit drug trafficking, which parallel the recommendations contained in the CMO. CICAD is being supported in these efforts by various OAS member states, UNDCP and ILANUD. In addition, support for training of police is provided by the Government of Canada, through Royal Canadian Mounted Police.

Education for Prevention. This line of action is one of the primary efforts by CICAD to reduce the demand for drugs by promoting comprehensive drug prevention programs in the schools of the hemisphere. Its strategy closely resembles the recommendations in Chapter 1 of the CMO and is designed to help youngsters deal with their problems without recourse to drugs, and to mobilize family and community support for the school prevention programs. Its plan of operations seeks to establish regional and subregional mechanisms of support for national efforts in drug abuse prevention activities.

Through four inter-American workshops and a hemisphere-wide meeting held in Quito, Ecuador in May 1990, the National Drug Commissions and Ministries of Education and Health of all member states were consulted on their needs. Based on these diagnoses, the Inter-American Program of Quito: Comprehensive Education to Prevent Drug Abuse was designed; it was adopted in June 1990.[44] It provides for inter-American support for national efforts in developing and applying appropriate curricula, training instructors, carrying out critical research and evaluation work, preparing teaching aids and audio-visual materials, and developing community and media linkages to disseminate appropriate anti-drug messages.

To implement the Program of Quito, four major subregional programs are now moving from the planning stage to implementation: one in Central America, including the Dominican Republic and Panama; the second in the Andean region; the third in southern South America, building on the Argentina-Uruguay Bi-National Program; and, the fourth in the English-speaking Caribbean. In the planning and implementation of these programs, the Inter-American Council for Education, Science and Culture (CIECC) and the Pan American Health Organization (PAHO) have joined forces with CICAD; and, the participation of UN and other multilateral bodies is actively encouraged. In addition, with the support of several OAS member states, hemisphere-wide support services are being mobilized to cooperate in the planning, execution and evaluation of project activities through socio-economic research, epidemiology, communications strategies and community mobilization.

In addition, a program to deal with the drug problem among the multitude of street children in the Andean countries has been initiated. Building on study financed by the IDB, this is the first step in developing a multi-country program to alleviate this problem.

Programs to involve young people directly in combatting drugs, called Youth Encounters, are being conducted in member states by the Inter-American Children's Institute (IIN). To date, the methodology, which seeks to mobilize youth leaders to combat drug abuse, has been tested in twelve Latin American and Caribbean countries with CICAD funds. Over 2,500 youth leaders and 100 national professionals have been trained.

Community Mobilization. This line of action is aimed at mobilizing non-governmental organizations in the member states—the media, corporations, the advertising community, private enterprise and private voluntary organizations—to support and/or fund private action to broaden public understanding of the drug problem and to cover essential prevention, treatment and rehabilitation services which the public sector cannot provide. CICAD initiated activities in this area in early 1989 with narcotics public awareness workshops, seminars for journalists and consultation with corporate and media heads from various member states. In addition, some country activities have moved into operation:

- A multi-country strategy for promoting community action against drug use has been developed with the support of the Centers of

Youth Integration of Mexico and the University of Oklahoma of the United States. The first application was in Argentina in 1990, followed by Central America in 1991. Brazil in 1992 was developing a similar program adopted to its needs.
- Consultant services to the National Drug Commissions on communications strategies for narcotics public awareness campaigns. In addition to country-oriented training attention is being given to developing models for multi-country research and development of communications strategies in cooperation with the International Center for Higher Communications Studies for Latin America (CIESPAL), at its headquarters in Quito, Ecuador.
- Teleconferences to facilitate cooperation among national and private anti-drug organizations throughout the Americas. The First Inter-American Teleconference was held on May 22, 1990, focusing on cooperative efforts by the media and the public and private sectors to produce and disseminate multi-media messages discouraging drug abuse. A cooperative university program, based on computer simulations, has also received CICAD support.

Uniform Statistical System. The Program of Rio calls upon CICAD to set up the Inter-American Data Bank.[45] It is now functioning, with a substantial data base. Much of data collected from OAS member states is not comparable because of differences in systems and criteria. Hence, CICAD is developing a Uniform Drug Statistical System for application in the region. In consultation with specialized agencies of several OAS member countries, the framework for the Uniform System has been designed, including cooperation in data collection and agreement on common definitions, procedures and systems for collecting, storing and publishing data. CICAD is now developing with the Governments of Mexico and Uruguay two subregional statistical centers to facilitate the application of the Uniform Drug Statistical System in the region. In this effort, close working relations with the UNDCP have been established to insure coordination and compatibility. The Japanese Government over the next three years will be providing financial support for the development of the System.

Inter-American Drug Information System. The Program of Rio also calls upon CICAD to set up an Inter-American Documentation Center. It is compiling a specialized collection of materials, publications and audiovisuals on the drug problem in the member states. One of its major objectives is to facilitate access by the member states to available information about the drug problem. In pursuit of the objective, it has sponsored the creation of the Inter-American Drug Information System (IADIS). Working with 13 regional and subregional entities, agreement has been reached on the initial design and the framework for its installation.[46] IADIS is now being installed and tested in eleven OAS countries. The Commission of European Communities is providing financial support for installing the first stage of the IADIS.

Both the Data Bank and the Documentation Center will form part of a regional network which, in cooperation with other international and regional public and private organizations, will not only better serve the needs of member states but also facilitate the active exchange of information and research on drugs.

To carry out the five priority lines of action, CICAD works with national drug commissions and supports multi-country initiatives which promote inter-country cooperation and have a multiplier effect. It works with both public and private entities. It is not a funding agency. It is a coordinator and facilitator. It provides regional support for national efforts, promotes exchange of information and experiences, and undertakes to seek financing for projects and activities that support its priority lines of action.

CICAD has also begun to study experiences through the world in eradication of illicit cultivation of coca leaf, poppy and marijuana and on strategies for alternative development. The need for finding longer term approaches to preventing and discouraging the production of such crops is a socio-economic, political and human priority of many governments. The Inter-American region is now seeking to assess techniques and results to date in order to help member governments and financial institutions identify the most promising for wide-spread application. The substantial flow of resources required to eradicate illicit cultivation can only be mobilized through the sustained investment of public and private financial institutions—and, their interest clearly depends on their confidence in the strategy and program to be carried out.

Like many other regional programs now operating around the world, that of CICAD is being adapted to meet the needs of the countries. In its concept and operations, it complements UNDCP efforts to help member states apply the Conventions and the CMO. As a result, CICAD has proposed to the UN the establishment of a joint programming mechanism to coordinate their respective plans of operations and to enhance the scope and quality of their support to member states.

Conclusion

Multilateral efforts to deal with the drug problem are based on the three United Nations Conventions now in force and on programs by worldwide, regional and subregional bodies. These efforts are for the most part relatively recent, and are evolving rapidly. All complement the primary agent in the fight, the national state. There is no supra-national authority to exact compliance by governments, enforce the Conventions or impose programs. The multilateral bodies are essentially persuaders and counselors.

Even in this discrete role, they have progressively played a significant role in combatting drug abuse and illicit trafficking, because of the transnational nature of this criminal enterprise. No national jurisdiction acting alone can effectively stop the flow of these addictive substances, and ever-closer cooperation is needed among and between countries if the problem is to be brought under control. That cooperation whether it be bilaterally or multilaterally negotiated must increasingly encompass an ever-larger circle of countries because of the exploding impact of this criminal activity and the resources available to the illicit trafficker.

The multilateral machinery available at world-wide, regional and subregional levels is especially suited to developing and sustaining necessary inter-governmental cooperation. The building of consensus and finding commonality of purpose affords all of the parties the opportunity for participation in the process and sharing in the responsibility. It may be a slow, sometimes arduous process; but, the transnational character of the problem, in a world of nation states, offers us no other reasonable alternative.

With the reorganization of the United Nations administrative machinery initiated over the past two years by the General Assembly, there is a unique opportunity for rationalizing the world-wide regional relationship and for enhancing the effectiveness of coordination and cooperation. The norms and structures for efficacious long-term multilateral support for national programs are essentially in place. Our challenge is to give them the dynamism and resources required for governments to work together and to progressively overcome today's drug crisis.

Notes

1. See Socio-Economic Studies for the Inter-American Specialized Conference on Traffic in Narcotic Drugs, OAS document OEA/SER.K/XXX.1, CEIN/doc 7/86, 1986, pp. 2–23.

2. Speech by Secretary General of the United Nations, Ambassador Javier Pérez de Cuellar, February 20, 1990, delivered at the opening session of the seventeenth special session of the General Assembly UN document A/S-17/PV1, pp. 9–16.

3. For historical information about and detailed legal analysis of the development of the international juridical framework, see Chattergee, S.K., Legal Aspects of International Drug Control, 1981, and Legal Aspects of the System to Regulate International Commerce in Narcotic Drugs on a Global Scale, an information document for the Inter-American Conference on Traffic in Narcotic Drugs, OAS document OEA/Ser K/XXX.1, CEIN.doc.9/86, 1986.

4. See United Nations Document E/CN.7/1991/1/Rev.1, of December 20, 1990, prepared for the thirty-fourth session in which the history and functions of the

Commission on Narcotic Drugs are summarized. The Commission was created by the United Nations Economic and Social Council (ECOSOC) in resolution 9 (I) of February 16, 1946, as the successor to the Advisory Committee on Traffic in Opium and Other Dangerous Drugs. The resolution specifies its functions as subsidiary to the Council and includes assisting it in supervising the application of conventions and agreements, advising it on all matters related to the control of drugs, preparing such draft conventions as may be necessary, considering changes in the machinery for international control of narcotic drugs and submitting proposals to the Council and carrying out such additional functions as the Council may designate. Also for statutory functions of the Commission, see Articles 5–8 of the Single Convention on Narcotic Drugs, 1961, as amended by the Protocol amending Single Convention on Narcotic Drugs, 1961, Articles 2–3 of the Convention on Psychotropic Substances, 1971; and Article 21 of the United Nations Convention Against Illicit Traffic in Narcotic Drugs and Psychotropic Substances, 1988.

5. Single Convention on Narcotic Drugs, 1961, as amended by the Protocol amending the Single Convention on Narcotic Drugs, 1961, Article 33.

6. Op. cit. supra, Article 35 (a).

7. Ibid.

8. Op. cit. supra, Articles 5, 9–20 on scope, composition and functions of INCB.

9. Op. cit. supra, Articles 35 and 36.

10. See Article 7 of the 1971 Convention on Psychotropic Substances.

11. See Article 5, Paragraph 2 of the 1971 Convention on Psychotropic Substances.

12. The Fourth Preambular clause of the 1988 United Nations Convention against Illicit Traffic in Narcotic Drugs and Psychotropic Substances.

13. Op. cit. supra 6, Article 2, 1.

14. Article 23 (a) of the 1988 United Nations Convention, op. cit. supra 12. Also see Article 22 for the specification of INCB functions under the 1988 Convention.

15. Op. cit. supra 8. Also see articles 2 and 16–19 of the 1971 Convention on Psychotropic Substances and articles 22–23 of the 1988 Convention for INCB functions specified in their administration.

16. Article 22 (a) of the 1988 United Nations Convention, cited in footnote 5. Also see Article 22 for the specification of INCB functions.

17. See United Nations Document A/39/646 of November 12, 1984, for a detailed description of the functions of UNFDAC.

18. See General Assembly resolution 45/179 of 21 December 1990, concerning the "Enhancement of the United Nations structure for drug abuse control."

19. For a detailed analysis of the originals of the ICDAIT and the contents of the CMO, see United Nations Publication, the Declaration of the International Conference on Drug Abuse and Illicit Trafficking and Comprehensive Multidisciplinary Outline of Future Activities in Drug Abuse Control, 1988, UN document ST/NAR/14, UN Sales Publication No. E.88.XI.I, ISBN 92-1-148075-2,.00900P.

20. The International Police Cooperation Organization (ICPO/INTERPOL) was founded in 1923 in Vienna, by national police organizations of 6 European countries and Egypt. It grew to 34 national organizations by 1938 and was reorganized after World War II and its headquarters moved from Vienna to Paris.

21. The Custom Cooperation Council (CCC) was created by the Brussels Convention of December 15, 1950, by the customs services of over 40 countries. It is headquartered in Brussels.

22. See resolution A/RES/S-17/2 of February 23, 1990, of the seventeenth special session of the United Nations General Assembly.

23. Op. cit. supra 20, for detailed description of the programs of the various Specialized Agencies, which have not changed substantially since 1984.

24. Op. cit. supra 20 for a summary of WHO anti-drug programs.

25. ILANUD was created in 1975 and is headquartered in San Jose, Costa Rica. See 1988 pamphlet published by ILANUD for summary of its program and activities.

26. Op. cit. supra 14.

27. Op. cit. supra 8 and op. cit. supra 15 on INCB functions.

28. The Sub-Commission was created by resolution 6(XXV) of the twenty-fifth session of the Commission of Narcotic Drugs and authorized by the Economic and Social Council (ECOSOC), in its resolution 1776(LIV) of May 18, 1973.

29. HONLEA for the Asia and Pacific Region was authorized by ECOSOC resolution 1845(LVI) of May 15, 1974.

30. The HONLEA for Africa was authorized by ECOSOC resolution 1985/11 of May 28, 1985; for Latin America, by ECOSOC resolution 1987/34 of May 26, 1987; and, for the European region, ECOSOC resolution 1990/30 of May 24, 1990.

31. For a summary for the Colombo Plan Activities, see P. A. Abarro, the Role of an Intergovernmental Regional Organization in Combatting Drug Trafficking, United Nations Bulletin on Narcotics, Vol. XXX/X, No. 1, January–March 1987, pp. 4–50.

32. For a summary of the ASEAN program, see O'Hara and Sallek, Recent Developments in Legislative and Administrative Measures in Countries of the Association of South-East Asian Nations to Counter the Illicit Traffic in Drugs, United Nations Bulletin on Narcotics, Vol. XXXIX, No. 1, January–March 1987, pp. 51–56.

33. Report of the Secretariat of the Council of Arab Ministers of the Interior to the thirty-third regular meeting of the United Nations Commission on Narcotics Drugs, January 1989.

34. For a summary of the work of the Pompidou Group, see N. A. Nagler, The Council of Europe Co-operation Group to Combat Drug Abuse and Illicit Trafficking in Drugs (the Pompidou Group), United Nations Bulletin on Narcotics, Vol. XXXIX, No. 1, January–March 1987, pp. 31–40.

35. For a summary of the ASEP program, see C. N. Cagliotti, Cooperation between South American Countries in the struggle against Drug Abuse and Illicit Drug Trafficking, United Nations Bulletin on Narcotics, Vol. XXXIX, No. 1, January–March 1987, pp. 61–68.

36. For an analysis of the actions of the Caribbean Community, see A. M. Sherman-Peter, Co-ordinated Countermeasures of Caribbean Countries against the Illicit Drug Traffic: Recent Developments and Prospects, United Nations Bulletin on Narcotics, Vol. XXXIX, No. 1, January–March 1987, pp. 69–78.

37. See the Declaration of Punta Arenas, Costa Rica, of December 17, 1990, signed by the Chiefs of State of the five countries, in which they resolved: "to create a permanent Central American Commission devoted to the eradication of the

production, consumption and abuse of narcotic drugs and psychotropic substances, trafficking therein and related crimes, especially money laundering and legalization of other types of proceeds and to set up a regional mechanism for exchanging information on these matters."

38. For the evolution of the Inter-American Program and the creation of CICAD, see Irving G. Tragen, Cooperation of Countries within the Organization of American States to Combat Drug Problems, United Nations Bulletin on Narcotics, Vol. XXXIX, No. 1, January–March 1987, pp. 57–60.

39. For texts of the Inter-American Program of Action of Rio de Janeiro Against the Illicit Use and Production of Narcotic Drugs and Psychotropic Substances, see Resolution AG/Res. 813 and 814 of the OAS General Assembly. OAS Resolution AG/Res. 813 (XVI-0/86) created CICAD.

40. For the text of the Declaration and the Program of Action of Ixtapa, see Resolution AG/Res. 1045 (XX-0/90) of the OAS General Assembly.

41. Op. cit. supra 39.

42. For more detailed information about the scope and contents of the CICAD Program, see: OAS document CICAD/doc. 286/91 of January 14, 1991.

43. See CICAD document CICAD/CR/doc. 17/88, Rev.1 of January 27, 1988 for report on meeting in San Jose, Costa Rica, in which the Legal Development Program was designed.

44. See CICAD/CIECC/doc. 33/90, rev. 1, for the description of the Inter-American Program of Quito: Comprehensive Education to Prevent Drug Abuse. Recent developments are covered in CICAD doc. 289/91 of February 1991.

45. See CICAD doc. 289/91, ad. 1, for development of the Uniform Inter-American Statistical System and the Inter-American Data Bank.

46. See CICAD doc. 289/91 for information on the development of the Inter-American Drug Information System and the Inter-American Documentation Center.

9

Drugs in Post-Communist Societies

Rensselaer W. Lee III and
Scott MacDonald

In recent decades, the international narcotics trade has profoundly affected the economies, social life, and political institutions of nations throughout the world. In some countries, especially in South America, narcotics syndicates have insinuated themselves in the upper reaches of the power structure, established territorial bases, altered the dynamics of national and regional power relationships, and revamped employment and foreign trade patterns. Narcotics industries and the political movements that they support are associated with the violent political and economic disintegration of states such as Lebanon, Peru, and Afghanistan. Drugs are a social catastrophe in the United States and other consuming countries, where abuse of illegal drugs drives or complicates a wide range of social ills, from violent crime to homelessness to joblessness to AIDS.

The former Soviet bloc countries occupy a vast Eurasian region stretching from Prague to Vladivostok, and they increasingly are a part of this dismal drug panorama. To be sure, Eastern Europe and the former USSR, now the loosely federated Commonwealth of Independent States (CIS), to date have incurred fewer adverse consequences of drug abuse and drug trafficking than many other countries. The bloc's relative isolation from the West precluded a significant influx of Western hard drugs such as cocaine, heroin, and crack. In the Communist world's controlled economic system, small and uncoordinated narcotics traffickers found little opportunity to accumulate vast wealth. The newly liberated nations of Eastern Europe and the CIS, however, are assuming the status of an important new frontier for the illicit drug traffic. The demise of communist totalitari-

---

A much condensed and unrevised version of this chapter was published in *Foreign Policy*, No. 90, 1993, pp. 89–107.

anism in the East, the transition from socialist to free market economies, and access to the global economy have kindled new incentives and opportunities for organized crime, including the narcotics industry. In addition, political liberalization and the easing of social controls have spurred urban young people and many others to experiment with mind-altering substances. The rise of narcotics industries is further bolstered by the uncertain economic conditions prevailing in much of Eurasia, as well as by weak law enforcement, permissive drug laws, unprotected frontiers, and porous financial systems.

Several recent developments illustrate the volatility of the Eurasian drug front. In Poland, a sophisticated amphetamine industry with well-established international connections coalesced in the late 1980s. Czechoslovakia and Hungary have become significant way stations for moving Turkish-controlled heroin into Western Europe. Colombian trafficking families established front organizations and courier networks in Eastern Europe, facilitating the penetration of Western European markets. A drugs-for-weapons link may have precipitated the initial stages of Yugoslavia's disintegration. The former Soviet Union is emerging as an important network of drug-producing and drug-consuming nations. Moscow's weakening (and now virtually nonexistent) hold over former Soviet Central Asia and that region's bleak economic prospects directly correlate with an apparently massive expansion of drug crop cultivation in the region. If current trends continue, Central Asia could assume the status of a significant world supplier of cannabis and opium products in the 1990s.

The Western governments have not devoted sufficient attention to such disturbing trends. Consumed by issues such as economic reform, ethnic strife, and disarmament, Western policymakers have failed to develop a coordinated antidrug strategy that addresses this vast and awakening region. To date, the total flow of U.S., European Community (EC), and United Nations (UN) narcotics assistance to the East probably totals not more than $7 million to $9 million—and most of that sum goes to Eastern European countries along the Balkan heroin route.[1] In comparison, in FY 1993, the United States allocated almost $7 million in such aid to one relatively peripheral trafficking country, Ecuador. From Washington's standpoint, narcotics problems in the post-Communist world quite simply rank as a non-priority. For instance, Poland, Hungary, Czechoslovakia, Yugoslavia, and the former USSR were not even on the list of 50 drug-producing and drug-trafficking countries published in the State Department's 1992 version of its annual *International Narcotics Control Strategy Report*, while minor trafficking countries such as the Ivory Coast, Senegal, and Nepal at least rated a page in the report. (The 1993 *Strategy Report*, not published as of this writing, is expected to list some former Communist nations.) The United States has not dedicated a DEA or State Department narcotics representative for any post-Communist country. A shift in U.S. practice seems warranted. The former Communist bloc countries collectively possess the potential to flood Western and U.S. markets during the 1990s with narcotics such as amphetamines, hashish, and opium derivatives. More important, the unrestrained growth of criminal narcotics enterprises in the East threatens the integrity of Eastern economic and governmental institutions, magnifies the potential for East-West conflict, and complicates the building of a stable post-Communist order in Eurasia.

The Dynamic Eastern Drug Industry

Post-Communist states offer extremely attractive possibilities for drug trafficking and for laundering of drug money. A variety of historical, attitudinal, legal, regulatory, and economic factors work to undermine drug law enforcement in these states. The legacy of Communism itself constitutes one important factor: The Communist system encouraged self-delusion if not the growth of narcotics enterprises. Former Communist leaders in the USSR and Central Europe adhered rigidly to the ideology that illegal drug trafficking is peculiar to decadent capitalist societies. As a consequence, police, public health officials, and financial authorities are largely unprepared to cope with an unfettered drug trade. As one Czechoslovak psychiatrist observed: "Under the previous government, certain social problems were purposefully ignored or simply suppressed to the point of non-recognition. Drug abuse is among those problems and just as we are learning the fine points of the free market system, we find ourselves newcomers to the role of fighting drug abuse and drug traffic."[2]

This political myopia permeates virtually all institutions. A narcotics official in Kyrgyzstan recalls that drug entries in crime reports prompted some members of the public to cross out the statistic with a red pencil and scrawl, "What drugs? We don't have a drug problem."[3] In the former Communist states, police generally acquired little experience in investigating trafficking organizations, recognizing narcotics, and tracking the flow of drug money. Health personnel usually were not trained to identify drug addiction symptoms, furnish appropriate care, or conduct epidemiological research. Furthermore, schools, employers, families, and the media did little to educate potential users about the health hazards associated with drug abuse, reflecting the prevailing belief among Communist educational and health authorities (especially in the Soviet Union) that antinarcotics propaganda actually is counterproductive and only stimulates curiosity about drugs, particularly among the young.

Second, antiquated drug laws prevail throughout much of the post-Communist world. Drug use is not a crime in Czechoslovakia, Poland, Kazakhstan, Turkmenistan and the Russian Federation. In Poland, penalties are not necessarily imposed for possession of large quantities of drugs. In 1989, for example, Polish police arrested three men for the sale of 17 kilograms of amphetamines, but the prosecutor could not prove that the drugs actually had changed hands. After a 2-year trial, the court dismissed the charges, although the prosecutor is appealing. As of early 1992, not a single Polish amphetamine trafficker had been convicted and imprisoned by a Polish court.[4] In Czechoslovakia, a major loophole in the current narcotics law apparently permits individuals to cultivate marijuana for botanical, horticultural, or aesthetic purposes—because "they like the shape of the leaves or the color of the flowers," as one Czechoslovakian police official stated—and marijuana seeds are freely sold in local shops.[5] In Poland and Czechoslovakia, extradition of citizens is specifically outlawed, thus preempting a vital judicial tool for authorities confronting the essentially transnational drug trade. Finally, in many post-Communist countries, weak or nonexistent conspiracy statutes preclude bringing drug criminals to justice. Although transporting and selling narcotics and planting narcotics crops are crimes unless authorized by the government, the rules of evidence virtually require that the perpetrators be caught in the act. As a narcotics official in Uzbekistan's Ministry of Internal Affairs notes about opium cultivation, "The organizers, the growers are not here in the field; they are back in the villages and to prove their involvement is impossible under the legal system."[6]

Not surprisingly, the authorities themselves exhibit a relatively relaxed attitude toward illicit drugs. One Polish Interpol official commented, "Fighting drugs is a low priority for us. Prosecutors, judges and even police regard this crime in the same category as petty theft. They do not recognize that trafficking poses a threat or danger to society."[7]

Third, drug law enforcement suffers from a lack of broad-based citizen support. The law enforcement tactics employed during the Communist era bred a deep and pervasive popular mistrust of the police throughout Central Europe and the CIS. Criminal investigations consequently are hampered if not hamstrung by the authorities' failure to recruit citizens as informants and to identify witnesses who will testify in court cases. Moreover, prosecutorial systems in countries such as Poland and Hungary offer little latitude for plea bargaining, so traffickers perceive little incentive to confess crimes, identify accomplices, or furnish details about their organizations.

Fourth, the general economic and political disarray displayed throughout the former Communist world imposes an additional constraint on drug law enforcement. For example, the Polish police budget declined 13 percent from 1990 to 1991, as the government's overall budget deficit rose more than 700 percent as a percent of GNP. The use of patrol cars reportedly is limited to 60 kilometers per day, and the police abandoned plans to modernize vehicles and purchase new car radios. Incredibly, only about 30 full-time drug enforcement police patrol the entire country, and their annual funding totals only about $100,000 to $200,000.[8] In the now-defunct Soviet Union, law enforcement is characterized by chaos, especially in the Central Asian states, which depended on Moscow for much of their antidrug manpower and resources. Critical shortages are common in basic equipment such as vehicles, bulletproof vests, herbicides, computers, and typewriters. Moreover, funds are seldom available to rent helicopters for aerial crop surveys or eradication missions. Because drug crops increasingly are sown in mountain or desert regions that are logistically inaccessible by raid, police forces are virtually helpless to prevent the proliferation of illegal plots.

Fifth, post-Communist states unfortunately offer an inviting target for criminals who want to abuse local financial systems as a stash for narcotics earnings and funds derived from other serious crimes. The CIS and most East European states do not criminalize money laundering, and the legal system does not incorporate procedures for investigating the origin of private sector funds. Banks are not legally required to report deposits, transfers, and withdrawals, and banking authorities have no incentive to screen their clients or report suspicious transactions. In Poland, the convertibility of local currency and the absence of controls on importing and exporting foreign exchange generate additional incentives for laundering drug profits.

Although Czechoslovakia and Hungary recently passed laws to control money laundering, such laws will be difficult to implement: Western accounting procedures are relatively new, and bank regulators and their enforcement counterparts are preponderantly inexperienced in conducting financial investigations. Inconvertible currencies in most post-Communist countries constitute a not insuperable barrier to traffickers' financial operations. (For instance, recent data document Hungarian bank accounts belonging to the late Medellín kingpin Jose Gonzalo Rodriguez Gacha and Cali trafficker Jose Santa Cruz Londoño.[9]) Moreover, increasing East-West economic integration and the stabilization of the ruble in the CIS undoubtedly will undermine the inconvenience of converting currencies. In addition, the tightening of banking laws throughout the European Community (EC) to conform to the EC's June 1991 policy directive on money laundering will encourage the transfer of drug funds into more loosely run Eastern institutions.

Drug Trafficking Trends

Recent trends in drug supply, drug abuse, and organized crime are summarized below.

Supply

The decay and collapse of Communism have generated new narcotics trafficking patterns in the East. For instance, the Balkan countries, especially Bulgaria and Yugoslavia, traditionally served as a transit region for narcotics moving between Turkey and Western Europe, but the supply chain now extends to Central Europe. Record quantities of cocaine and heroin apparently are being conveyed through Hungary and Czechoslovakia. Although small by U.S. standards, these shipments represent a dangerous upward surge. The relaxation of custom controls in the late 1980s and early 1990s and the military conflict in Croatia, Slovenia, and Bosnia have prompted Turkish, Iranian, and Yugoslav traffickers—who dominate the overland heroin trade in Europe—to ship more heroin northeastward through Hungary and Czechoslovakia and from there across the Czechoslovakian-German border. As an indication of this trend, German heroin seizures along the Czechoslovakian-German border exploded from 8.5 kilograms in 1989 to 670 kilograms in 1991. Moreover, such seizures increased as a proportion of total heroin impounded by German customs, from 5 percent in 1989 to 65 percent in 1991.[10] Furthermore, Colombian trafficking organizations associated with the Medellín and Cali cartels, apparently are contemplating using Poland, Czechoslovakia, Hungary and even Russia as staging areas for smuggling cocaine to Western Europe. Such a route is exotic and undoubtedly expensive, but cocaine's European selling price of $50,000 to $55,000—compared to $15,000 to $20,000 in the United States—makes the option one that traffickers can easily afford.

Northeastern Europe is evolving into a source region for amphetamines, but Poland by far ranks as the most important producer and exporter of these substances. (A methamphetamine called Pervitin is produced in Czechoslovakia, but only minor quantities are exported.) Techniques for manufacturing amphetamine sulfate were introduced directly from the Netherlands, according to Polish Interpol officials.[11] (Holland's amphetamine industry ranks as the largest in Europe.) This successful transfer probably transpired sometime in the early 1980s; by the middle of the decade, Polish traffickers were beginning to export these drugs, according to European narcotics experts. Polish chemists improved on the techniques of their Dutch teachers, and Polish amphetamines currently embody the highest drug quality in Europe, with purity levels often ranging from 97 percent to almost 100 percent.[12] According to the Swedish Amphetamine Profiling Project, a center that analyzes the chemical signature of amphetamine sulfate seized in Europe, 20 percent of the amphetamines captured in Western Europe in 1991 were of Polish origin, compared to only 6 percent between 1985 and 1989.[13]

The former Soviet Union can be characterized as both a narcotics-producing and narcotics-consuming nation. Indeed, the country is virtually self-sufficient in narcotics. Heroin and cocaine imports from the West are escalating, but still represent a negligible share of the former Soviet market, although the CIS's increasing economic integration with the West could modify this equation considerably. As one MVD official in Moscow, Valentin Roshchin, explained, "If ruble convertibility is achieved, a tremendous flood of drugs could pour toward us."[14] The CIS has not yet acquired the status of a significant exporter of illicit drugs. However, one former Soviet official conceded in 1990, "The geographic scale of contraband drugs and the transit of drugs across our territory are expanding."[15] Drug cargoes from Southwest Asia (the Golden Crescent) and Southeast Asia (the Golden Triangle) travel across former Soviet territory by air, rail, and truck en route to Western Europe and North America. Most of the drugs move by train, hidden in the 150,000 containers that annually pass through the CIS.[16]

The former Soviet Union encompasses a gigantic base of raw materials necessary for the production of illicit drugs: Huge extensions of mostly wild marijuana, possibly more than 1 million hectares, reportedly are growing throughout CIS territory. A United Nations team visiting Central Asia in the spring of 1992 was informed that some 200,000 hectares of marijuana were thriving in Kazakhstan and Kyrgyzstan—about five times the recorded marijuana cultivation in the rest of the world—and that an additional 1 million hectares may be germinating in Russia. Central Asian marijuana, which reportedly tests for a high tetrahydracannabinol (THC) content, frequently is processed into hashish, one of the most commonly used drugs in the CIS. In addition, an estimated 3,000 to 5,000 hectares of illegal opium poppies are cultivated in Central Asia, mostly in Uzbekistan, Tadjikistan, and Turkmenistan.[17] And a type of poppy with lower morphine content, the so-called maslichny or oil-bearing variety, thrives in southern Russia and the Ukraine. Although Central Asia does not hold a monopoly on drug crops, the region's high-quality drugs are a significant factor in urban illicit drug markets in Russia and probably in other European CIS states. According to a ranking Ministry of Internal Affairs (MVD) official in Moscow, some 40 percent of the poppy straw, some 80 percent of the cannabis derivatives, and nearly all of the opium confiscated by police in Russia during 1992 originated in the Central Asian republics.[18] The narcotics relationship between these states and Russia is somewhat comparable to the one between Latin America and the United States. Since the collapse of the USSR, which obliterated Moscow's direct control over Central Asia's law enforcement institutions, the parallel is becoming ever more evident.

Drug crop cultivation is exploding in Central Asia in response to both dismal economic conditions and rising demand for drugs, especially in the European sections of the CIS. For example, the chief of the antinarcotics unit of the Uzbek Ministry of Internal Affairs reports a 10-fold increase in the number of poppy sowings in that republic in the past 3 years. "We see that the planted area has expanded, and at the same time that life is more expensive and the economy is getting worse," says another official in the same unit.[19] Traffickers are financing some of this new cultivation by hiring peasants and sometimes entire villages to plant and protect the crops. Poppy cultivation offers enormous economic returns. In mid-late 1992, a hectare of Uzbek opium poppies translated into a gross annual income of at least 2,000,000 rubles (between $5,000 and $8,000)—approximately 20 times the earnings from a hectare of cotton and 150 times the income from a hectare of grapes. Not only peasants but also members of the upper echelons of society seemingly covet a piece of the action. In one Uzbek oblast, prominent citizens such as the head of a public catering establishment and the deputy director of an asphalt plant were discovered growing opium poppies during a Moscow-run crop eradication campaign ("Operation Poppy") in 1990.[20]

Such trends might well be unstoppable. On the one hand, after the Union dissolved, Moscow ceased funding counternarcotics operations, including aerial map surveys and crop eradication campaigns in Central Asia. Governments in that region lack the resources and probably the political will to continue such programs, at least at the same level of intensity. On the other hand, Central Asia's grim economic conditions—poverty, expanding populations, high unemployment, and physical isolation from world markets—probably will propel even larger numbers of Asians into the lucrative opium business. Interestingly, hard-pressed Central Asian governments also have evaluated opium, albeit legal opium, as a potential source of revenue. Both Kyrgyzstan and Kazakhstan have contemplated introducing official cultivation of opium, and in Kyrgyzstan, an agonizing public debate raged from early 1991 to early 1992. The governments of three out of Kyrgyzstan's five oblasts and some national-level officials support a plan for establishing plantations on 9,000 hectares. This plan would earn the country perhaps $10 million to $15 million annually at current legal opium prices (assuming optimal growing conditions) and even more if the opium was converted to morphine and pharmaceuticals. Opium in fact was cultivated on Kyrgyz state farms as late as the early 1970s, but the practice led to corruption. As much as 40 percent of the crop was stolen and sold through criminal channels to addicts in Kyrgyzstan and other republics.[21] In 1974, the USSR halted state production of opium, and Kyrgyzstan's plantations, which at one time extended over 7,000 hectares and employed 20,000 people, were cut down. Opponents of the scheme—including various domestic groups, Russia, and almost the entire international community—argued that traffickers would infiltrate the new plantations and make off with a portion of the opium crop. Bowing to pressure, the government of Kyrgyzstan shelved its opium project in January 1992.[22] Yet, the issue probably will survive—especially if desperate farmers connive with financially strapped local governments to make ends meet by cultivating illegal opium.

Drug Abuse

Abuse of nonalcoholic drugs long has plagued Eastern Europe and the former USSR, although discussion of the subject officially was discouraged until late in the Communist era. Patterns of drug abuse thus developed in isolation from the international narcotics market. The principal Western hard drugs—heroin, cocaine, crack, and LSD—seldom are available in post-Communist countries. In contrast to the Western pattern, addicts often procure or manufacture their own drugs rather than buying them on the black market. The pattern of drug abuse varies somewhat by country. Homemade poppy derivatives, especially injectable compounds made from poppy straw or opium, are common in Poland, Russia, the Ukraine, Turkmenistan, Tadjikistan, and Uzbekistan. Marijuana and hashish are particularly prevalent in Kyrgyzstan, Kazakhstan, and Russia. Ephedrine-based amphetamines (actually methamphetamines) are gaining popularity in Russia, the Baltic states, and Czechoslovakia. However, Poland's high-quality amphetamines, produced from the chemicals benzylmethylketone and phenyl 2 propinol, are almost all exported.

No reliable data are available on the number of people abusing drugs in Eastern Europe. This is hardly surprising: The former Communist regimes in Eastern Europe viewed drugs essentially as an affliction of capitalist societies and thus did not encourage epidemiological research on the subject. No national household surveys on drugs were conducted, and no national data banks were established. Consequently, health authorities possess no overall understanding of the nature and scope of drug consumption.

Yet, drug abuse apparently has reached serious proportions in some former Communist states. Although the number of Poles treated in hospitals and outpatient facilities is relatively small (only 6,700 in 1989), a senior health official estimates the drug-abusing population at anywhere from 50,000 to 300,000.[23] Approximately 80 percent of patients hospitalized for drug abuse are addicted to a poppy straw extract called *kompot*, a kind of liquid heroin, usually of low purity, which is injected intravenously. (Approximately 7,000 hectares of low-grade papaver somniferum, opium poppy, are legally cultivated in Poland for seeds. Farmers illegally sell the straw—the dried bulbs and upper stems of poppy plants—to addicts.) *Kompot* is limited by a short shelf life, cannot be easily transported over long distances, and has not stimulated a market in the West. Drug addiction in Poland, however, does produce spillover effects that trouble Western health authorities. Needle sharing among addicts and unsanitary practices in the street sale of *kompot* have contributed to the rapid spread of AIDS in Poland. For example, many addicts buy from street dealers who sell the drug from large bottles by the cubic centimeter. The same bottle serves as many as 100 addicts, who insert syringes and extract the required doses. According to 1990–1991 health statistics, approximately 1 in 12 Polish drug addicts is infected with the AIDS virus, and more than two-thirds of all HIV-infected people use drugs.[24] Because Poland now is open to the outside world, the not unlikely prospect of an AIDS epidemic in that country would almost certainly accelerate the spread of the disease in other parts of Europe.

The CIS states have not forged a consensus on the total number of users. Recent police estimates range from 1.5 million to 7.5 million for the former Union. Soviet health authorities tabulate addiction rates by counting everyone who used a treatment facility during the past 5 years; these rates vary substantially by republic, reflecting both cultural patterns and drug availability. For example, in rural Turkmenistan, opium consumption is traditional: The drug is prescribed for stomach ailments, distributed at weddings and other celebrations, and administered to unruly children. Consequently, Turkmenistan's addiction rate in 1990 totaled 94.8 per 100,000 people, quadruple the all-Union average of 23.7 and quadruple Russia's rate of 19.1. Uzbekistan, probably the former Union's largest opium producer, reports only 20.6 addicts per 100,000. The Ukraine, a major producer of poppy straw, tallies the second highest addiction rate in the former Soviet Union—41.3 addicts per 100,000.[25]

Some indicators suggest that drug use in the former Soviet Union is rising rapidly. Between 1985 and 1990, the number of drug addicts as a percentage of the Soviet population multiplied by more than 70 percent, according to the USSR Ministry of Health Statistics. Gorbachev's ill-conceived anti-alcohol campaign in 1985–1987 was designed to reduce violent crime (alcohol figures in about 70 percent of the murders committed in the USSR) and to regain lost workforce productivity, but probably contributed to expanding drug use. An unfortunate and unforeseen outcome of the campaign was driving many young people to consume drugs. Many young Soviets became familiar with drug use during the Afghanistan war, providing a conduit for the large quantities of Afghan opium and hashish entering the Soviet Union and later stimulating increased production of these narcotics in the Central Asian republics. In the Slavic republics, the especially rapid growth in drug addiction rates in the mid-

and late 1980s ranged from 90 percent in the Russian Republic to 320 percent in Byelorussia.[26] According to Moscow's head narcologist, Edward Drozdov, the percentage of Moscow secondary school students who sampled drugs increased from 6.4 percent in 1986–1987 to 16.5 percent in 1992. According to Drozdov, in some of Moscow's professional technical schools, 100 percent of the student body has experimented with narcotics.[27] The drug abuse scenario likely will deteriorate further: A decision by the Russian parliament in December 1991 to remove criminal penalties and fines for nonmedical use of drugs—functionally an attempt to legalize use—will almost certainly foster the spread of narcotics in the Russian federation.

Comparatively speaking, Central Asia exhibits a fairly serious drug abuse problem. In four Central Asian republics—Kazakhstan, Kyrgyzstan, Uzbekistan, and Turkmenistan—drug abuse rates in 1990 exceeded those in Russia and most other former Union republics. However, the rates apparently are swelling more slowly in Kazakhstan and Uzbekistan, and Kyrgyzstan and Turkmenistan actually recorded declines in addiction rates from 1985 to 1990. Tadjikistan stands out as the anomaly in the group: The addict population is relatively much smaller than Russia's, but is growing somewhat more rapidly. At the same time, drug production—or at least commercial processing of opium poppies—apparently is rising at an alarming rate in Central Asia, primarily to serve the expanding ranks of consumers in the European region of the former USSR. However, as one Uzbek narcotics official notes, "With the opening of ties to the West, now it is possible that the narcotics will reach the West in exchange for hard currency."[28]

Organized Crime

Organized drug crime in a sense has arrived in post-Communist states. Criminal organizations are acquiring the capability to transport drugs across regional and national boundaries. International trafficking organizations are gaining footholds in the region, a development that ultimately will enhance the sophistication of local trafficking. Finally, the drug trade is producing seven significant political and economic effects on post-Communist societies. Polish, Colombian, Yugoslav, and intra-CIS trafficking groups exemplify these trends, in effect representing the new face of organized drug crime in Eastern Europe and the CIS.

Poland's amphetamine industry constitutes the most sophisticated indigenous narcotics enterprise in the post-Communist countries. Judging from the extremely high purity of the final amphetamine sulfate product, the Polish amphetamine production process characterizes a sophisticated operation. Criminal groups apparently have first-class laboratory equipment and highly qualified chemists at their disposal. (Polish Interpol officials believe that traffickers may have access to legal laboratories in universities and scientific research institutions.) Polish amphetamine gangs are fairly rudimentary by international standards. Unlike Colombian organizations, they exhibit little permanent structure, lack a core of salaried employees, are not vertically integrated from production through foreign distribution, and tend to be multiline organizations that engage, for example, in auto and art theft, counterfeiting, and drug trafficking. Moreover, the traffickers can ship drugs to markets in Germany and the Scandinavian countries, procure essential chemicals such as benzyl methylketone, and even clandestinely manufacture the chemicals in Poland. Finally, traffickers are adept at keeping the authorities at bay. "We know the location of the amphetamine laboratories in the Praga district of Warsaw," reports one Polish Interpol official. "But by the time we get there, the chemicals and drugs will be gone."[29]

Like successful trafficking organizations elsewhere, Polish amphetamine gangs are starting to buy into the legal economies. According to Polish Interpol, traffickers in Poland apparently have invested in fish processing, publishing, photo processing, purchasing, and agribusiness enterprises. The police reported that amphetamine traffickers bought a vegetable farm and an associated canning plant with the idea of smuggling amphetamines out of Poland in the cans.[30] Outside of Poland—especially in Germany and the Scandinavian countries—amphetamine gangs operate through a kind of Polish pipeline, a broad network of resident Polish citizens or former Polish nationals who serve as critical links in the wholesale trade, taking delivery of drugs from Poland, storing them, and reselling them to local distributors. The foreign connection is as important to Polish drug smuggling gangs as the estimated 1 million Colombians living in the United States are to the activities of the so-called Colombian cartels—or the 2 million Turks living in Europe are to Turkish heroin-smuggling families. Of course, the Polish pipeline can move any type of drugs into Western markets—Central Asian hashish, Afghan heroin, or even Colombian cocaine.

Ominously, international trafficking organizations are trying to coopt Central European nationals into smuggling. The strategic objectives are easily discernible: widening avenues of penetration into Western European markets and reducing the visibility and exposure of the parent organization. The authorities associate Colombians, Turks, and Nigerians with organized drug trafficking, making them tempting targets for customs officials at national borders.

Colombian trafficking organizations most clearly exemplify this trend. For example, the Cali cartel tried to recruit Polish couriers to smuggle cocaine across the Polish-German border. The Colombians also reputedly are developing ties with Polish amphetamine trafficking networks, again to diversify pathways for shipping cocaine to the West. For instance, in October 1991, Polish customs officials at Warsaw International Airport arrested a Colombian nurse, Julia Stella Cruz Oviedo, who was carrying 600 grams of cocaine in 75 vials in her stomach. A subsequent police interrogation disclosed that Cruz Oviedo was linked to the so-called Cali cartel and that she had instructions to deliver the cocaine to a Polish courier who would then transport the cocaine to Germany across the Polish-German frontier.[31] In Czechoslovakia, Colombian traffickers established warehouses and shipping companies, probably using such enterprises as fronts for receiving cocaine shipments. Last September and October, two 100-kilogram loads of cocaine secreted in bean shipments were impounded in Poland and Czechoslovakia. The cocaine was routed to a Czechoslovakian-Colombian agricultural import company—YAROS—based in Prague, for further transshipment to the Netherlands. A Colombian national and, interestingly, two former intelligence officers from the Czechoslovakian security forces jointly owned[32] the shipping company—perhaps a harbinger of the future profile of organized crime in the East.

The Yugoslav trafficking organizations have fostered strife and anarchy. Yugoslav heroin dealers now actively operate in a number of European countries, including Switzerland, Italy, Austria, and Germany. Nonetheless, the Yugoslav nationals constitute a special case—some of the groups apparently are motivated by political as well as business priorities. Specifically, Yugoslav trafficking groups apparently served as vehicles for financing and equipping separatist movements in Yugoslavia. Many if not most of the Yugoslavs arrested in Europe in 1990 were Croats and ethnic Albanians, the latter from Serbia's Kosovo province. Croatia, of course, has more or less gained its independence, and many Kosovo Albanians are now seeking freedom from Serbian domination, possibly as a prelude to anschluss with Albania. Switzerland's Minister of Justice learned last October that Kosovo Albanians purchased semiautomatic weapons in Bern and Basel, using the proceeds from heroin sales in Switzerland.[33] An analysis of other reports suggests that the weapons were either sold to Croat separatists or supplied to Kosovo's Front of Resistance and National Liberation of Albanians, a splinter group that then aimed at bringing Kosovo out of Albania and joining it with Yugoslavia.[34] The Yugoslav arms-for-drugs link functions as a controlling precedent. Any ethnic splinter group might want to turn to narcotics trafficking to finance its separatist or irredentist ambitions. Other ethnically mixed countries that are source or transit countries for narcotics—Russia, Czechoslovakia, Uzbekistan, and Kyrgyzstan, for instance—view such a prospect as very disturbing indeed.

The criminal landscape in the CIS countries also features organized drug gangs. For example, interregional criminal organizations have emerged to transport Central Asian drugs into the Slavic CIS countries. Central Asians themselves typically do not perform this role. Rather, outsiders—mainly Caucasian groups such as Azerbaidjanis, Chechens, and Georgians—travel to Central Asia, purchase the drugs from local dealers, and distribute them in Moscow, St. Petersburg, Kiev, and other major cities. Several years ago, individuals or small, uncoordinated groups managed the production and sale of narcotics in major Soviet cities. Today the market is much more highly structured. In a 1990 *Pravda* interview, a Moscow police official was asked, "How does the drug mafia differ from ordinary sellers of marijuana and hashish?" The official replied:

> First, there were occasional deals, one on one. Second, a person involved in drugs combined within himself both the manufacturer and the buyer and even the seller. That was three or four years ago. Everything is different now. All the elements characteristic of the drug mafia are inherent in the drug delivery and sales organization: demarcation of roles, profound secrecy, and also the use of hiding places, passwords, and the hiring of guards.[35]

In a retail drug organization, different members assume varying responsibilities, such as transporting drugs to points of sale, identifying buyers, hiding drugs, collecting payments, informing buyers of the location of the drugs, and furnishing security. Such gangs—which sometimes boast modern transportation, weapons, and communication equipment—pose a major challenge for the usually undermanned, underequipped, and underfunded police forces in major CIS cities.

Sophisticated production facilities for processing narcotics are still relatively rare in the CIS. Most manufactured drugs are still made at home, usually in the user's own kitchen. However, as one MVD spokesman noted in August 1990: "The appearance of synthetic drugs in illegal circulation is increasingly being recorded. And this means that underground laboratories using industrial equipment and chemical reagents are operating in the country."[36]

Such operations have been detected in St. Petersburg, Moscow, Riga, Baku, Perm, Rostov, Tomsk, Vladivostok, and other CIS cities. Most of these illegal laboratories produce methamphetamines or methadone. Emulating Polish operations, chemists and laboratory workers from universities or government research organizations manage these facilities. Rather curiously, heroin refining is virtually nonexistent, even in the opium cultivation zones of Central Asia—however, this virtual vacuum probably cannot be sustained. Central Asia's growing economic ties with its Moslem neighbors—including experienced narcotics producers such as Turkey, Iran, Pakistan, and Afghanistan—will offer a conduit for transferring refining and trafficking expertise throughout the region. Indeed, drug dealers in countries such as Turkey and Iran—which punish drug offenses harshly—may see the poor and weak Central Asian states as an attractive ancillary site for large-scale heroin production.

Finally, organized drug criminals are making inroads into post-Communist societies. On the economic front, some private or cooperative commercial ventures established since the beginning of Gorbachev's *perestroika* campaign in 1985 are acting as convenient legal covers for laundering drug money. This corruption created apprehension about the privatization process of privatization itself. For example, in a 1992 interview with an ABC news team, Russian MVD official Valentin Roshchin described narco-investment as follows: "It taints the character and future of free enterprise; it subverts it. The criminal element is in a position now where it can buy out a lot of property previously owned by the people. So drug money speaks louder here than anywhere in the world."[37]

Corruption of the bureaucracy also is worsening, especially in the poppy cultivation zones of Central Asia. For example, leading drug dealers in Uzbekistan reportedly hold positions in the government bureaucracy, in state economic enterprises, and (before 1992) in Communist party organs. Alternatively, traffickers can bribe local officials, although protection payments did not always achieve the desired results when Moscow was running "Operation Poppy" campaigns. For example, in July 1991, the Soviet MVD's elite Dzerzhinski division detected a large field (between 2 and 3 hectares) in Uzbekistan's Samarkand oblast. Swooping down on the field, the team was greeted by an angry peasant who asked, "Why did you come here? We already gave money to the raion (district). Wasn't it enough?"[38]

The organized criminal groups dealing in narcotics regard the USSR's collapse and the emergence of the CIS as the best of all possible worlds. Moscow's relations (at least formal relations) with MVD antidrug units in Central Asia have virtually vanished. The CIS retains a common economic space and almost transparent borders—although Russia reportedly intends to monitor its boundaries with other CIS states more closely—but the sovereign member states have yet to implement a common program for combatting drug trafficking. Substantive cooperation still must be negotiated on matters such as interdiction, joint investigations, crop eradication, antidrug legislation, and extradition. In effect, traffickers can roam freely around the commonwealth, but the authorities are not free to pursue them. Moreover, in the near absence of customs controls, shipping drugs from Tashkent to Arkhangelsk, for example, is virtually risk free. The Central Asian states are hypersensitive about their newly gained sovereignty and recoil from giving the Russian police information about local trafficking groups or drug shipments in progress. Finally, a new class of untouchables has risen from the ruins of the Soviet empire. For example, in Moscow, Azerbaidjani clans control an estimated 80 percent of the retail narcotics market. Yet, the brain centers of these families—the organizers and financial controllers of this traffic—reside in Azerbaidjan. In the absence of an extradition agreement between Russia and that country, the Azerbaidjani kingpins effectively are beyond the reach of Moscow authorities. [39]

Policy Implications

Confronting increasingly out-of-control drug traffic, police and public health officials everywhere from Warsaw to Bishkek desperately crave large infusions of antidrug assistance from Western nations, especially the United States. The Eastern wish list is vast: They want helicopters, herbicides, vehicles, crop substitution programs, Western advice on improving their criminal legal codes for narcotics, U.S. advice on tracking the flow of illegal drug money, and foreign assistance in coordinating epidemiological surveys and testing and producing drugs that seem to show promise in treating addicts.

Such appeals have not elicited much of a Western response thus far. The region has received miserly antinarcotics assistance, and Washington—mired in an expensive and unproductive cocaine war in the Andes—views drugs in post-Communist societies as exotic and essentially tangential to U.S. interests.

However, the West and the United States should begin taking notice. The potential drug scenarios themselves are disturbing. The former USSR—by virtue of its size, geographic location, and potential for cultivating drug crops—likely will become a significant exporter of narcotics during the 1990s. Because of its proximity to the Golden Crescent countries, Central Asia almost certainly will serve as a staging area for moving narcotics from many different regions—South America, Central Asia, and the Golden Crescent.

Nonetheless, compared to other sectors of the world—Southeast Asia, South America, Mexico—the problem apparently is relatively manageable. Trafficking organizations in the post-Communist world have not yet acquired the technical capabilities and distribution linkages common in groups such as the Colombian cartels, the Turkish heroin clans, or the Chinese triads. Heroin refining has not yet caught on in former Soviet states. Although the gigantic marijuana stands in the CIS would daunt even the most determined eradicators, the Central Asian opium production of some 3,000 to 5,000 hectares apparently is on a par with the cultivation of

Colombia or Lebanon—not with that of major producers such as Burma and Thailand. Drug dealers have not yet bought into the upper reaches of the bureaucracy and the political system. No "Samarkand cartel" operates paramilitary armies and controls vast reaches of Uzbekistan's territory. Yet, as Bem Bambayev, a major in the Uzbek MVD Criminal Investigation Division, remarked, "If this disease is not choked while it's young, it will expand and grow. It will grow if we do not get the necessary help."[40] The chief of the Kyrgyz MVD's antinarcotics unit, Aleksandr Zelichenko, observed, "It is very worthwhile to invest money in our republic so that you do not have a second Colombia or Bolivia on your hands."[41] Perhaps these officials have a point. Certainly the marginal effect of sending narcotics-related assistance to Uzbekistan would be much greater than sending the same resources to the Andean countries, where coca covers an area of more than 200,000 hectares, $500 million in U.S. funding since 1989 has failed to make a dent in cocaine production, and leading drug dealers stroll in and out of prison cells at their convenience.

Although the emergence of a sophisticated Eurasian narcotics industry clearly threatens Western Europe, the risk to the United States is at first glance less obvious. However, the following prospects afford little room for U.S. complacency. First, if regions such as Central Asia assume the status of major opium, heroin, and cannabis producers, the worldwide supply of such drugs undoubtedly will rise significantly. Central Asia currently could flood the world market with marijuana and hashish if better transportation and marketing arrangements were negotiated. In the near-term, Central Asians—or Turks, Iranians, Pakistanis, or other enterprising outsiders—could easily build heroin refineries in Central Asia. The concomitant burst of cheaper and purer heroin ultimately would find its way to the streets of New York, Los Angeles, Washington, and other U.S. cities—directly or indirectly. For example, if the supply of Central Asian heroin to Western Europe displaces Golden Crescent and Golden Triangle heroin, those traditional producers likely would channel their oversupply into the existing distribution network in the world's largest potential market, the United States.

Second, more than any other part of the former Soviet Union, Central Asia urgently requires external development assistance in any form—a circumstance that has created new and exciting financial opportunities for international organized crime. Traffickers are responding eagerly, exploiting the abysmally weak law enforcement in the East to establish a new network of smuggling routes, money-laundering operations, cultivation and production centers, and—as Eastern currencies become increasingly convertible—consumer markets. Moreover, these international players are not exclusively European and Eurasian. For example, Colombian and Nigerian traffickers who currently serve the U.S. market are gaining a foothold in Eastern Europe. If successful, such diversification can only enhance the profits, reach, and power of these already lethal international enterprises, which surely would flex their new economic muscle in Latin America and the United States.

Third, the United States cannot afford to ignore the geostrategic implications of a dominating drug industry in post-Communist Eurasia. For instance, Central Asia stands not only as the most prominent narcotics producer in the CIS, but also as a centuries-long crossroad for competing national and ethnic interests. Drugs and associated trafficking operations consequently fuel an already incendiary political dynamic now commonly characterized by ethnic clashes, boundary disputes, and religious challenges to state authority. In addition, opportunistic neighbors such as Russia, China, Iran, and Turkey might further undermine Central Asian stability by trying to exploit the social and military vacuum produced by the collapse of the USSR. Unlike their Latin American counterparts, however, Central Asian states have access to sophisticated conventional weapons, and Kazakhstan retains an ominous nuclear arsenal. At its worst, the resulting strife would inexorably demand U.S. attention. Could we overlook a Central Asian cycle of violent political and economic disintegration comparable to the narcotrafficker-fomented crises in Lebanon, Peru, and Afghanistan? Would the U.S. national interest be well served by the emergence of a narcocratic rogue state in Uzbekistan or nuclear power Kazakhstan? How might we react if nuclear materials and dangerous weapons from decaying Russian and Central Asian Defense establishments fell into the hands of international drug criminals?

Fourth, the escalating infiltration of fledgling Eastern financial systems by drug traffickers represents a clear and present danger to Western commercial institutions, including the U.S. banks and corporations operating in the region. The narcotics industry's money laundering enterprises in countries such as Poland can instantaneously wire drug trafficking profits to U.S. branch banks and financial repositories worldwide. The integrity of the international financial system is at risk because of the potential contamination by illegal drug profits, despite recent measures to improve accountability in international banking transactions and thus reduce counterparty exposure. Moreover, the unimpeded international flow of narcodollars would further obstruct struggling law enforcement officials.

To be sure, geography dictates policy: The evolving drug industry in the post-Communist world probably will play a more central role in supplying drugs to Western Europe than to North America. Still, large exports of hashish and ultimately heroin from former Soviet states would directly or indirectly flood U.S. markets, especially on the West Coast. Furthermore, the global dimensions of the narcotics problem require sharing the burden. Washington is trying to induce wealthy European nations and Japan to increase contributions to global antinarcotics programs, including the drug war in the Andes, primarily a U.S. concern. For geographic or political reasons, U.S. bilateral programs admittedly might not be the most appropriate vehicle for funneling antinarcotics assistance to some post-Communist countries. For example, in Central Asia, institutional agencies such as the United Nations Drug Control Program (UNDCP) might pursue this goal most effectively. However, even here, Washington ran in the wrong direction—the Bush administration planned to slash its 1992 contribution to UNDCP by a huge 44 percent.[42] In contrast, the Clinton administration's request for fiscal year 1994 narcotics control contributions to international organizations was more than double that of fiscal year 1992 levels.

Despite such constraints and caveats, U.S. interests are too powerful—and world-class players too few—to disregard the emerging narcotics industry in the former USSR. The United States must consider a range of cutting-edge and traditional antidrug policy strategies, including but not limited to imposing conditions on aid packages, supporting crop eradication and substitution, and furnishing financial technical expertise. For example, when the United States signs an aid agreement, such assistance should depend on the prospective recipient documenting legal and law enforcement reforms such as criminalizing money laundering, making drug trafficking a major offense, strengthening law enforcement tactics, and cooperating with other law enforcement agencies bilaterally or through organizations such as Interpol. The United States also could influence conditions on multilateral aid by using its leverage with institutions such as the International Monetary Fund and the World Bank.

Because the drug trade can be viewed as a socially perverse response to fundamental functions of supply and demand, crop eradication and substitution programs could be a key component of U.S. policy. If we intend to discourage Central Asian farmers from cultivating opium and to encourage their cooperation in eradication programs, we must offer them an alternative livelihood. Even successful eradication programs cannot prevent peasants from recultivating formerly lucrative crops such as opium unless they can turn to viable crops, gain acccess to Central Asian markets, and sell their produce for a profit.

Financial systems in the CIS are rudimentary and would benefit from a wide variety of technical assistance, including advice on needed legislation, basic accounting standards, current supervisory practices, and techniques for investigating financial crimes. As Valentin Roshchin noted in an interview last May with ABC News, "One of the most acute problems we will have to address soon is money laundering of funds received from the West. We have no laws to deal effectively with the problem."[43] Although the G-7 Financial Action Task Force is assessing Eurasian needs, the more crucial step is advanced training for bankers, financiers, and associated government regulators. In addition, wherever possible, we should encourage countries to implement asset forfeiture programs, thus creating an additional incentive for Eurasian government agencies to cooperate with their Western counterparts.

In the end, both the United States and Western Europe hold compelling political interests in restraining the expanding drug trade in the East. A flood of opiates, amphetamines, cocaine, and other drugs from the lawless reaches of Eurasia could prompt Western counties to erect new trade and customs barriers and retard the European economic integration from the Atlantic to the Urals that General de Gaulle envisioned. A deluge of narcotics also could undermine the economic integration process in the European Community, in the wake of removal of trade and finance barriers.

Moreover, the spread of drug trafficking and other forms of organized crime in Central Europe and the CIS—stark symbols of post-Communist social decay and political incompetence—could generate widespread pressure for a return to authoritarian rule or at least for a suspension of privatization and economic liberalization programs. When a narcotics official such as Valentin Roshchin contends that Russia's emerging capitalist sector is tainted by drug dealers, he is articulating a state of mind about his country's entire economic and political direction.

Finally, the stable and legitimate development of societies evolving from Communist rule is in the best interests of all countries. Yet, this development is not a foregone conclusion. The former Soviet republics, economically poor but well endowed with narcotics crops, seem especially vulnerable to political and economic penetration by drug dealers and their criminal cohorts. Societies dominated by such forces will not be reliable partners for building a new post-Communist order in Eurasia. Given such prospects, Washington should closely monitor developments in the newly liberated region from Eastern Europe to the Pacific Ocean, build antinarcotics coalitions when appropriate, and assist Russia, Central Europe, and Western Europe as they shape responses to an increasingly dangerous drug dynamic. When Western aid programs help the CIS counter money laundering, addiction, rampant crime, and other drug-related problems, such programs also indirectly bolster the case for democracy and free markets in these formerly communist countries.

In short, U.S. policymakers who view the evolution of a thriving CIS drug industry as tangential to our primary interests are simply misguided. The window of opportunity for formulating an effective policy is rapidly narrowing: The narcotraffickers suffer from no crisis of will and are moving decisively to augment their economic base. If we shortsightedly fail to act, drug abuse in the United States—and the worldwide economic and political power of organized crime—will rise in parallel to previously unimaginable heights.

Notes

1. To date, main Western donors to post-Communist countries have been, in order of importance, the German government, the United Nations Drug Control Program and the British government.

2. Pavel Bem, Chief Doctor at the Center for Drug Addict Cure in Prague. Speech to the Conference on Drug Abuse in Paris on April 18, 1991, p. 1.

3. ABC News. Interview with Aleksandr Zelichenko. In: *Transcripts of Interviews with Law Enforcement Officials in Russia, Kyrgyzstan, and Uzbekistan*. May-June 1992, p. 4. [Hereafter: *Transcripts*.]

4. Telephone interview with Polish Interpol Headquarters in Warsaw, conducted by Lee in Washington, D.C., on March 4, 1992.

5. Interview with the Czechoslovak Narcotics Commission in Prague, conducted by Lee on January 23, 1992.

6. Interview with Bem Bambayev, *Transcripts*, p. 12.

7. Telephone interview with Polish Interpol Headquarters in Warsaw, conducted by Lee in Washington, D.C., on March 4, 1992.

8. Interview conducted by Lee at Polish Interpol Headquarters in Warsaw on January 16, 1992. Also: Margaret Watson. "Opiates, Amphetamines, and AIDS in Poland." *Radio Free Europe Research Report No. 9*. Radio Liberty. 1992, p. 8.

9. U.S. Department of State, Bureau of International Narcotics Matters. *International Narcotics Control Strategy Report 1991*. Washington, D.C.: U.S. Department of State. March 1991, p. 383. Also: Elaine Shannon. "New Kings of Coke." *Time*. July 1, 1991, p. 28.

10. Bundeskriminalamt (BKA). Wiesbaden, Germany. Telefax. March 20, 1992.

11. Interview conducted by Lee with Polish Interpol officials in Warsaw on January 16, 1992.

12. Interview conducted by Lee with UN officials from the UN Drug Control Program in Vienna, Austria, on January 9 and 10, 1991.

13. Interview conducted by Lee with BKA officials in Wiesbaden on December 9, 1991.

14. V. Urvantsev. "Will We Curb the Drug Business?" *Pravda*. November 23, 1990, p. 6.

15. A. Illesh. "Skol'ko u Nas Narkomanov." *Izvestia*. August 29, 1990, p. 6.

16. V. Skripnik. "The 'Diplomat' Operation." *Rabochaya Tribuna*. May 17, 1990, p. 3.

17. UN International Drug Control Programme. "Special UNDCP Fact-Finding Mission in Seven Republics of the Commonwealth of Independent States." April 2 to May 2, 1992, pp. 3–4. (Hereafter: *UN Report*.) The opium estimate was furnished by MVD officials in Moscow and Tashkent in interviews in May and December 1992.

18. Interview conducted by Lee with Valentin Roshchin, head of the Moscow Interregional Bureau for Narcotics Control, in Moscow on May 13, 1992.

19. Interview with Major Bem Bambayev, Uzbek MVD Department for Drug Trafficking and Drug Abuse. *Transcripts*, p. 11. Interview conducted by Lee with Alisher Dzhurayev, chief of the same unit, on April 29, 1992.

20. Vladimir Berezovskiy. "Will Uzbekistan Turn Into Another Colombia?" *Nezavisimaya Gazeta*. July 9, 1991, p. 6. Peter Fuhrman. "Lethal Harvest." *Forbes*. July 6, 1992, p. 45. Interview conducted by Lee with Vyacheslav Tarbeev. Press Office of the President of Uzbekistan, December 30, 1992.

21. B. Kalachev and N. Osipov. "Kolumbiiskii Sindrom Srednei Asii." *Moskovskie Novosti*. October 6, 1991, p. 6.

22. Interview conducted by Lee with Kyrgyz narcotics officials in Bishkek on April 20 and 21, 1992.

23. Watson, op. cit., p. 2.

24. Statistics furnished by Maria Dziedzic, Adviser to the Minister of Health, during an interview at the Ministry of Health in Warsaw on January 14, 1992.

25. Statistics furnished by the Soviet Ministry of Health, All-Union Institute of Narcology, in September 1991.

26. Ibid.

27. T. Chebakova. "Narkomafia Raskruchivayet Spiral' Gryaznovo Biznesa." *Rossiiskaya Gazeta*. April 24, 1992, p. 4.

28. Interview with Bem Bambayev, *Transcripts*, p. 13.

29. Interview with a Polish Interpol official, conducted at the Marriott Hotel in Warsaw on January 17, 1992. Ewa Wilk. "Amphetamina—Smierc Na Eksport." *Spotkania*. December 4, 1991, pp. 24–27.

30. Interview conducted by Lee with Polish Interpol official in Warsaw on January 16, 1992.

31. Ibid.

32. Information from interview with DEA officials at The Marriott Hotel in Vienna, Austria, on January 24, 1992. Interviews with UNDCP officials in Vienna on January 10 and 11, 1992.

33. "Yugoslavia: Balkan Route Fuels War." *The Geopolitical Drug Dispatch*. Paris. November 1991, p. 1.

34. See, for example, the following sources. "Reports Link Drug Trade, Croatian Guns Deal." *Tanjug*. (In English.) 0759 GMT, December 12, 1991. "Ethnic Albanian Plot Uncovered in Kosovo, Says Serbia." Reuters: The Reuter Library Project. December 19, 1991. "Interpol General Assembly Without Illusions as Regards Combatting Drug Trafficking." *Neue Zuerchen Zeitung*. November 19, 1991, p. 7.

35. Urvantsev, op. cit.

36. A. Illesh. "Skol'ko u Nas Narkomanov?" *Izvestia*. August 29, 1990, p. 6.

37. Interview with Valentin Roshchin, *Transcripts*, p. 31.

38. Aleksandr Pogonchenkov. "Prazdnik Obshchei Bedy." *Moskovskii Komosomolets*. March 18, 1992, p. 2.

39. As a result, the narcotics trade and other illicit enterprises in Moscow controlled by these crime lords continue to flourish.

40. Interview with Ben Bambayev, op. cit., *Transcripts*, p. 14.
41. Interview with Aleksandr Zelichenko, *Transcripts*, p. 8.
42. Jeffrey Laurenti. "The U.S. Retreats in the War on Drugs." *The Christian Science Monitor*. April 30, 1992, p. 10.
43. *Transcripts*, p. 30.

10

The Limits and Consequences of U.S. Foreign Drug Control Efforts

Peter Reuter

For twenty years programs aimed at reducing the production and export of illicit drugs in foreign countries have played a major role in the rhetoric of drug control policy in the United States, though they have never accounted for much more than 5 percent of total federal expenditures. Since 1970 drug control has often been the dominant issue in U.S. relationships with the Andean region and, at times, with Mexico, Pakistan and Turkey.

The effort to control drug production overseas has generally been viewed as ineffective and perhaps even counterproductive, both for the producing nations and for U.S. diplomacy. Certainly, drug production in the traditional source countries has grown apace, notwithstanding increased funding for drug control provided by the United States and Western Europe to those nations. Mexico, the most co-operative of the source countries, continues to produce record amounts of heroin and marijuana, while Asian opium production grows by leaps and bounds.[1] The production and export of cocaine from the Andean region, the primary focus of concern throughout the 1980s, seems to continue almost unabated into the early 1990s. The decline following the August 1989 Colombian government crackdown against the Medellín cartel, precipitated by the cartel's assassination of the leading presidential candidate, turned out to provide only a brief hiatus. In part this reflects the fact that the crackdown was intended to diminish the threat of the cartel to government authority rather than to reduce cocaine production.

This chapter is adapted from an essay of the same title that appeared in *The Annals of the American Academy of Political and Social Sciences* 3521, May 1992. Support for the preparation of this chapter was provided by the Ford and Weingart Foundations through grants to RAND's Drug Policy Research Center. Robert MacCoun offered helpful suggestions.

U.S. pressures for source country governments to act aggressively against the cocaine industry can be counterproductive if they raise hostility to the central government. That has been a particular concern in Peru, where the Sendero Luminoso guerillas have been able to establish themselves as an alternative authority in the major coca growing area.

Pessimism about source country control programs, as they are generally known, is fairly widespread.[2] Indeed, outside of official documents it is difficult to find the slightest sign of optimism. However, much of that pessimism reflects the failure of the United States to persuade the governments of the major cocaine and opium producers to attempt serious implementation of production controls. For both political and economic reasons, though mostly the former, these governments have been reluctant to take actions against an industry that has become regionally, and sometimes nationally, important. The (usually implicit) belief of program advocates is that, if the producer governments could be persuaded to properly implement control efforts, substantial reductions in the production of illegal drugs would result.

The argument of this chapter goes beyond that, at least for Andean cocaine production.[3] It suggests that the failure of source country control may lie not so much in the difficulties of program implementation as in the basic structure of the drug industry. It seems unlikely that eradication, crop substitution or any related effort aimed directly at coca growing and cocaine refining in Peru, Bolivia and Colombia will make a significant difference to total Andean cocaine production, though it may affect the distribution of cocaine production among these countries.

The next section presents a framework for analysis of source country control efforts. This is followed by a description and assessment of the kinds of programs that have been used to control drug production and exports in the Andean region. The final section discusses, in a highly speculative manner, the issue of why, in the face of continuing lack of success and increasing awareness of the systemic nature of that failure, source country control programs continue to play a major role in the rhetoric of drug policy.

Analytic Framework: Risks and Prices

The analysis here uses an approach that can be labeled "risks and prices."[4] Its basic assumption is that supply-side programs focusing on parts of the distribution system distant from the consumer can only affect the price paid by the consumer. Such programs cannot restrict the physical availability of cocaine in the United States There are simply too many farmers, refiners, exporters and smugglers for enforcement to directly limit the amount available for U.S. consumption to, say, 100 tons per annum. The question then is how the international programs affect the risks and other costs of drug suppliers and how that in turn will affect retail prices in the United States.

Each kind of supply-side program (except for enforcement against retail markets[5]) directly affects a particular sector of the cocaine production/distribution system. For example, crop eradication raises the risks and costs faced by farmers; that should be reflected in the prices that refiners have to pay for leaf in order to induce farmers to stay in the business. Refinery destruction, by raising the risks and costs of refiners, should increase the difference between the price refiners pay for leaf and the price they receive from exporters when they sell the refined product. Similarly, interdiction raises the risks and costs of smugglers and should increase the difference between import and export prices. Programs may have indirect effects on other sectors[6] but the primary effect is sector specific.

The important consequence is not the induced change in returns received by participants at different points in the distribution and production system but on the final price paid by consumers. As the price of smuggling services rises, it is reasonable to assume that there will be an increase in the retail price of the drug. Though that may have slight effect in the short-run on consumption of addicted users, it may have a more substantial long-term effect by reducing the rate at which new users become heavy users, just as the effect of increases in cigarette taxes shows up primarily in reduced teenage smoking rates.[7]

We assume that price increases at one stage of the production or distribution is passed on essentially additively; e.g., an increase of $1,000 in the landed price of cocaine will raise the final price by $1,000 plus a modest amount representing increased inventory and risk-associated costs for those down stream. In effect, the assumption is of competition in each phase of distribution, with the mark-up determined not as a percentage of the purchase price but by the risks and other costs of operating at that level of the market. Caulkins[8] presents an alternative model in which the price increases are multiplicative; i.e., a 10 percent increase in the landed price of cocaine will generate roughly a 10 percent rise in the retail price. Though Caulkins produces suggestive evidence of proportionality in historical prices within the United States, the model's assumptions about distributor behavior are counter-intuitive and the evidence is not persuasive with respect to leaf and export prices.

Prices

An analysis of the price of cocaine at different points of the production and distribution system suggests the inherent limits of international programs, particularly those that focus on the farm sector. Table 10.1 presents

TABLE 10.1 Cocaine Prices Through the Distribution Chain (per pure kilogram equivalent, 1988)

At the farm	$750.00
Export (Colombia)	$2,000.00
Import (Miami)	$15,000.00
Wholesale (1 kilogram in Detroit)	$23,000.00
Ounce (Detroit)	$47,000.00
Retail (1 gram unit)	$135,000.00

the price chain for 1988, the most recent year for which I have prepared this analysis. The figures are very rough; for example the price of leaf required to produce a kilogram of cocaine may be anywhere between $500 and $1500.[9] Nonetheless, three points are very clear and not likely to be affected by any measurement problems. Certainly they have been true for other years in which these price chains have been estimated.

First, leaf production accounts for an absolutely trivial share of the final price of cocaine to U.S. consumers; probably much less than 1 percent of that price. Second, even by the time the cocaine reaches the point of export the price is still less than 5 percent, indeed perhaps only 2 percent, of the retail price. Third, smuggling costs (including the profits of smugglers) account for less than 10 percent of the retail price. Most of the cost of getting drugs to users is accounted for payments to dealers near the end of the distribution system, probably because they bear most of the risks (both from the criminal justice system and from competitors).[10] Only if international programs can dramatically increase the risks and costs of these upstream components of the cocaine industry will they be able to make a difference in the United States. The following sections suggest why such a difference is unlikely to be attained.

Source Country Programs

It is useful to start by examining why cocaine consumed in the United States is both grown and refined in the Andes rather than in the United States. Ecological factors may be taken as of minor importance, given that (contrary to popular myth) coca can be grown in a variety of climatic and agricultural conditions; the primary source of coca for the legal markets of the late 19th century were commercial plantations in Java[11] and the U.S. government grew coca in Florida, for medicinal purposes, during World War II.[12]

Two elements probably explain the location of production. First, the factors involved in production and refining are relatively cheap there. For example, Bolivian farmers charge very little for their labor, compared to their American counterparts; Greenfield[13] cites a daily wage of about

$3.50 in the Chapare in 1988, probably less than the hourly wage of most U.S. farm labor. Their alternative earnings opportunities are very weak. Greenfield also notes that coca growing is labor intensive; labor costs account for about 75 percent of first year costs.

Second, the risks imposed by source country governments are very modest. Farmers face little risk of having their crops destroyed; eradication, excluding "set-aside" purchases by the Bolivian government, has never reached even as high as 5 percent of coca cultivation in any of the Andean countries. Refiners and distributors face even less risk of going to prison, though in-country seizures of refined drugs have gone up substantially. Despite concerns that convicted drug dealers face too slight a prospect of prison time in the United States, dealer risks of incarceration are almost certainly much higher here than are grower/refiner/distributor risks in the Andes. A combination of corruption, intimidation and indifference explain the lack of stringency in enforcement against the bulk of those involved in drug production. Coca fields in the United States would face substantial risks from crop eradication efforts.

Programs aimed at reducing Andean exports of cocaine to the United States can be divided according to which participant they target: farmer, refiner and trafficker. Each has distinctive limitations; space limitations permit analysis here only of the first two.

The Farm Sector

The programs aimed at coca farmers included the coercive (eradication) and the persuasive (crop substitution and land retirement). We eschew description of program details[14] and focus on the evidence as to their effectiveness.

Eradication. Throughout the 1980s the primary goal of the Bureau of International Narcotics Matters of the U.S. State Department has been to induce the source countries to accept the necessity for eradication programs. Despite these efforts, none of the Andean countries have permitted spraying of coca fields and the U.S. government in 1991 seems to have lowered its emphasis on this program.

Could farmer costs be greatly increased through eradication? The experiences of the few intense eradication programs do not justify much optimism. Mexican opium growers were subject to an effective aerial eradication effort in the mid-1970s. At the time they were growing their poppies in large, open and accessible fields, in a relatively compact three province area.[15] Aided by a lengthy and severe drought, the program was initially successful and reduced the production of opium in Mexico, all of which was destined for the U.S. heroin market. Since the distribution channels from other production sources could not readily expand, this had a significant impact on American heroin consumption. Note that Mexico accounted for no more than 5 percent of world opium production.

Within five years, though, the Mexican industry had reestablished itself, with smaller fields, located in more remote areas and better protected from aerial spraying. Opium growing had also now spread well beyond the original three Northern provinces. Indeed, by the late 1980s substantial production was occurring over the southern Mexican border, in Guatemala. Though Mexican opium farmers had higher production costs than their Asian counterparts (with 1988 farmgate prices of $4,000 per kilo, compared to $1,000 in Burma) this does not seem to have led to any significant increase in the price of U.S. heroin. The production cost difference was more than counterbalanced by lower international transportation costs.

More successful has been the eradication program aimed at American marijuana producers. These growers have adapted to the increasing intensity of the domestic eradication effort, moving their plants indoors (thus lowering their exposure) and using better growing techniques to increase per acre yields. But farmgate prices, even adjusted for higher THC content and inflation, have risen, perhaps substantially.[16] The growers may have been pushed to the margin of technological feasibility.

These experiences suggest the likely effects of a sustained and intense eradication campaign against the coca industry. Very exposed areas such as the Upper Huallaga Valley in Peru or the Chapare region of Bolivia, where coca is grown in large open fields, may essentially be eliminated from coca growing. More will be grown in areas, such as the Amazonian jungle, in which eradication is much more expensive and difficult. No doubt the leaf price will rise as farmers have to use less productive land, varieties of leaf with lower content of the desired alkaloid, and spend more time getting the leaf to refiners, etc. It seems highly unlikely, however, that it will rise enough to increase U.S. cocaine prices noticeably. A tripling of the leaf price, so that $3,600 were needed to purchase the leaf for a kilogram of cocaine, would still increase cocaine prices in the United States by less than 2 percent.

It is of interest to consider whether coca eradication could produce the medium-term disruption in U.S. markets achieved by the Mexican program. Two differences seem important. First, a good deal of coca is grown for markets other than the United States; big cuts in production would lead to less use of coca products in the source countries rather than the United States, since demand there is more sensitive to leaf price changes. If reports from Brazil and Colombia about local consumption of refined products there are correct, then that may be a substantial quantity.[17] The rising share of Latin cocaine product apparently destined for European markets also presents a potential buffer for U.S. consumers.[18] In contrast, there was never evidence of significant Mexican heroin or opium consumption. Second, production is more dispersed, making it more difficult to eliminate most of it in a short period of time. A "pre-emptive" strike against the exposed areas is unlikely to cause disruption comparable to that achieved in Mexico in the mid-1970s. As just suggested, the development of jungle production in Brazil, where the plants are under triple jungle canopy, adds to the difficulty now faced by the eradicators.

Crop Substitution. Faced by the daunting political realities of programs that deprive large numbers of peasants of their livelihood, the Andean governments have chosen in recent years to stress non-coercive programs to persuade farmers to shift from coca to legitimate crops. These programs, called crop substitution, also have the attraction of generating additional funds from donor countries; Bolivia has been particularly effective in attracting these funds.[19]

Evidence on the effectiveness of crop substitution programs is slender but discouraging. These programs have been tried for almost twenty years, mostly under the auspices of the United Nations Fund for Drug Abuse Control (UNFDAC). Most of the programs have been hampered by adverse operational conditions; for example, the relatively promising UNFDAC efforts aimed at Afghanistani opium production in the late 1970s came to an end when the central government lost control over the growing areas following the Soviet-led coup in Kabul. Only in Thailand have the programs claimed much success and the rapid increase in Burmese production, serving the Thai heroin market at lower cost, probably explains the decline in indigenous opium production.

Analysis also suggests that crop substitution programs offer no more long-term promise than eradication as a method for reducing the flow of cocaine to the United States. They assume that, through provision of improved infrastructure, subsidized fertilizer/irrigation, perhaps even price supports, legitimate crops can be made attractive to the peasant farmers who are currently growing coca leaf.[20] That in turn assumes the price of coca leaf will stay fixed. However, the elasticity of demand for cocaine in the United States with respect to the price of leaf in Bolivia is essentially zero.[21] Cocaine refiners will be willing to pay very much more for coca leaf if they need to and will be able to fully pass on that increase to U.S. consumers with only negligible reduction in consumption. Peasant farmers will be better off with substitution programs that improve their productivity but the flow of cocaine will be only very slightly diminished.[22]

Land Buy-out. The Bolivian government has implemented a hybrid program, offering to pay coca farmers for taking land out of coca production. The price per hectare was set at $2,000 and in 1990 for the first time a significant number of hectares were indeed taken out of production.

There are two weaknesses to this program. First, the effect of the program is to set a floor on the earnings of coca farmers. If the return from coca falls low enough, then $2,000 becomes an attractive price for a hectare. In effect, the risks of putting land into coca cultivation are reduced, with the promise of $2,000 minimum payback. The second problem arises from the fact that the coca plant has a long productive lifetime but has lower yields after the tenth, perhaps even the seventh year (Greenfield, supra). At some point, the coca plant's yield falls to a level that makes the $2,000 payment attractive. Spedding states that "Most of the fields offered for eradication are already choked by weeds or too old to be of any value."[23]

In principle, both problems are soluble. The program could be restricted to land in coca cultivation before a certain date, thus not affecting incentives for new cultivation. The second problem could be eliminated by a similar limitation on the age of the plants eligible for purchase. However, these solutions require that the government can create a register of coca lands and keep track of plant age. Without the co-operation of the peasantry, which is well organized in Bolivia to resist undesired government intrusions, neither is feasible.

Refinery Destruction

Since the mid-1980s, as the limitations of crop eradication have become more obvious, the United States government has promoted programs aimed at destruction of cocaine refineries. Thus the U.S. Army, at the invitation of the Bolivian government, sent in troops and equipment in the summer of 1986 to assist Bolivian military and police units eliminate local refineries (Operation Blast Furnace). The U.S. government also regularly reports the number of refineries destroyed in source and transshipment countries.[24]

The rationale for these programs is that they will lower the demand for illicit leaf, by raising refiners' costs and eliminating refining capacity, and thus lower leaf price. With lower leaf price peasants will have less incentive to grow coca. At the same time these programs have the considerable attraction of not imposing direct costs on peasant farmers. Thus they generate less political unrest.

Alas, there is again less to this than meets the eye. Cocaine refineries are not like oil refining plants; they need involve no significant capital plant, frequently being constituted instead of very simple equipment, located in a primitive shack. This was the kind of facility turned up by Blast Furnace. They are easily and cheaply replaced. Refinery destruction is probably little more than the elimination of a specific location for a short period of time.

The official enthusiasm for refinery destruction bears some similarity to the American military attitude toward the destruction of Viet Cong "arms factories" in the early 1960s; these factories were in fact very ad hoc and temporary structures, using indigenous and scrap materials to fabricate primitive light weaponry. Neil Sheehan, in his recent book on the Vietnam war[25] notes that field U.S. officers had "the impression that the words 'Viet Cong hamlet' and 'VC arms factory' conjured up in [the general's] mind World War II images of a German barracks and a munitions plant" (p. 111). Some major cocaine refineries have been found, with true barracks and landing fields, but forcing refiners to be more covert offers no prospect for raising refining costs to a noticeably higher share of the retail price, given that small refiners do successfully compete in the industry currently.

Operation Blast Furnace is a case in point. The immediate effect of the operation was indeed a decline in leaf price; according to press reports, leaf price fell by 70 percent. However, consistent with rapid restoration of refining capacity, leaf price had risen to almost 90 percent of its earlier level six months after the completion of Blast Furnace.

Refiner margins are very small; perhaps no more than $1,000 per kilogram. Assume that a refinery destruction program was so successful that refiners had to process two kilos of leaf for every one that made it to the point of export. Even with generous assumptions about risk aversion, that might raise the refining margin from $1,000 to $4,000. The same logic that points to the low probability of being able to achieve major increases in retail prices through raising leaf production costs applies here as well.

Conclusion

Source country programs, whether they be crop eradication, crop substitution or refinery destruction, hold negligible prospect for reducing American cocaine consumption in the long-run. This conclusion does not rest on the well-known frailties of the source country governments, particularly that of Peru. Even if the Peruvian government were less corrupt, more stable and more efficient, an intense eradication program is likely, at best, to cause a short-term interruption in the flow of cocaine to the United States. Forcing farmers to plant in smaller and less accessible fields would make a negligible difference to the U.S. consumer. Similarly, even if the source country governments were able to provide the stable local conditions needed for delivery of the services necessary to make alternative crops viable in the major growing regions, it would not reduce the availability of coca leaf to refiners. Crop substitution programs involve, in effect, a bidding war between the government on one hand and cocaine refiners on the other; even if refiners have to raise the price they pay for leaf by 200 percent to persuade sufficient farmers to continue to raise coca, total U.S. demand will be negligibly affected. The same analysis applies to programs that reduce barriers for source country's legitimate products in the United States;[26] these are likely to do no more than redistribute coca production among the source countries.

Why do these programs continue to generate political support? The programs have demonstrably failed in the past. A recent House of Representatives Appropriations Committee report noted that "despite U.S. efforts to provide economic assistance to Andean countries, the fact remains that coca growing and processing remains a major and seemingly irreplaceable element in the economics of Peru, Bolivia and Colombia. Nobody has come up with a viable strategy to transform this economic dependence and as such the political will of the various governments to continue to fight the 'drug war' is ever changing."[27] There is also considerable unease with the implementation of the programs. For example a recent report of the Inspector General of the State Department[28] noted the Bolivian government had appointed some corrupt officials to key drug control positions.

The arguments presented in this article have acquired broad currency in the debates of recent years.[29] The government of Peru, the primary coca leaf producing country, is barely functioning at all. The transfers of U.S. money to aid farmers who are currently producing drugs that have devastated American cities does not have much popular appeal, particularly when farm programs in the United States are being cut. Yet the President's Fiscal Year 1992 budget proposed significant increases in the funding of international control programs; from $307 million in FY 1990, they were slated to rise to $612 million in FY 1992.[30]

I suggest that there are three reasons for this continued popularity. First, there is a need to appear to be doing something about every aspect of the drug problem. Even if all the evidence and analysis points to the inefficacy of these programs, Congress and the President cannot readily abandon the rhetoric of two decades, unless alternative methods for source country control can be found. But that explains only why the programs continue, not why they grow. Here I think we need to look at the dynamics of program budgets: a rising budgetary tide lifts all boats. The expansion of drug control expenditures at the federal level has raised spending on all these programs, the successful and the unsuccessful alike.

Second, foreign initiatives have a peculiar attraction for presidents. They provide opportunities for highly visible meetings in which the president is not merely a politician, allocating money to bureaucrats, but the leader of the nation taking responsible action in the world as a whole. Even now, the amounts being spent in the Andes constitute a modest share of the federal drug control budget. For a few hundred million dollars the President achieves a prominence that few similar sized domestic programs can provide.

Third, the possibility of success cannot absolutely be ruled out. The success of the Mexican opium spraying program, even though 15 years old, still lives as a vivid example of what can happen under the right conditions. Little enough analytic attention has been given to these issues that any proponent of source country control efforts can bring up that success as evidence for the merit of continued overseas efforts. Opponents can not readily find analyses that point to the special conditions distinguishing that case from the ones currently being considered.

Moreover, these programs do have real effects, even if not usually on U.S. drug consumption. They can have substantial impact on the source countries themselves. Crop eradication programs may increase the power of guerilla movements by increasing peasant hostility toward the central government; that is of particular importance in Peru. Crop substitution programs on the other hand may help the central government increase its authority. Given that these programs seem likely to be an enduring part of U.S. foreign policy, and unlikely to help the United States, primary attention should be focused on choosing programs that do the least harm overseas.

Notes

1. National Narcotics Intelligence Consumers Committee, *Narcotics Intelligence Estimate*, Washington, D.C., 1990.

2. Among recent prominent statements of this pessimism are Bruce Bagley, "Colombia and the War on Drugs," *Foreign Affairs*, Fall 1988, and Rensselaer Lee, "Why the United States Cannot Stop South American Cocaine," *ORBIS*, Fall 1988. For a more complex view see *Seizing Opportunities: Report of the Inter-American Commission on Drug Policy*, Institute of the Americas and the Center for Iberian and Latin American Studies, University of California, San Diego, June 1991.

3. The conclusions of this chapter are close to those of an earlier analysis that dealt primarily with opium control: see Peter Reuter, "Eternal Hope: America's Quest for Narcotics Control," *The Public Interest*, Spring, 1985.

4. A detailed account of this approach is given in Peter Reuter and Mark Kleiman "Risks and Prices: An Economic Analysis of Drug Enforcement," in Michael Tonry and Norval Morris (eds.), *Crime and Justice: An Annual Review of Research*, Vol. 7, Chicago, 1986. For refinements, see Jonathan Cave and Peter Reuter, *The Interdictor's Lot: A Dynamic Model of the Market for Drug Smuggling Services*, Santa Monica, CA, RAND, 1988; and Mark Kleiman and Kerry Smith, "State and Local Drug Enforcement," in Michael Tonry and James Wilson (eds.), *Drugs and Crime*, Chicago, University of Chicago Press, 1990.

5. The distinctive feature of enforcement against the retail transaction is that it imposes costs directly on the customer, not reflected in the price that is paid to the

dealer. See Mark Moore, "Achieving Discrimination in the Effective Price of Heroin," *American Economic Review*, Vol. 63, May 1973.

6. For example, interdiction may affect the price of leaf. Interdiction both raises retail prices, reducing final demand, and the amount of leaf needed for a given final demand (because it raises the amount of cocaine shipped per kilogram consumed). The second effect is likely to outweigh the first under most assumptions about the relevant parameters. See Peter Reuter, Gordon Crawford, and Jonathan Cave, *Sealing the Borders: The Effect of Increased Military Involvement in Drug Interdiction*, RAND Corporation, Santa Monica, CA, 1988.

7. See Eugene Lewitt and Douglas Coate, "The Potential for Using Excise Taxes to Reduce Smoking," *J. of Health Economics*, Vol. 1, 1989.

8. Jonathan Caulkins, *The Distribution and Consumption of Illicit Drugs: Mathematical Models and Their Policy Implications*, unpublished Ph.D. dissertation, MIT, Cambridge, MA, 1990.

9. The range represents in part the enormous variation in leaf prices. In Bolivia, since 1986, the range within a year in the Cochabamba region of Bolivia is at least 1 to 5.

10. The explanation for this observation probably lies in the fact that low level dealers have to spread their risks over a small quantity of cocaine relative to that over which smugglers and high level dealers spread their risk. Hence the mark-up per gram, in absolute dollars, will be highest at the low end of the trade.

11. Richard Ashley, *Cocaine: Its History, Uses and Effects*, Warner Books, New York, 1975.

12. Ronald Siegel, personal communication.

13. Greenfield, *Bolivian Coca: A Perennial Leaf Crop Subject to Supply Reduction*, unpublished Ph.D. dissertation, University of California, Berkeley, 1991.

14. Little detailed research is available on these programs. See Rensselaer Lee, *White Labyrinth: Cocaine and Political Power*, New Brunswick, NJ, Transaction Press, 1989.

15. For details about this early period see Richard Craig, "Operation Condor: Mexico's Anti-Drug Campaign Enters a New Era," *J. Interamerican Studies and World Affairs*, August 1980.

16. Published DEA reports point to only modest increases in potency adjusted prices in recent years. Anecdotal evidence suggests that the official prices now substantially understate actual prices; there are also reports of bouts of scarcity in various cities.

17. This assumes that Brazilian and Colombian demand is more elastic than U.S. demand with respect to leaf price. The demand curves may be the same but the retail price is more sensitive to leaf price in countries where dealer risks are low.

18. European border seizures of cocaine exceeded 15 tons in 1990, comparable to the 1983 levels in the United States. Yet data on European cocaine consumption point to a market that is still quite small.

19. See, for example, *National Strategy for Alternative Development*, 1990, an English-language document produced by the Presidency of the Republic of Bolivia, that argues for large infusions of capital from overseas.

Limits and Consequences of U.S. Drug Control Efforts 221

20. These programs can have perverse effects. Sanabria claims that the introduction of a road into the Cochabamba region, intended to facilitate the marketing of legal produce, instead helped provide cocaine traffickers with a landing strip for their small planes. H. Sanabria, *Social and Economic Change in a Bolivian Highland Valley Peasant Community: The Impact of Migration and Coca*, unpublished Ph.D. dissertation, University of Wisconsin, Madison, 1989; cited in Greenfield supra.

21. Even if U.S. demand for cocaine is elastic with respect to retail price, that price is very insensitive to changes in leaf price.

22. Note though that such programs may affect where coca is grown in the Andean region. A successful crop substitution program in Bolivia would raise the price of coca in Bolivia and motivate refiners in Colombia to purchase more leaf in Peru.

23. A. L. Spedding, "Coca Eradication, A Remedy for Independence?—With a Postscript," *Anthropology Today*, Vol. 5, No. 5, October 1989.

24. See the annual *International Narcotics Control Strategy Report*.

25. Neil Sheehan, *John Paul Vann and the Bright Shining Lie*, New York, 1989.

26. The Colombian government complained bitterly in 1989 when the United States refused to help improve access for Colombian textile exports at the same time that large quantities of aid were being provided by the United States to assist in fighting the Medellín cartel.

27. U.S. House of Representatives *Report on Foreign Operations, Export Financing and Related Programs Appropriations Bill, 1993*, Washington, DC, June 18, 1992.

28. U.S. Department of State, Office of the Inspector General, *Drug Control Activities in Bolivia*, Audit Report 1-CI-030, October 1991.

29. See, for example, *Operation Snowcap*, Report of the House Government Operations Committee, 1990.

30. Office of National Drug Control Policy, *National Drug Control Strategy*,Washington, DC, 1991, p. 140.

About the Contributors

Kevin Healy is a grant officer for the Inter-American Foundation, a congressionally funded foreign aid agency. He has worked in that capacity for the past fifteen years in the countries of Bolivia, Peru, and Ecuador. Prior to that, he worked with a social science research team from Georgetown University in Paraguay and was a Peace Corps Volunteer in Peru. Dr. Healy is the author of a book on rural development in Bolivia and has published numerous articles on grassroots development in the Andean region, the impact of coca and cocaine production in Bolivia, and indigenous social movements. Dr. Healy has degrees from the University of Notre Dame, Georgetown University, and Cornell University, where he received his doctorate in developmental sociology.

Rensselaer W. Lee III is president of Global Advisory Services of Alexandria, Virginia, a firm that consults on international economic and political issues for the U.S. government and private industry clients. He is concurrently an associate scholar at the Foreign Policy Research Institute in Philadelphia, Pennsylvania. Dr. Lee is the author of *The White Labyrinth: Cocaine and Political Power* and of numerous articles on the drug trade and other international problems. He has testified several times before congressional committees and has appeared on national television shows such as ABC's "Good Morning America," ABC's "Nightline," "CBS Evening News" and the Cable News Network.

Melvyn Levitsky is a career Foreign Service Officer who was appointed Assistant Secretary of State for International Narcotics Matters (INM) in June 1989. In this capacity, Assistant Secretary Levitsky has played a central role in developing and implementing U.S. government's foreign counternarcotics policies and programs. He has directed the State Department bureau responsible for planning, implementing, and overseeing the administration of the International Narcotics Control Program under the authority of the Foreign Assistance Act. Mr. Levitsky and his staff have advised the Secretary of State and other U.S. government principals on international drug control, as well as providing programmatic direction to U.S. missions abroad. INM represents the United States at UN and other international drug control organizations and coordinates the relevant international drug control programs of all U.S. government agencies.

Since entering the Foreign Service in 1963, Mr. Levitsky has had broad foreign policy experience, serving in Germany, Brazil, and the Soviet Union and as Ambassador to Bulgaria from 1984 to 1987. His Washington assignments have included Director of the Office of UN Political Affairs between 1978 and 1982 and Deputy Assistant Secretary of State for Human Rights and Humanitarian Affairs in 1982. From 1983 to 1984, Mr. Levitsky was the Deputy Director at the Voice of

America. Prior to becoming the Assistant Secretary for INM, Mr. Levitsky served as Special Assistant to the Secretary and Executive Secretary of the Department, in which capacity he worked closely with Secretary of State George Shultz.

Donald J. Mabry, professor of history and associate dean of the College of Arts and Sciences at Mississippi State University, has written extensively on the Latin American narcotics trade, including editing and contributing chapters to *The Latin American Narcotics Trade and U.S. National Security*. His primary interest is the use of U.S. military in antinarcotics efforts. His other books are *Mexico's Accion Nacional*, *The Mexican University and the State*, and, with Robert Shafer, *Neighbors—Mexico and the United States*.

Scott MacDonald is an international economic advisor at the Office of the Comptroller of the Currency in Washington, D.C. In that capacity, he has worked on international economic and financial issues, including money laundering. He received a B.A. from Trinity College in Hartford, Connecticut; an M.A. from the University of London's School of Oriental and African Studies; and a Ph.D. in political science from the University of Connecticut. He has served as the Chief International Economist at Maryland National Bank and at Connecticut National Bank and has published widely, including *Dancing on a Volcano: The Latin American Drug Trade* (1988); *Mountain High, White Avalanche: Cocaine and Power in the Andean States and Panama* (1989); and was a coeditor, with Bruce Zagaris, of *International Handbook of Drug Control* (1992).

David F. Musto, who is a professor in the Child Study Center, a professor in psychiatry, and a professor in the history of medicine, has been a member of the Yale faculty since 1969. His research has centered on social history, particularly the development of policies involving alcohol, narcotics, AIDS, the family, and mental health. Dr. Musto has investigated many areas touching on history and medicine and was a member of the White House Strategy Council on Drug Abuse Policy during the Carter administration. He is also a member of the Advisory Panel on Technologies for Understanding the Root Causes of Substance Abuse and Addiction, Office of Technology Assessment, Congress of the United States.

Dr. Musto has published widely in professional journals and is particularly noted for his study of drug policy, *The American Disease: Origins of Narcotic Control*, published first in 1973 and in an expanded edition in 1987. His essays on social issues appear in the general media such as *The New York Times*, *The Wall Street Journal*, *The Los Angeles Times* and *The Washington Post*, and he is often sought as a commentator on social policy by news magazines and television networks.

Raphael F. Perl is a specialist in international narcotics policy with the Congressional Research Service of the Library of Congress in Washington, D.C. He is the author of numerous congressional and academic publications on narcotics policy issues, including *International Narcotics Control and Foreign Assistance Certification: Requirements, Procedures, Timetables, and Guidelines* (U.S. Senate, Committee on Foreign Relations 1988). Mr. Perl earned a B.S. in Foreign Service as well as a J.D. from Georgetown University. He is a graduate of the U.S. Army J.F.K. Special Warfare Center's Foreign Area Officer Program and a graduate of the National War College. He is a regular participant in international drug policy fora within the academic and governmental community.

About the Contributors

Peter Reuter is senior economist in the Washington office of RAND and codirector of RAND's Drug Policy Research Center. He earned his Ph.D. in economics at Yale University and was guest scholar at the Brookings Institution before joining RAND in 1981. His initial research dealt with the organization of criminal activities, resulting in the publication of *Disorganized Crime: The Economics of the Visible Hand* (1983).

Since 1983, Dr. Reuter has worked primarily on drug policy issues, publishing a number of papers and studies on drug enforcement, including *Sealing the Borders*, a study of the effects of increased interdiction, and *Money from Crime: A Study of the Economics of Drug Dealing in Washington, D.C.* His current research focuses on European drug policies. Dr. Reuter testifies regularly before Congress and gives numerous seminars to policy audiences.

Irving Tragen has been the executive secretary of the Inter-American Drug Abuse Control Commission (CICAD) of the Organization of American States since its creation in 1987. He has been a member of the G-7's Chemical Action Task Force and participated in expert groups on various aspects of the drug problem in Europe and Asia as well as in Latin America, the Caribbean, and North America. Dr. Tragen is a specialist on Inter-American Affairs whose experience spans forty-eight years. As a career U.S. Foreign Service Officer from 1953 to 1980, he served in seven countries including assignments in the Alliance for Progress and as U.S. AID Director in Bolivia, the Central American Common Market, and Panama. In the late 1970s, he was the Deputy U.S. Representative to the OAS and Ambassador to the Inter-American Economic and Social Council and the Inter-American Council for Education, Science, and Culture. He is a lawyer by profession, with a J.D. from Boalt School of Law of the University of California–Berkeley and post-graduate legal studies at the University of Chile.

William O. Walker III is professor of history at Ohio Wesleyan University. During 1992–1993, he served as senior research associate in the North-South Center and as visiting professor in the Graduate School of International Studies, both at the University of Miami. He is the author of *Drug Control in the Americas*, rev. ed. (1989) and *Opium and Foreign Policy: The Anglo-American Search for Order in Asia, 1912–1954* (1991). He is editor of *Drug Control Policy: Essays in Historical and Comparative Perspective* (1992) and has published numerous articles on U.S. drug policy. In 1988, he was awarded a Social Science Research Council–John D. and Catherine T. MacArthur Foundation Fellowship in International Peace and Security.

David L. Westrate, Assistant Administrator for Intelligence of the Drug Enforcement Administration (DEA), is responsible for the management of the entire range of DEA intelligence activities worldwide. Mr. Westrate previously served as the Assistant Administrator for Planning and Inspection, where he managed all planning, security, inspections, and integrity matters for DEA. He has also served for five years as the Assistant Administrator for Operations with worldwide responsibility for DEA's day-to-day enforcement activities. Heading the Operations Division, he was instrumental in establishing many DEA domestic and international enforcement programs. Mr. Westrate has testified before the U.S. Congress on numerous occasions on drug law enforcement issues during the past decade. He is a graduate of Michigan State University's Criminal Justice Program, and he served in the U.S. Marine Corps.

About the Book

Controlling illegal trafficking in narcotics is a complex challenge. Dilemmas for policymakers abound. Despite new measures adopted by the international community that have led to tactical victories, the flow of illicit drugs into the United States continues largely unabated, and worldwide production of opium, marijuana, and coca continues to grow dramatically.

In this timely work, specialists from government, academia, and the private sector debate recent U.S. foreign drug policy—its origins, its elements, its implementation, and its prospects for success. Serious conflicts between U.S. international narcotics policy and U.S. foreign policy contribute to the dilemmas inherent in curbing global drug trafficking: Interdicting drugs interrupts the free flow of goods, people, and wealth across international borders.

International political and economic instabilities, especially political breakups and ethnic strife in former police states, complicate U.S. foreign drug policy. Because U.S. antidrug goals can bring political disruption and economic loss to countries where narcotics production is economically and socially entrenched, the United States must cooperate with an international antinarcotics coalition of producer, transit, and consumer nations, operating within the context of their perspectives and priorities while trying to achieve competing U.S. foreign policy goals.